NEW SERIES • VOLUME IX

COSTERUS

Essays in
English and American
Language and Literature

Rodopi

1978

RICHARDSON THE NOVELIST

RICHARDSON THE NOVELIST: THE PSYCHOLOGICAL PATTERNS

by

GERALD LEVIN

Rodopi

1978

Acknowledgement is made to the following publishers for permission to quote from the works listed:

Sigmund Freud Copyrights Ltd., The Institute of Psycho-Analysis, and The Hogarth Press Ltd., for permission to quote from *The Standard Edition of the Complete Psychological Works of Sigmund Freud*, translated and edited by James Strachey.

Excerpted from "'A Child Is Being Beaten': A Contribution to the Study of the Origin of Sexual Perversions" and "The Economic Problem in Masochism," Volume 2; excerpted from "Contributions to the Psychology of Love. A Special Type of Choice of Object Made by Men" and "Some Character-Types Met With in Psycho-Analytic Work," Volume 4, in *The Collected Papers of Sigmund Freud*, edited by Ernest Jones, M.D., authorized translated under the supervision of Joan Riviere, published by Basic Books, Inc., Publishers, New York, by arrangement with The Hogarth Press Ltd. and The Institute of Psycho-Analysis, London.

Reprinted from "Richardson's *Pamela*: Conflicting Trends," *American Imago*, Vol. 28, No. 4 (1971) by Gerald Levin; by permission of Wayne State University Press.

Reprinted from "The Symbolism of Lawrence's *The Fox*," *CLA Journal*, XI (December, 1967); by permission of *CLA Journal*.

Cover: Henk Schippers

Printed in the Netherlands
ISBN: 90–6203–410–1

To Lillian

The vast, unexplored morality of life itself, what we call the immorality of nature, surrounds us in its eternal incomprehensibility, and in its midst goes on the little human morality play, with its queer frame of morality and its mechanized movement; seriously, portentously, till some one of the protagonists chances to look out of the charmed circle, weary of the stage, to look into the wilderness raging round.

– D. H. Lawrence, *Study of Thomas Hardy*

Table of Contents

PREFACE

The extent of the commentary on Samuel Richardson the man, in this study of his four novels, is that they provide indirect proof of Edmund Bergler's theory that psychic masochism is a necessary condition of genius, and of Theodor Reik's similar view. This theory tells us nothing, however, about specific traits or complexes in the individual. Therefore, I do not suggest that Richardson identified emotionally with the sadistic behavior of some of his male characters, or that he exhibited in his personal life or his published statements masochistic traits I shall analyze. Not enough is known about Richardson to draw such conclusions; and even if more were known, the novels do not require a biographical context for their interpretation, as for example do many of Conrad's stories and novels. Instead my concern is with Richardson the novelist – with how he created his characters, drawing on what must have been an acute understanding of people and their world, as well as on unknown sympathies and personal qualities.

Clearly, the Richardson who emerges in the moralizing letters and pages in the novels is often at odds with the Richardson readers past and present have discovered in the depiction of character – and this discrepancy has long affected criticism of the novels. To many readers and critics Richardson is an incessant moralizer and even pious hypocrite, to others an acute social historian and psychologist. Mario Praz's once influential view that the novels exhibit "unctuous pietism" and a "sensual, turgid background," the constant moralizing serving as a disguise for "situations of heightened sensuality," represents perhaps the most negative opinion.[1] D. H. Lawrence's reference to Richardson's "calico purity and his underclothing excitements" is well known.[2] However, the view that Richardson was a naive artist,

1. *The Romantic Agony,* second edition (London: Oxford University Press, 1970), pp. 98-99.

2. *Phoenix: The Posthumous Papers of D. H. Lawrence,* ed. Edward D. McDonald (London: William Heinemann, 1936), p. 552.

confused and imitative of popular genres in his worst pages and unconscious of means and effects in his best, is no longer widely held, though he has not been wholly exonerated from the charge of occasional moral obtuseness, vanity, and insensitivity. Recent studies by Margaret Anne Doody and Mark Kinkead-Weekes, following the lead of Alan D. McKillop, Frederick W. Hilles and other earlier critics, show quite the opposite. Nevertheless, the image of Richardson as a morally insensitive, pompous amateur sticks in the minds of readers. For many *Pamela* and its sequel are read as an amusing sport, or as a basis for enjoying Fielding's *Joseph Andrews* and *Shamela*; *Clarissa* is read usually in abridgement, and is uncertainly admired – given its enormous critical reputation; *Sir Charles Grandison* is largely ignored (to my knowledge, no popular edition or abridgement has appeared in this century).

The intellectual problem in Richardson, as critics have dealt with it, is related to the biographical. To redeem Richardson from ridicule and censure, sympathetic critics have depended mainly on the novels to show his keen awareness of the social and religious currents of thought in his time, and of novelistic and dramatic traditions, which he shaped to his own needs. But there is still disagreement over Richardson's basic view of human nature. Recent critics point to the influence of Puritan ideas and sympathies, the liberal influence of Latitudinarian Christianity, and general eighteenth century ideas of "sentiment" and innate good feeling and the social affections – a rather different view from those who stress Richardson's debt to eighteenth century materialistic philosophy.[3] Eaves and Kimpel state the intellectual problem perfectly: "Richardson is one of the clearest cases in literature of the difference between the imaginative mind and the speculative mind."[4]

The psychology of Richardson's characters, in the major tradition of criticism, has been analyzed mainly as a function of these backgrounds, or in light of Richardson's own stated intentions. Two

3. Margaret Anne Doody, *A Natural Passion: A Study of the Novels of Samuel Richardson* (Oxford: Clarendon Press, 1974), pp. 246-47, 166-72; Cynthia Griffin Wolff, *Samuel Richardson and the Eighteenth-Century Puritan Character* (Hamden, Connecticut: Archon Books, 1972), pp. 179-80, 206-07; T. C. Duncan Eaves and Ben D. Kimpel, *Samuel Richardson, A Biography* (Oxford: Clarendon Press, 1971), Chapter 22; Praz, pp. 98-99.

4. *Samuel Richardson,* p. 618.

recent and distinguished studies of the characters depart somewhat from this tradition. Morris Golden examines them as psychological types apart from the dramatic movement of the novels that Kinkead-Weekes traces almost page by page. Analyzing Clarissa within the psychological framework that Richardson himself provides, Kinkead-Weekes concludes that "Richardson clearly understood how much lay hidden in the mind that the daylight consciousness either repressed or failed to understand . . . but which dreams, or derangement, could reveal."[5] And he finds in many pages of *Clarissa* a depth of characterization that is not to be found again in the English novel until this century. Kinkead-Weekes also sheds important light on revisions in *Clarissa* that darken the character of Lovelace in the third edition – and thus on Richardson's creative method. Eaves and Kimpel have also added to our understanding of this method in their distinguished biography.[6]

A tradition of psychological criticism different from these critics tends to ignore or give little attention to the social, religious and literary backgrounds. The language of this criticism has been Freudian – as it is in this study of the novels. In general, psychoanalytic criticism tends to treat fictional character as a construct of psychical qualities, usually assumed to derive from the writer himself. This approach was pioneered by Freud, who, in his great essay "Creative Writers and Day-Dreaming," argues that the creative writer "splits" his ego into many component egos in the process of composition. Controversial psychoanalytic studies of Poe and other writers have sought to identify these components and reconstruct from them the inner character. Freud's later essay "Character Types Met With in Psychoanalytic Work" shows how fruitful this constitutive approach can be, applied toward character alone without attending to the writer.[7]

5. *Samuel Richardson, Dramatic Novelist* (Ithaca: Cornell University Press, 1973), p. 231.

6. Kinkead-Weekes, "*Clarissa* Restored? ", *Review of English Studies* (New Series), 10 (1959), 156-71; Eaves and Kimpel, "The Composition of *Clarissa* and Its Revisions before Publication," PMLA, 83 (1968), 416-28; *Samuel Richardson, A Biography,* Chapters 5, 10, 14. In considering the character of Lovelace in *Clarissa,* Kinkead-Weekes stresses the revisions occurring after publication of the first edition; Eaves and Kimpel stress the process of revision occurring before. Their views are not incompatible, as we shall see.

7. Gerald Levin, *Sigmund Freud* (Boston: Twayne Publishers, Inc., 1975), Chapter 5.

In analyzing Richardson's characters I have followed this latter approach. More specifically, I have given attention to the dislocations of character existing at two "levels" in the work – the surface plot and the underlying fantasy, which in Richardson are not always consistent with one another; for Richardson is not always a fantasist in creating his characters. I do, however, regard the novels – including *Pamela* and its sequel – as more unified psychologically than has been recognized. In general, I have departed from certain psychoanalytic critics in regarding the deeper level of fantasy as primary in our experience of the character, when in fact such an underlying fantasy exists in the characterization.

In many paragraphs I have written about characters as though they were consistent, living psychological beings, though such analysis proceeds always by analogy, which implies differences between reality and fiction as well as similarities. I have kept in mind that no single approach accounts totally for a character. The interests of the novels are various, never single, and I have not tried to account for all of them. My concern is with the psychological patterns.

In the first chapter I outline the psychological approach to be taken. Following analysis of the four novels in light of Freud's theory of masochism and related theories, I consider the "sentimental" treatment of character and action that Richardson bequeathed to later writers; I also consider the relationship between sentimentality and sadism – first suggested by Goethe – and the problem of character in fiction, generally, in light of these various ideas. In the concluding chapter on Richardson and D. H. Lawrence I give attention to the special problems of psychological realism, and characters of modern psychological fiction.

Most of this book was written and parts of it were published (in different form) before the appearance of the studies by Margaret Anne Doody, Cynthia Griffin Wolff, and Mark Kinkead-Weekes. I have made acknowledgment to ideas of theirs used in revising the manuscript for publication; I owe a particular debt to Kinkead-Weekes's account of the dramatic action of *Clarissa.* Judith Wilt's article, "He Could Go No Farther: A Modest Proposal about Lovelace and Clarissa," PMLA, 92 (January 1977), appeared too late for me to discuss.

I am grateful to the editors of the following journals for permission to reprint the following articles in revised and expanded form:

"The Symbolism of Lawrence's *The Fox,*" *CLA Journal,* XI (1967); "Richardson's *Pamela*: 'Conflicting Trends,'" *American Imago,* XXVIII (1971); "Lovelace's Dream," *Literature and Psychology,* XX (1970); and "Character and Fantasy in Richardson's *Sir Charles Grandison,*" *Connecticut Review,* VII (1973). I am grateful also to Wayne State University Press for permission to reprint the article, "Lovelace's Dream." I owe special thanks to my colleague, John Phillipson, University of Akron, for advice on an earlier draft of this study.

Chapter One

THE PROBLEM FOR CRITICISM

1

A puzzling aspect of Richardson is the indefinite yet compelling sense of fatality that governs his major characters, with the possible exception of Sir Charles Grandison. Though the social and religious contexts of the idea of fate in the eighteenth century are well known, fatality and a peculiar determinism in Richardson, and in addition the gross disparity between fortune and deserts, remain mysterious. The social subordination of women and the conventions governing their behavior, family structure and domestic arrangements, Puritan norms of character and moral responsibility – these are indispensable to an understanding of plot and details of character. Yet neither singly nor together do these contexts and norms account for Richardson's distinctive treatment of character and development of plot, both of which are shaped by a never fully stated conception of fatality.

Perhaps the most remarkable instance of it occurs in the third quarter of *Clarissa.* Following her escape to Hampstead from a London house in which Lovelace has kept her confined (the house is in fact a brothel), Clarissa is tricked into returning to the city in the company of hired women posing as Lovelace's aunt and his cousin, Lady Betty and Charlotte Montague. Lovelace insists on making a stop at the house from which Clarissa had escaped, and waiting in the carriage Clarissa's apprehension increases. She realizes that she is to be lured back into the house, and she feels helpless to save herself. Her fears shortly become a reality: she is drugged by Lovelace's accomplices and helped out of the carriage and into the house, in which later the same night she is finally raped. Though Clarissa has resisted Lovelace's advances successfully in previous scenes, the rape seems to be foreknown and unavoidable.

In his letter to his friend Belford the same day, Lovelace exults in how he tricked Clarissa: "I'll teach the dear charming creature to emulate me in contrivance! I'll teach her to weave webs and plots against her conqueror! I'll show her, that in her smuggling schemes she is but a spider compared to me, and that she has all this time been spinning only a cobweb!"[1] Clarissa's own account to her friend Miss Howe, weeks later, stresses her feeling of paralysis and doom:

> But think, my dear, what a dreadful turn all had upon me, when, through several streets and ways I knew nothing of, the coach slackening its pace, came within sight of the dreadful house of the dreadfullest woman in the world, as she proved to me. . . .
>
> Dreadfully did my heart then misgive me: I was ready to faint. Why this terror, my life? You shall not stir out of the coach – but one question, now the fellow has drove us this way. . . .
>
> My heart misgave me beyond the power of my own accounting for it; for still I did not suspect these women. But the antipathy I had taken to the vile house, and to find myself so near it, when I expected no such matter, with the sight of the old creature [the keeper of the house, Mrs. Sinclair], made me behave like a distracted person. . . .
>
> Again the pretended Miss Montague urged me; standing up as ready to go out if I would give her room. Lord, my dear, said she, who can bear this crowd? What will people think?
>
> The pretended lady again pressed me, with both her hands held out – Only, my dear, to give orders about your things.
>
> And thus pressed, and gazed at (for then I looked about me), the women so richly dressed, people whispering; in an evil moment, out stepped I, trembling, forced to lean with both my hands (frightened too much for ceremony) on the pretended Lady Betty's arm – O that I had dropped down dead upon the guilty threshold! (III, 364-67)

A few pages later Clarissa describes the moments before the rape, and finishes with these words:

> I remember I pleaded for mercy. I remember that I said *I would be his – indeed I would be his* – to obtain his mercy. But no mercy found I! My strength, my intellects, failed me – and then such scenes followed – O my dear, such dreadful scenes! – fits upon fits (faintly indeed and imperfectly remembered) procuring me no compassion – but death was withheld from me. That would have been too great a mercy! (III, 371)

"What a fatality, my dear, has appeared in your case, from the very

1. *Clarissa,* Everyman edition (London: J. M. Dent, 1932), III, 191. Subsequent references in the text are to this edition.

beginning till this hour! ", Miss Howe writes, on receiving this letter (III, 377). Clarissa indeed has had intimations of her fate even before she leaves her parents' house, tricked by Lovelace, and with him makes a slow journey to London. Though earlier she has only vague suspicions of his true character, she dreams that Lovelace has discovered her complicity in a plot against him by members of her family, and kills her: "I thought he made them all fly into foreign parts upon it; and afterwards seizing upon me, carried me into a churchyard; and there, notwithstanding all my prayers and tears, and protestations of innocence, stabbed me to the heart, and then tumbled me into a deep grave ready dug, among two or three half-dissolved carcasses; throwing in the dirt and earth upon me with his hands, and trampling it down with his feet" (I, 433). The dream foreshadows later events, culminating in Clarissa's second (and successful) escape from the London house, and soon afterwards her death. Whatever guilt she bears in leaving her parents' house to avoid marriage to a man she despises, and in failing to perceive the character of Lovelace to whom she imprudently entrusts her safety, nothing she has done is deserving of the suffering she endures. Nor does Richardson allow the reader to believe that the rape is punishment for imprudent acts. Yet Clarissa not only regards her suffering as deserved but accepts it as destined. Her pious comment, in one of her last letters, that roses do not grow without thorns (IV, 277) is typical of her general attitude toward life. Puritan guilt and pious reflection contribute to these feelings but do not fully explain their intensity.

It is equally surprising that Mr. B., Pamela's abductor, truly aggressive in his feelings though he is clumsy in his attempted assaults upon her, should characterize the rape he intends to perform as "the dreadful time of reckoning" – as if some vicious quality in Pamela or act that she has performed deserves nothing less.[2] Pamela no doubt contributes to this impression, for she looks for causes of her torment in personal qualities that, like Clarissa's, are not represented as vicious. During her captivity she responds in this typical way to a letter of B.'s: "I sat ruminating, when I had a little come to myself, upon the terms of this wicked letter: and had no inclination to look into my own. The bad names, *fool's plaything, artful creature, paint-*

2. *Pamela,* Everyman edition (London: J. M. Dent, 1962), I, 178. Subsequent references in the text are to this edition.

ed bauble, gewgaw, speaking picture, are hard words for your poor Pamela; and I began to think whether I was not a very naughty body, and had not done vile things. . . . Then how dreadful are the words, he will *decide my fate* in three weeks! " (I, 142) Consistent with these fatalistic and unmotivated self-accusations, her behavior after B. gives up his pursuit and proposes marriage is almost immediately submissive: Pamela acquiesces in whatever interpretation B. wishes to make of her character. Readers have found many of her statements hypocritical, as in her response to B.'s suggestion that she has reason to feel resentment against one of his servants, Mrs. Jewkes, who abused and struck her: "Sir . . . you are so kind that I ought to forgive every body; and when I see that my happiness is brought about by the very means I once thought my greatest grievance, I ought to bless those means, and forgive all that was disagreeable to me at the same time, for the great good that hath issued from it" (I, 269). Her moral confusion is perhaps most evident in this later passage:

> Henceforth let not us poor short-sighted mortals pretend to rely on our own wisdom; or vainly think, that we are absolutely to direct for ourselves. I have great reason to say, that, when I was most disappointed, I was nearer my happiness: for had I made my escape, which was so often my chief point in view, and what I placed my heart upon, I had escaped the blessings now before me, and fallen, perhaps, headlong into the miseries I would have avoided. And yet after all, it was necessary I should take the steps I did, to bring on this wonderful turn: O the unsearchable wisdom of God! (I, 276-77)

A number of explanations have been offered for statements like these; one is that the feminine code in Richardson's time forbade the woman to admit love for a man until he had proposed marriage (Richardson states the essentials of this view in a widely-read *Rambler* paper in 1751).[3] It remains to be explained why, then, so many of the first readers of the novel missed this point. Even if one grants that Pamela has courted the treatment she receives from B. and his servants – and it is difficult to find convincing evidence for this interpretation – there is clearly no established relationship between the promised reckoning and the deserts of hypocritical behavior. The threat of rape is punishment for willful or scornful behavior – or the

3. Ian Watt, *The Rise of the Novel* (Berkeley: University of California Press, 1962), p. 167; cf. p. 155.

rejection of an ardent lover – only in fantasy. Pamela's intense fatalism is deeply invested in fantasy; left unexplained in the novel, it takes on the appearance of hypocrisy.

The passages quoted suggest that Richardson's women suffer from an indefinite guilt that must be expiated; the motives of guilt are usually vague and tentative. The notable instance in *Sir Charles Grandison* is one of the dual heroines, Lady Clementina della Porretta, who becomes temporarily deranged after she refuses Grandison's proposal of marriage. More so than Pamela, Clementina is a figure of fantasy, little credible in comparison to the other heroine of the novel, the English Harriet Byron, and to Grandison's willful sister Charlotte. Clementina's loss of Grandison is associated with beating fantasies and death wishes; at one point in the novel she dreams of stumbling over Grandison's body in an orange grove.[4] Toward the end of the novel, she recovers and tells Grandison that her derangement was God's punishment for her pride and that she must submit to His justice. Her motive in refusing Grandison's proposal, however, clearly has nothing to do with pride; the ostensible reason is that she cannot marry a Protestant, but something else interests Richardson. His demonstration that her sacrifice of Grandison and the cruel treatment she suffers during her derangement have ennobled her character is the central interest, and suggests a fantasy similar to that underlying Pamela's statements and actions.

The social inferiority of women and their proper subordination to fathers, brothers and husbands are specified norms in the four novels. Pamela states the normative view in the sequel, in referring to the Biblical injunction that, owing to the curse on Eve's disobedience, the woman is not to "usurp authority over the man" and is subject to her husband (II, 206). This explanation is at best partial; for Richardson's men often express identical feelings of guilt and anxiety. Lovelace is haunted by a fatality that not only drives him to an act of rape but also hunts him to the grave. "Fate, I believe, in my conscience, spins threads for tragedies, on purpose for thee to weave with" (IV, 450), he writes Belford. His dying words to Clarissa's cousin Morden return to this theme: "There is a fate in it! . . . a cursed fate! – or this could not have been! But be ye all witnesses that I have provoked my destiny . . ." (IV, 529). Similar feelings

4. *Sir Charles Grandison* (London: Oxford University Press, 1972), Part 2, Volume III, 241. Subsequent references in the text are to this edition.

occur in the whole novel. In *Grandison,* Harriet Byron's abductor Sir Hargrave Pollexfen – whose aim is marriage, not rape – is later wounded in France, in the course of aiding Bagenhall in an attempted seduction, and at the end of the novel, stricken with remorse, dies. Richardson dramatizes his death, his self-recrimination echoing Lovelace:

> My despondency is, must be, of the blackest kind. It is blacker than remorse: It is all repining; but no repentance; I cannot, cannot repent . . . . Lord! Lord! Lord! what a hand have I made of it, for the last three or four years of my life! who might have reached Threescore-and-ten with comfort! whereas now, at Twenty-eight, I am on the very brink of the grave. It appears to me as ready dug: It yawns for me: I am neither fit to die, not to live. My days are dreadful: My nights are worse: My bed is a bed of nettles, and not of down. Not one comfortable thought, not one good action, to revolve, in which I had not some vile gratification to promote! Wretched man! It is come home to me, with a vengeance. (3, VI, 142-43)

The nemesis that pursues Richardson's men and women alike, bringing pain and infrequent blessing and happiness, is difficult to explain entirely through social conventions and through the Puritan code that insists on the punishment, equally, of sexual libertinism and unconscious wishes. More than one critic has noted a discrepancy between surface pieties and underlying tensions against which Richardson needed to defend strongly. A. M. Kearney, commenting on the occasional confusion of voices in *Pamela,* suggests that the formal qualities of the epistolary style tend to refine the "inflaming" scenes: "No one in fact was as conscious of indecency in literature as Richardson, though his very preoccupation with it suggests some ambivalence."[5]

Examined in light of psychoanalytic ideas, the fatality that haunts Richardson's characters becomes much less mysterious. We shall see that it resembles the fate associated with the Oedipus complex, and more generally is associated with the incestuous object-choices men and women undergo in the course of maturation.[6] Freud uses the word *Fate* with a larger meaning in mind: his reference is to the

5. "Richardson's *Pamela*: The Aesthetic Case," in John Carroll, ed., *Samuel Richardson: A Collection of Critical Essays* (Englewood Cliffs, New Jersey: Prentice-Hall, 1969), p. 31.

6. Sigmund Freud, "A Child Is Being Beaten," *Standard Edition of the Complete Psychological Works* (London: The Hogarth Press, 1954-74), Volume XVII, 168. Subsequent references to Freud in the text are to this edition ["S.E."].

primitive and mythological. Yet the feelings represented in their much different contexts are much the same. The formulation especially pertinent to Richardson occurs in Freud's important essay of 1924, "The Economic Problem of Masochism," to which we will return frequently in this study. The essential idea is the following: With the increasing severing of relations between the child and his parents, their imagos are joined with those of other authority figures, including heroic people that the child wishes to emulate. Fate is the ultimate figure of authority: "The last figure in the series that began with the parents is the dark power of Destiny which only the fewest of us are able to look upon as impersonal" (S.E., XIX, 168). These relationships are responsible for the several kinds of masochism in people, and Freud's analysis of these kinds sheds light on qualities noted in Richardson's characters. More specifically, the fatality which governs their lives is consistent with what Freud distinguishes as "moral masochism." In contrast to "erotogenic" and "feminine masochism," moral masochism tempts the person to sin and draws upon him "the reproaches of the sadistic conscience . . . or by chastisement from the great parental power of Destiny" (S.E., XIX, 169). Freud concludes: "In order to provoke punishment from this last representative of the parents, the masochist must do what is inexpedient, must act against his own interests, must ruin the prospects which open out to him in the real world and must, perhaps, destroy his own real existence" (S.E., XIX, 169-70).

Though Freud implies that masochism need not be neurotic – an important qualification in speculating about the psychological insight of a writer – the weight of his concern is with the neurotic and the pathological. To summarize his view of masochism briefly, the child overcomes the Oedipus complex by introjecting the parental imagos, joining these imagos to those of the other figures mentioned. These imagos comprise the desexualized moral imperatives instituted in the superego. Moral masochism is essentially a regression to the Oedipus complex, the result of which is the unconscious resexualization of morality. Though the moral masochist denies himself pleasure and endures suffering at the hands of Fate, Destiny, or God, the underlying motives of his behavior are Oedipal and therefore strongly sexualized – like those of feminine masochism, to be discussed shortly. Whatever disagreement there is among later psychoanalytic writers on the origin and significance of moral masochism (one prevailing theory is that masochism originates in pre-genital disturbances), these writers agree with Freud's general characterization.

But one important addition to the general theory should be noted. Reik and Grunberger observe that the docility commonly found in masochistic behavior disguises unconscious hostility and defiance. Reik states that though the masochist talks as if he is defeated he refuses to be so; he has made himself invincible by surrendering completely to authority and learning to endure privation and to exhaust the will of those who aggress against him. His total acquiescence renders his aggressors impotent.[7] Here may be the explanation for the strange mixture of qualities in Pamela that have been mistaken for hypocrisy.

Related to moral masochism in at least two of Richardson's characters, B. and Lovelace, is feminine masochism. The feminine masochist, Freud states, imagines himself in situations characteristic of women: among these are giving birth and performing the passive role in sexual intercourse. He differs from the moral masochist in the overtly erotic content of fantasies:

> We have sufficient acquaintance with this kind of masochism in men . . . derived from masochistic – and therefore often impotent – subjects whose phantasies either terminate in an act of masturbation or represent a sexual satisfaction in themselves. The real-life performances of masochistic perverts tally completely with these phantasies, whether the performances are carried out as an end in themselves or serve to induce potency and to lead to the sexual act. (S.E., XIX, 161-62)

Evidence of these trends in Richardson's characters is discovered primarily in complex displacements or fantasies and dreams (in *Clarissa*), and secondarily in voyeuristic behavior (in B. and Lovelace and their accomplices) which suggests a close identification with their victims. According to another psychoanalytic writer, Otto Fenichel, the voyeur is fixated on experiences that produce castration dread and exhibits "the hunger for screen experiences, that is, for experiences sufficiently like the original to be substituted for it; but differing in the essential point and thereby giving reassurances

7. Theodor Reik, *Masochism in Modern Man* (New York: Farrar and Rinehart, 1941), p. 164; Bela Grunberger, "Psychodynamic Theory of Masochism," in Sandor Lorand, ed., *Perversions: Psychodynamics and Therapy* (New York: Gramercy Books, 1956), pp. 192-93.

that there is no danger."[8] It is not surprising that several critics of Richardson offer a similar explanation in discussing implied attitudes toward his characters and elicited responses. Watt's comment on *Clarissa* is typical: "Richardson's impersonal and anonymous role allowed him to project his own secret fantasies into a mysterious next room: and the privacy and anonymity of print placed the reader behind a keyhole where he, too, could peep unobserved and witness rape being prepared, attempted and eventually carried out. Neither the reader nor the author were violating any decorum . . . ."[9]

I shall try to show that the enormous power of Richardson's depiction of rape and its consequences, in *Clarissa,* and the much different exploration of related themes in *Pamela* and *Grandison,* derive from the sexualization of morality in moral masochism. His plots are energized by a series of nuclear fantasies Oedipal and masochistic. Other fantasies consistent with these are found in *Grandison,* and join this novel to the earlier three in important ways not recognized by critics.

The much debated sentimentality of Richardson's novels may be profitably examined in light of psychoanalytic ideas. In general, the sentimental novel of the later eighteenth century is concerned mainly with the emotional experience of the characters, which is assumed to reveal their true selves. Richardson is undoubtedly sentimental by this definition. Debate has centered rather on whether the eighteenth century sentimental view of inborn good feeling or benevolence – a view that developed in opposition to the Puritan and Stoic distrust of the emotions – is to be found in Richardson. The novels suggest that Richardson held intellectually to the view that good feeling is potential in people but must be educated and held in check; Grandison expresses this view more than once, and in Clementina and other characters we see the consequences of disordered feeling. A recent critic argues persuasively that the intensive portrayal of emotional experience from moment to moment is consistent with and probably was influenced by eighteenth century Puritan ideas: "All of life was, in some sense, a religious trial . . . hence the heroines, like their Puritan forerunners, tended to dwell upon the particulars of any given event. The anxiety which attaches particu-

8. *The Psychoanalytic Theory of Neurosis* (New York: W. W. Norton, 1945), p. 348.

9. *The Rise of the Novel,* p. 199.

larly to the seductions is a perfectly standard response to what was generally viewed as the most dangerous temptation man had to confront; it was important to record each such temptation because each was a possible occasion of sin."[10]

Psychoanalytic theory helps us to refine the characterization of Richardson as a sentimental novelist: we find in the novels the investment of moral and feminine masochism in plots that develop the intensely emotional experience of the characters. Either in the main or in subplots erotic feeling is courted and inevitably punished, the pursuing nemesis of predator and victim depicted according to familiar eighteenth century Puritan ideas.

These trends further suggest a relationship between sentimentality and sadism. Indeed, we find in Richardson, and in later writers as various as Goethe, Dickens and Lawrence, a typical treatment of character and a typical structure or plot that suggest a special genre of the psychological novel. We shall consider this new treatment of character and plot later in this study. The idea of fatality, which we have been examining, continues to be of concern to psychological novelists – to Lawrence particularly – and, as we shall see, helps to explain the intense repetitiveness that joins the rhythm of *Sons and Lovers* to *Clarissa* and other sentimental novels.

2

Psychological studies of the novels have turned on assumptions about Richardson the man – on the depiction of the characters as a revelation of Richardson's ideas (Golden is a notable exception). A popular view of psychological critics is that Richardson created sadistic men with whom he sometimes identified (as we noted, Golden calls attention to the masochism of Lovelace and other male characters, but stresses the apparent sadism of the "bold young men"). Ian Watt's view that Clarissa is the masochistic female who complements the sadistic male is typical. Leslie Fiedler similarly comments that Clarissa is "a projection of male guilt before the female treated as a mere sexual object," and he identifies Lovelace and Clarissa as "the male principle and the female, savior and Devil, aristocracy and bourgeoisie . . . the head and the heart – what we would call now super-

10. Wolff, *Samuel Richardson and the Eighteenth-Century Puritan Character*, p. 23.

ego and . . . id."[11] Even critics whose approach to Richardson is historical rather than psychological call attention to his frequent ambivalence.

Modern rhetorical criticism has made us aware that discovery of the man behind the work is a difficult job, perhaps an impossible one. The most thorough exposition of the difficulties is that of Wayne Booth, who shows that the "implied author" as he prefers to call him must be distinguished from the actual writer. Not only cannot the feelings and attitudes of the writer be the same from work to work, but he may reveal a self in his various writings that he cannot reveal in ordinary life.[12] Still, the effort to characterize the writer behind the work is a preoccupation of critics. Discovering the "meaning" of a work depends on a definition of the work's "self" or "persona" in relation to implied values.

Rhetorical theories and approaches that seek to do this and thereby solve the problem of "meaning" range from the New Critical definition of meaning as a total disclosure of the "norms" of the work (the thrust of W. K. Wimsatt's essay on the "concrete universal") to Booth's neo-Aristotelian conception of the "implied author," and Kenneth Burke's "symbolic action" – a structure identifiable with the motives of the author: "Now, the work of every writer contains a set of implicit equations. He uses 'associational clusters.' . . . There is no need to 'supply' motives. The interrelationships themselves *are* his motives. For they are his *situation*; and *situation* is but another word for *motives.*"[13]

In his essay on "anaesthetic criticism," Frederick Crews advances beyond these ideas. The author, Crews suggests, is a "represented mind" – not to be discovered exactly in the writer's biography, and to be understood best as a kind of "negative capability," limited by inevitable personal conflicts that arise in the process of composition: "The ego-state suffusing the work must borrow heavily from the 'countercathected system' – that is, the cluster of defenses preventing inadmissible actions and expressions – that make up the

11. *The Rise of the Novel,* pp. 232, 237; *Love and Death in the American Novel* (New York: Criterion Books, 1960), pp. 41, 34-35.

12. *The Rhetoric of Fiction* (Chicago: University of Chicago Press, 1961), pp. 73-74.

13. *The Philosophy of Literary Form* (New York: Vintage Books, 1957), p. 18.

author's habitual character, and his career will escape redundancy only to the degree that he can vary his defenses."[14] Biographical and historical information provide at best negative evidence, limiting and qualifying generalizations about the writer and his work.

Rhetorical critics agree that biographical information, when available, is always difficult to assess. The usual assumption in biographical studies is that all information at hand is pertinent to the problem under investigation. In the same way, historical studies concerned with the writer's mind and imagination tend to assume that his employment of genres or contemporary philosophy (eighteenth century Deism or twentieth century existentialism) entails his perception, understanding and personal engagement. Studies concerned with the creative process combine both of these approaches in assuming that the writer's imagination can be discovered in the transformations and changes of source materials; as in John Livingston Lowes' famous study of Coleridge, imagination is identified with the process by which the fusion of materials occurs.

Psychoanalytic critics early attempted to read the mind of the writer directly from the work – a practice sponsored by Freud in his essays on Leonardo and Dostoevsky, and carried further by Ernest Jones, Marie Bonaparte and others, with debatable success. And much more was made of the transformations and creative process; for Freud, in describing these by analogy with the dream-work, named what Romantic critics throughout the nineteenth century had made mysterious – in defining the imagination by analogy with the presumed faculties of religious experience. Freud did something even more significant: he looked to the reader for an understanding both of the writer and of his characters – more specifically, to the defenses which the reader erects in the course of experiencing the literary work, defenses which the writer must deal with, if not overcome. Indeed the structure of the literary work is read out of these defenses. This rhetorical approach is proving a more useful one.

To be more specific, Freud joins author and reader psychology in his consideration of psychopathological drama, in his essay "Psychopathic Characters on the Stage," and in his general comments on art in the later essay "Creative Writers and Daydreaming." In psychpathological drama, he suggests, the hero becomes ill, in con-

14. Frederick Crews, ed., *Psychoanalysis and Literary Process* (Cambridge, Mass.: Winthrop Publishers, 1970), p. 20.

trast to other heroes in drama; he is not ill from the beginning of the play. Hamlet is his example. At the point of illness reader and character psychology join. The audience, disposed to the same neurosis as the character, becomes ill in the course of identifying with the passional suffering of the hero. (S.E., VII, 309) Freud, in the later essay, treats the author as the spectator of his own work; dividing his ego into "many part-egos," he personifies "the conflicting currents of his own mental life in several heroes" (S.E., IX, 150). This splitting, he states in his even later essay on "the uncanny," creates a feeling of uncertainty over whether the writer has drawn us into the real world or into "a purely fantastic one of his own creation" (S.E., XVII, 230). It is the underlying patterns of the work that readers intuit: and to "overwhelm" us with the representation of "secret motives," the artist employs a rhetoric of concealment. Freud states in the essay "Some Character Types Met With in Psychoanalytic Work": "It is in fact a case of multiple motivation, in which a deeper motive comes into view behind the more superficial one. Laws of poetic economy necessitate this way of presenting the situation, for this deeper motive could not be explicitly enunciated. It had to remain concealed, kept from the easy perception of the spectator or the reader; otherwise serious resistances, based on the most distressing emotions, would have arisen, which might have imperilled the effect of the drama" (S.E., XIV, 329).

The defenses of the literary work – particularly in those genres which tend to deal with distressing emotions – are of increasing concern to the psychoanalytic critic. In his reference to "the significance of fixed genres with their coded assurance that psychic activity will be patterned and resolved along familiar lines," Crews suggests how the writer's handling of a particular genre may be analyzed. Crews adds: "For this very reason, however, art that strives for originality is always restless within its formal borders and frequently generates new forms."[15]

A related and important problem for criticism is the kind of transformation that occurs in the reader. This consideration is basic to Norman Holland's analysis of literary experience, in his important study of reader psychology. Holland suggests that the job of the structure of the literary work is to manage anxiety so that the reader achieves the greatest possible enjoyment of the fantasy. His for-

15. Ibid., pp. 20-21.

mulation of this idea is a development of Freud's important insight: "The literary work, through what we have loosely termed 'form,' acts out defensive maneuvers for us: splitting, isolating, undoing, displacing from, omitting (repressing or denying) elements of the fantasy. Meaning, whether we find it or supply it, acts more like a sublimation: giving the fantasy material a disguised expression which is acceptable to the ego, which 'makes sense.' "[16] Like Crews, Holland treats genres as "defensive patterns." These contribute important features to the literary structure. Another feature is discovered in the conflicting trends that generate anxiety and at the same time relieve it.

The rhetorical problem is surely the most complex that the psychological critic of Richardson faces. For characters are shaped according to the expectations of his readers, by the defenses he felt impelled to make, and by the possibilities of fantasy he intuited in the character types provided by the genres he had chosen to work with. Margaret Anne Doody finds in the Richardson novel "the rhythm of constriction-expansion" – a rhythm shaped by the expectations as well as by the inherent form of the epistolary novel.[17] The epistolary narrative, into which Richardson fitted the characters typical of early eighteenth century tragic drama, made possible a progressive development of character and thereby what Doody refers to as an "image of freedom": the character finds himself alone, facing his emotions and his real self.[18]

We shall see that, though Richardson shaped his plots and fitted his character to a general design, his characterization is often an improvisation of qualities fitted to the fantasy of the moment and subsequently rationalized.[19] This qualification means that the novels cannot be read as finished wholes. For example, it is not possible to state finally whether B. has meant to harm Pamela or whether Lovelace dies repentant; it is possible only to distinguish trends of character fitted, not always consistently, to a general action. Even the

16. *The Dynamics of Literary Response* (New York: Oxford University Press, 1968), p. 189.

17. *A Natural Passion: A Study of the Novels of Samuel Richardson,* p. 63.

18. Ibid., p. 11.

19. George Sherburn has analyzed particular changes that occurred in the surface rendering of character, in " 'Writing to the Moment': One Aspect," in *Samuel Richardson: A Collection of Critical Essays,* pp. 152-60.

intellectual content of the novels – the lectures and little sermons of Pamela and Grandison on education, luxury, dress and other such topics – seem improvised. One of their purposes is to define social relationships, not to advance the plot; when this is their sole purpose, they are unimportant to the action. Such improvisation of character forces Richardson to employ a rhetoric of concealment which rationalizes the deeper interests of character and action. Clearly, a traditional genre, with its fixed interests, plot devices and rhythms, promotes this rationalization and an increasingly free character development.

Richardson was compelled by the fictional genre he had adopted to follow the course of feelings of his narrators. But he was also compelled to do more, as Mrs. Barbauld noted in her life of Richardson which introduces the correspondence:

> That letters should be written at all times, and upon every occasion in life, that those letters should be preserved, and altogether form a connected story, it requires much art to render specious. It introduces the inconvenience so much felt in dramatic writing, for want of a narrator; the necessity of having an insipid confidant to tell the circumstances to that an author cannot relate in any other way. It obliges a man to tell of himself, what perhaps no man would tell; and sometimes to repeat compliments which modesty would lead him to suppress: and when a long conversation is repeated, supposes a memory more exact than is generally found. Artificial as it therefore is, still as it enables an author to assume, in a lively manner, the hopes and fears, and passions, and to imitate the peculiar way of thinking of his characters, it became fashionable, and has been adopted by many both at home and abroad . . . .[20]

In other words, the epistolary novel called for an art of concealment and made possible for writers a special identification with their characters. The strategies needed to tell the story provide, then, a particularly rich opportunity to explore the "defensive strategies" of interest to the psychologcial critic.

How much can a rhetoric of concealment tell us? What is it likely to imply? In C. P. Snow's *The New Men,* a remarkable study of the psychology of English nuclear scientists, the narrator Lewis Eliot reflects on the character of his brother, a scientist who has become aware of the destructive possibilities of atomic energy: "He was more moved than Mounteney who, despite his cantankerousness, was a

20. *The Correspondence of Samuel Richardson,* ed. Anna Laetitia Barbauld (London, 1804), Volume I, xvii.

gentle man, to whom any kind of cruelty seemed like a visitation from another planet. Mounteney had never had to struggle with a sadic strain in his own nature. It is men who have had to struggle so who hate cruelty most."[21] To state the paradox in relation to the moralizing novelist, systematic moralizing is frequently a compensatory activity – a defense against unknown inner qualities. Certainly, the letters and novels reveal these occasional qualities: an acute sensitivity to criticism, seen in Richardson's eagerness to respond to charges against his characters (often at considerable length); his capacity for self-ridicule; an acute sensitivity to and hatred of pain and mental anguish. But this is all that can be said or known.[22]

Some or all of these qualities are of course found in gifted writers who immerse themselves in the suffering of their characters. Edmund Bergler suggests that the writer of what he terms "full talent" deals with "the most decisive human motivation: unconscious psychic masochism." Indeed the conflict he undergoes is basically "undigested masochistic passivity" associated with infantile experiences with the mother. *"Objective psychological truth" coincides with the subjective defense needed by the writer in his struggle with his nature at the moment he writes.*[23] K. R. Eissler reaches a similar conclusion in his study of Goethe: the more intense masochism of the artist of genius produces a lessened defense against pain. The work of art is his main defense, once the pain becomes so great that it must be resisted. In resisting pain through creative activity, the genius differs from the moral masochist, who succeeds in enduring suffering by unconsciously resexualizing it.[24]

These are general characterizations of the creative artist, not per-

21. *The New Men* (New York: Scribner's, 1954), pp. 85-86.
22. Richardson wrote to Lady Bradshaigh towards the start of their friendship: "And from this odd, this grotesque figure, think you, Madam, that you have any thing to apprehend? Any thing that will not rather promote than check your mirth? I dare be bold to say (and allow it too) that you would rather see this figure than any other you ever saw, whenever you should find yourself graver than you wish to be." John Carroll, ed., *Selected Letters of Samuel Richardson* (Oxford: Clarendon Press, 1964), p. 136.
23. "Writers of Half-Talent," *American Imago,* 14 (1957), 155; *The Writer and Psychoanalysis* (New York: Doubleday, 1950), pp. 81, 238.
24. *Goethe: A Psychoanalytic Study* (Detroit: Wayne State University Press, 1963), p. 1384.

sonal ones. The limits of interpretation are evident in the conclusions about Richardson that we began with. It is surely significant that, according to Freud, fantasies sadistic in form may be masochistic in their gratification (S.E., XVII, 190-91). If this statement is true, then the sadistic trends which Richardson's critics have focused on may be superficial; the characters and their situations may have been imagined masochistically. The idea of fatality, illustrated earlier, indeed suggests what Reik terms the masochistic "flight forward" to a dreaded event as a way of allaying anxiety. The specific defenses that we find in the novels – and the idea of fatality is one of these – can be analyzed; but what the defense was for Richardson personally we cannot know.

The defenses and trends of character to be analyzed suggest the following: Surface character is often a "defensive maneuver" – to use Holland's phrase – a way of exploring (sometimes through negation, at other times displacement and condensation) erotic themes common to men and women. Whether arising from qualities in Richardson or absorbed from a diverse culture, his rigorous moralism is, intellectually, a quasi-primitivist view to which he consistently adheres: the good man – the feeling man – stands in opposition to a calloused society, damaged by its surrender to erotic experience and its attendant cruelties, and needing reform.

In Richardson's characters feelings of guilt disguised as an aggressive piety become the instrument of Fate – indeed, are identified with it – in the surface plot. The coincidence of this conception of Fate with the much different fatality of the nuclear fantasy that energizes the plot produces the remarkable form of the novels. In this coincidence of a Puritan nemesis and fantastic cause and effect, morality resexualized at the deeper level of experience, the social critic and the psychologist in Richardson meet.

Chapter Two

"CONFLICTING TRENDS" IN *PAMELA*

1

A peculiarity of *Pamela* is that, for a time after B. abducts his dead mother's maid-servant, keeps her a prisoner in his house in Lincolnshire, attempts to rape her, then seems to undergo a change of heart and proposes marriage, Richardson keeps alive the possibility that he has arranged a mock-marriage. B.'s character remains somewhat unknown; the reader is never quite certain of what he will do.

Though inflamed with love, B. regards Pamela as a "subtle, artful gypsey" (I, 17), a "little hypocrite" who has "all the arts of her sex; they were *born* with her" (I, 24). Given this view of her character, we have no reason to question why he feels justified in pursuing her by any means. He has reason, indeed, to believe that Pamela is not indifferent to him. B. makes several advances to her at his mother's house in Bedfordshire, forcing kisses upon her, putting his hand on her bosom and tearing her gown, and spying upon her: Pamela writes: "I just remember I got into the room; for I knew nothing further of the matter till afterwards; for I fell into a fit with my terror, and there I lay, till he, as I suppose, looking through the keyhole, espied me upon the floor, stretched out at length, on my face . . ." (I, 20). Despite these threats, Pamela finds reasons not to leave the house and return to her parents – at one point questioning the housekeeper, Mrs. Jervis: "but do you think if I was to ask to stay, that he is sorry for what he has done? – aye, and *ashamed* of it too; for I am sure he ought, considering his high degree, and my low degree, and that I have nothing in the world to trust to but my honesty" (I, 29).

That Pamela is half-dreaming of a proper relationship with her employer is suggested, in the scenes in Bedfordshire, by her reporting the cook's remark that she has the "fine face" of a lady and may come to something (I, 31). In a later scene she reflects on the vagueness of love: "Is it not strange that love borders so much upon hate? But this wicked love is not like the true virtuous love, to be sure: *that* and *hatred* must be far off as *light* and *darkness.* And how must this hate have been increased if he had met with a base compliance, after his wicked will had been gratified! " (I, 40) In the course of these scenes, she delays her departure on the excuse that she requires proper clothes to return to her parents and needs time to make them herself. Perhaps realizing that her delay is deliberate, B. feels teased and is increasingly driven by frustration and rage. His exchange with Pamela over the clothing reveals the tensions of the moment: "You may well . . . turn away your cursed face; I wish I had never seen it! " (I, 36) When she appears in her new clothing, his temper is inflamed further; he tells Mrs. Jervis that Pamela is a slut with the power of witchcraft: "I offered to go away; for I believe he wanted me to ask to stay in my place, for all this his great wrath; and he said, 'Stay here, stay here, when I bid you! ' and snatched my hand. I trembled, and said, 'I will! I will! ' for he hurt my fingers he grasped me so hard" (I, 36).

Shortly afterwards, he hides in a closet, in the room she is sharing with Mrs. Jervis, and springs upon her as she undresses, with Mrs. Jervis about to fall asleep on the other side of the bed: "I pulled off my stays, and my stockings, and all my clothes to an under-petticoat; then hearing a rustling again in the closet, 'Heaven protect us! But before I say my prayers I must look into this closet.' And so was going to it slip-shod, when, O dreadful! out rushed my master in a rich silk and silver morning-gown" (I, 49). His ambush proves unsuccessful, for Pamela screams and faints. The intensity of the scene – in particular, the seriousness of the threat to Pamela is reduced by the presence of Mrs. Jervis, whom B. threatens to throw out of the window. Nothing will happen while she is in the room. Richardson thus negates the fears he has aroused through a rather clumsy device of plot. This scene, and others like it in Bedfordshire, are important in preparing the reader for the Lincolnshire scenes – in which, for example, Pamela is threatened with being stripped of her clothes. In other words, Richardson is warning that Pamela is to become increasingly defenseless. Clumsy as his efforts in Bedfordshire may seem, neither B. nor the attempt he makes are comical in effect.

Immediately after this encounter, he arranges her abduction, imprisons her in the house in Lincolnshire, subjects her to rough treatment at the hands of his servants, begins to relent in his pursuit after a second unsuccessful attempt upon her, and finally proposes marriage. Though these scenes occupy less than a fourth of the novel, they are the most intense, bringing Pamela at one point to thoughts of suicide:

> God forgive me! but a sad thought came just then into my head! – I tremble to think of it! My apprehensions of the usage I should meet with, had like to have made me miserable for ever! O my dear, dear parents, forgive your poor child; but being quite desperate, I crept along, till I could raise myself on my staggering feet; and away limped I! – What to do, but to throw myself into the pond, and put a period to all my griefs in this world! – But O! to find them infinitely aggravated (had I not, by the Divine Grace, been withheld) in a miserable *eternity*! (I, 149)

Once B. begins to relent, the threat of rape (not merely ardent pursuit) should give way to new interests; indeed, the intensity of Pamela's reflection on suicide prepares the reader for this turn. Yet Richardson continues to play on fears of rape. Thus, after B.'s first hesitant proposal and his statement to Pamela that she "pray for the continuance of this temper" (I, 193), she receives a warning of a possible mock-marriage, in a letter dropped by a gypsy (actually written by B.'s steward Longman). The letter states that B. plans to hire a ruined attorney to impersonate a minister and perform the marriage ceremony (I, 198). Though no such person comes to the house, B.'s admission before the wedding that he did plot such a mock-marriage does not put the matter to rest. Though Pamela has reason to trust the minister, Mr. Williams, B.'s secrecy about the ceremony, which he insists on having performed in the house presumably to spare Pamela social embarrassment, and her slight but continuing apprehension that she is being deceived, keep these tensions faintly alive.

So does the sudden appearance soon after the ceremony of B.'s hot-tempered sister, Lady Davers, who is vehement in her suspicion that the marriage is irregular. The matter seems laid to rest only when B. assures his sister that the marriage is legitimate and thanks God that he came to abhor the plot against Pamela. (I, 380) B.'s secrecy, it should be noted, has nothing to do with Richardson's possible objection to ostentatious marriage ceremonies: B.'s scruple is rather to be explained by the turns of fantasy that mark these early and later pages.

But other tensions remain. In the course of a violent quarrel with his sister over the marriage, he berates Pamela for stooping to her and interfering in the argument: "how dare you approach me, without leave, when you see me thus disturbed! Never for the future come near me, when I am in these tumults, unless I send for you" (I, 393). Though his anger immediately subsides, partly because his frightened sister grows conciliatory and begs him to forgive Pamela, the episode warns that B. may still be dangerous.

Richardson's willingness to play on these fears, once Pamela's fortunes begin to rise, and so interrupt the rhythm of the novel, clearly shows that motives are to be understood at the level of dream and fantasy. The threat of rape is allowed to persist, and yet as in nightmare is forestalled. Indeed Richardson early in the novel alleviates anxiety about the outcome when he interrupts the narrative with the comment that Pamela wrote her letters as a journal, for a time "that she might afterwards thankfully look back upon the dangers she had escaped" (I, 82). The scenes that follow build in intensity, yet the reader's knowledge that no real harm will come to Pamela dampens it somewhat.

Other problems presented by the novel seem less intractable when we examine them in this light. A notorious problem is Pamela's inept efforts to escape from the house in Lincolnshire; to cite one notorious example, she thinks too late of using a ladder she observes resting against the garden wall. Another is the moral confusion on which so much critical attention has been focused – chiefly Pamela's seeming willingness to rationalize her situation and perform moral turnabouts. Before B. appears at the Lincolnshire house, she reveals in a letter that she is prepared to listen to proposals:

> O good Sir! I too much apprehend that *your* notions of honour and *mine* are very different from one another: I have no other hope but in your continued absence. If you have any proposals to make me that are consistent with your honourable professions, in my *humble* sense of the word, a few lines will communicate them to me, and I will return such an answer as befits me. But what proposals can one in your high station have to make to one in my low degree! I know what belongs to your exalted station too well, to imagine that any thing can be expected but sad temptations, and utter distress, if you come down: you know not, Sir, when I am made desperate what the wretched Pamela *dares do*! (I, 120)

Much later in the novel, when B. suggests that his servant Mrs. Jewkes, who mistreated Pamela, went beyond his orders in striking her, Pamela admits to having been "a little provoking," and asks him not to order the woman out of her sight: "when I see that my happiness is brought about by the very means I once thought my greatest grievance, I ought to bless those means, and forgive all that was disagreeable to me at the same time, for the great good that hath issued from it" (I, 269). Later, in the course of planning to share her good fortune with others, she comments on the change in B., his "kindness and fondness for me," and she adds:

> I am very glad of it; for it would rejoice me to be an humble means of making all mankind so; and, oh! what returns ought I not to make to the Divine goodness! and how ought I to strive to diffuse the blessings I experience, to all within my knowledge! – For else, what is it for such a worm as I to be exalted? What is my *single* happiness if I suffer it, niggardlike, to extend no further than to myself? But then, *indeed,* do God Almighty's creatures act worthy of the blessings they receive, when they make, or endeavour to make, the whole creation, so far as in the circle of their power, happy! (I, 325)

Many readers have been appalled or amused by Pamela's willingness to fall in with her wicked master's plans once he has proposed marriage. Her pious statement that she has been marked to share her good luck with those less fortunate makes the ways of God seem strange indeed.

We mentioned Watt's explanation of her seeming hypocrisy: Pamela is governed by a code that forbids her to admit her feelings for B. before he proposes and forces her to regard his sexual advances as horrifying. Watt refers to the "striking horror of any sexual advance until the conjugal knot is tied."[1] The contradictions in her feelings and behavior are more credible, however, in the dreamlike atmosphere and action of the early scenes in Lincolnshire. The reason Pamela does not seriously try to escape is that the logic of the everyday Bedfordshire world is irrelevant to her situation. The world of Lincolnshire, the entire forty days of her confinement have the feeling of nightmare: grazing cows become charging bulls; servants are seen as ogre-like warders in the employ of an invisible master, who when he appears after a long delay acts unpredictably and issues terrifying warnings. Richardson's imagination is fully active in these scenes; erotic themes are explored, at the same time that Richardson prepares to negate, in part by suggesting a better side to B.: "He clasped me to him with great ardour, and said, 'Hide your

1. *The Rise of the Novel,* p. 155.

dear face in my bosom, my beloved Pamela! your innocent freedoms charm me! – But then say, how well – what? " (I, 193)

Some of the "defensive maneuvers" that Richardson employs are consistent with Freud's theory of negation, a cornerstone of his formulation of mental life. The essential idea is that repressed ideas can become conscious only through their denial. The repression is taken account of and unblocked, but is not accepted. Thinking and feeling are at odds. (S.E., XIX, 237-39). Thus Pamela's erotic feelings can be expressed only by being transformed into pious reflection. For this reason, too, her actions verge on impotence. Trying to climb over the garden wall, she finds the bricks giving way and receives a blow on the head, also injuring her shins and an ankle. She remains on the ground for several minutes; fails two or three times to get up; discovers bruises, a hip and shoulder stiff and aching, and her head bleeding. Yet Richardson makes almost nothing of these injuries; they seem hardly to have occurred. Long after the threats to her virtue and physical being have vanished, a sense of emotional impotence remains. Pamela's predictable apprehension about the wedding night – in her words afterwards, of that "guest, that, however welcome, as now my duty teaches me to say, is yet dreadful to me to think of" (I, 311) – is not a sufficient explanation of her feelings. Before the ceremony, dressed in a white gown that was B.'s mother's, she slips and almost sprains her ankle (no mention here of earlier injuries), and is helped down the stairs by her former warder and enemy, Mrs. Jewkes: "She gave me very good words, and begged me to go: I got up: but my knees beat so against one another, I was forced to sit down again. At last I held by her arm, and, passing by Abraham, I said, 'This ugly slip, coming down stairs, has made me limp; so I must hold by you, Mrs. Jewkes. Do you know what alterations there are to be in the chapel, that we must give our opinions on them?' " (I, 308) The episode recalls Freud's statement that in dreams falling is "a way of describing a surrender to an erotic temptation" (S.E., V, 395).

Though the mode of comedy in later scenes and in the sequel will increasingly dominate, the scenes leading up to the marriage ceremony and the subsequent appearance of Lady Davers are in the tragic mode, chiefly to negate and ultimately deflect the erotic interests aroused and intermittently developed.

The dream-quality and ambivalence of these scenes helps to explain another difficulty of these pages – B.'s apparent sadism. For we see him almost entirely through Pamela, who exaggerates the menace of those characters who do his bidding and who appear unmenacing after tensions have been relieved. Though the voices in *Pamela* shift without explanation, as A. M. Kearney indicates, Richardson manages these altering perceptions of Pamela masterfully.

The essence of Pamela's fantasy in the Lincolnshire scenes is degradation, culminating in B.'s kissing and talk of torture and his threat to strip off her clothing if she does not show him her papers: "But I can tell you of as good a punishment. If a criminal won't plead with us here in England, we *press* him to death, or till he does plead. And so, Pamela, that is a punishment that shall certainly be yours, if you won't tell without" (I, 207). Discrepancies in his characterization – not associated with a fantasy such as this – continue into the sequel. Richardson knew that he had overdrawn the character, for later in the novel and in the sequel he rationalizes or denies B.'s sadism. Thus toward the end of the sequel Pamela insists to Mrs. Towers that her husband was never a "common town rake" and that his reformation resulted from his "sense" and "fine understanding" (II, 457). This is precisely the view B. takes of himself immediately after the attempted rape: he has never been "a very abandoned profligate" or done anything vile, he asserts; otherwise he would have gratified his passion for her instead of displaying remorse and pity. What should matter is that Pamela is as "inviolate a virgin" as when she entered his house (I, 188). Yet later he refers to his former life, implying that his career as a libertine had been extensive: "O how heartily I despise all my former pursuits, and headstrong appetites! What joys, what true joys, flow from virtuous love; joys which the narrow soul of the libertine cannot take in, nor his thought conceive! – And which I myself, whilst a libertine, had not the least notion of! " (I, 322)

These discrepancies might be taken to harm the characterization irreparably. Yet they do not. Though the possibility of further cruelty is intimated in B.'s flashes of strong temper, and previous offenses are hinted at later, like another reformed rake – Belford in *Clarissa* – he is not *shown* to succeed in rape. This is the decisive consideration, as is the virginity of the woman.

Richardson's willingness to disturb the emotional current and follow the turns of fantasy accounts in part for these conflicting trends of character. Though diverse in nature, they are represented through materials that prove finally compatible, as the relationship between Pamela and B. is worked out. Still, one constant of character can be distinguished. The persistence of strongly sadistic qualities in B. suggest a type encountered by Freud: the person in whom sadistic qualities disguise a feminine masochism with which genital activity is uneasily joined. This activity is shown in sadistic images and motifs and therefore appears to be dominant. In B. this trend of character is suggested in a series of displacements occurring in the first half of the novel. By contrast, the increasingly passive role that B. plays in the remainder of the novel and in the sequel may be interpreted as masochistic, with a suggestion of latent defiance.

To review Freud's theory of masochism in more detail: feminine masochism is based on primary, erotogenic masochism ("lust of pain") which passes through stages of libidinal development. These include the wish to be beaten by the father (in the anal-sadistic stage), castration fear (in the phallic stage), and fantasies associated with women (in the genital stage) – among these performing the woman's role in coitus and child bearing. Though sexual wishes seem to be absent in moral masochism and suffering appears to be endured for its own sake, the moral component of the experience – the conviction that the suffering is deserved – has actually been sexualized. Feminine masochism, like moral masochism, results from a failure to overcome the Oedipus complex through normal transference of libido to substitute love objects; it is essentially a regressive wish to enjoy sexual intercourse with the father, this wish serving as a means of overcoming the threat posed by the father in the child's earlier longing for the mother. The beating fantasies typical of feminine masochism are disguised expressions of this second wish. (S.E., "The Economic Problem of Masochism," XIX, 157-70) In " 'A Child is Being Beaten' " Freud suggests that the feminine masochist is sometimes able, tenuously, to join his masochism with genital activity (S.E., XVII, 196). Later psychoanalytic writers, as we noted earlier, suggest that feminine masochism may disguise defiance and hostility. This possibility has bearing on B.'s conduct.

B.'s enactment of what seems feminine masochistic fantasies combine with actions designed to overcome psychical impotence;

this state of mind is suggested indirectly by his declared aversion to marriage and his frequent misogynic statements, thus his comment on Pamela's letter to Parson Williams, who tried to help her: "The man who thinks a thousand dragons sufficient to watch a woman, when her inclination takes a contrary bent, will find all too little: she will engage the stones in the street, or the grass in the field, to act for her, and help on her correspondence" (I, 239).

Since Richardson does not provide inside views of B. in this part of the novel or extensive ones later (as he does of Lovelace, whose dreams and fantasies are fully disclosed), more direct evidence is discovered in his apparent voyeurism evident in the Bedfordshire bedroom scene and most obvious in the intense interest he takes in Pamela's journal. Even more significant are displacements of character, achieved through a duplication of episodes in Bedfordshire and Lincolnshire.

The chief of these displacements is the identification of B. with Mrs. Jewkes, his agent in the abduction, and before his appearance at the house on the thirty-sixth day of Pamela's confinement, his surrogate as her tormentor. In Golden's words, "B.'s alter ego,"[2] Mrs. Jewkes is a composite of many qualities, some of which increase and diminish in importance as the action progresses. In the early scenes she appears a strongly masculine figure. When Pamela first encounters her, during the journey to Lincolnshire, the woman imitates B.'s behavior in the opening scenes: "every now-and-then she would be staring in my face, in the chariot, and squeezing my hand, saying – 'Why, you are very pretty, my silent dear! ' And once she offered to kiss me. But I said – 'I don't like this sort of carriage, Mrs. Jewkes; it is not like two persons of one sex.' She fell a laughing very confidently, and said – 'That's prettily said, I vow! Then thou hadst rather be kissed by the other sex! I-fackins, I commend thee for that" (I, 91).

Her sexual interest in Pamela is not, however, developed in the scenes that follow: Richardson instead focuses on her sadistic qualities. She strikes Pamela several times, or threatens to strike her; after one hard slap, she kisses her as a sign of reconciliation (I, 108-09). She is described in these scenes as "broad, squat, pursy"; she has a "huge hand, and an arm as thick as my waist, I believe,"

2. *Richardson's Characters,* p. 18. For a contrasting view of B., see Mark Kinkead-Weekes, *Samuel Richardson, Dramatic Novelist,* 21-22, 49-53.

and "her brows grown down over her eyes." Pamela adds: "She has a hoarse man-like voice, and is as thick as she's long: and yet looks so deadly strongly, that I am afraid she would dash me at her foot in an instant, if I was to vex her" (I, 97). As we shall see, she resembles Mrs. Sinclair in *Clarissa,* Lovelace's accomplice in abduction and rape, whose eyebrows according to Lovelace are "erect, like the bristles upon a hog's back," and who pouts her "blubber-lips, as if to bellows up wind and sputter into her horse-nostrils" (*Clarissa,* III, 195-96).

Colbrand, B.'s Swiss servant, is described in the same exaggerated terms, and exhibits the same qualities: "He has great staring eyes, like the bull's that frightened me so; vast jaw-bones sticking out; eyebrows hanging over his eyes; two great scars upon his fore-head, and one on his left cheek; two large whiskers, and a monstrous wide mouth; blubber lips, long yellow teeth, and a hideous grin" (I, 145). The fiery-eyed bull with which she identifies Colbrand recurs when two grazing cows are imagined as bulls: "Here is the spirit of my master in one bull, and Mrs. Jewkes's in the other: now I am gone, to be sure! " (I, 132) Recovering from her fright, she realizes her mistake. With Mrs. Jewkes sleeping beside her, she dreams that Colbrand and B. have come to her bedside to assault her, and awakens in terror (I, 145). Her fear of rape is heightened by Mrs. Jewkes's later statement that B. plans to marry her to Colbrand and buy her from him on the wedding day. Even before her fears have been aroused, she expresses concern that a mock-marriage has been planned to ruin her (I, 156).

Cut off from the protections of society (the parson, Mr. Williams, proving ineffectual) and intensely fearful of her warders, she comes to identify B. with Mrs. Jewkes. Walking in the garden in one scene, she stops to fish in the pond; on hooking a carp, she tells Mrs. Jewkes that she has been thinking of herself: "I was comparing you and myself to my naughty master. As we hooked and deceived the poor carp, so was I betrayed by false baits; and when you said, 'Play it, play it,' it went to my heart to think I should sport with the destruction of the poor fish I had betrayed . . ." (I, 113). This momentary identification perhaps explains her ambivalence; more specifically, her willingness to pacify a woman she has abundant reason to hate cannot be explained through fear alone. Nor does she continue to protest strenuously when Mrs. Jewkes sleeps in her bed (without seeking to molest her).

B.'s identification with Mrs. Jewkes is most obvious in the climactic scene to which these events lead – the attempted rape. This scene is almost exactly the counterpart of the Bedfordshire bedroom scene which, I suggested, prepares for the tensions Richardson now explores fully. Disguising himself in the gown and petticoat of Pamela's maid, an apron over his face and shoulders – feminized sufficiently that Pamela is able to describe him as trembling like an aspen leaf – he lies down on the other side of Pamela. Clasping her waist, he seizes one arm while Mrs. Jewkes, the "vile procuress," grasps the other. When Pamela realizes what is happening, B. is driven to frenzy: "But he kissed me with frightful vehemence; and then his voice broke upon me like a clap of thunder, 'Now, Pamela,' said he, 'is the dreadful time of reckoning come, that I have threatened.' I screamed out in such a manner, as never any body heard the like. But there was nobody to help me; and both my hands were secured, as I said. Sure never poor soul was in such agonies as I" (I, 178). Mrs. Jewkes urges the young man to proceed:

> Said he, "One word with you, Pamela; hear me but one word; and hitherto you see I offer nothing to you." – Is this *nothing*," said I, "to be in bed here? To hold my hands between you! I will hear, if you will instantly leave the bed, and take this villainous woman from me! "
>
> Said she (O disgrace of woman kind!) – "What you do, Sir, do: don't stand, dilly dallying. She cannot exclaim worse than she has done; and she'll be quieter, when she knows the worst." (I, 179)

When B. puts a hand on her bosom after offering to withdraw if Pamela agrees to his proposals, she faints. Awakening, she finds her tormentors sitting on either side of the bed, frightened by her cold sweating. The scene builds to a second attempt, with the same results. Nothing in the treatment is comical:

> And will you, Sir," said the wicked wretch, "for a fit or two, give up such an opportunity as this? – I thought you had known the sex better. She is now, you see, quite well again! "
>
> This I heard; more she might say; but I fainted away once more, at those words, and at his clasping his arms about me again. When I came a little to myself, I saw him sit there, and the maid Nan, holding a smelling-bottle to my nose, and no Mrs. Jewkes. (I, 179-80)

The scene also has its counterpart in *Clarissa,* both in Lovelace's plan to take Miss Partington's place in bed, should Clarissa permit her to sleep in her room, and during the rape, in the course of which Mrs. Sinclair seeks to frighten the drugged girl. This similarity is powerful evidence of the important role of displacement in Richardson's imagining of his male characters.

Typical of the feminine masochist, who seeks pain at the hands of the loved one, B. is drawn to Pamela because she has aroused his "tumults" – by showing interest in him and at the same time resisting his advances. Once the interest of the novel begins to shift from Pamela's sufferings to the possibility of marriage, the nature of his interest in her changes and new patterns of conflict emerge. B. wishes now to alter his relationship and establish what Victor Smirnoff terms "the masochistic contract." Such a contract provides "a certain immutable setting" for the receiving of pain. Smirnoff adds: ". . . the conditions imposed are an essential part of the masochistic position: the masochist is not looking for a consenting accomplice, eager to inflict pain or to torture the victim. There is an analogous demand on the sadist's part, who does not want his victim to submit too readily to the pleasure of being tortured or abused. . . . there is no complementary agreement between the sadistic and the masochistic desire."[3] The "certain immutable setting" is one implication possibly of the long series of rules governing conduct in marriage that B. submits to Pamela. To understand these new patterns, we must turn to the sources of feminine masochism – incestuous feelings and their representation in the novel.

3

These patterns center in what seems to be B.'s altered conception of the role that Pamela is to play in his life. Stated briefly, she is to become an instrument of pain in her exalted new role of wife-mother. This is conceivably why he gives up his plan of making her his mistress.

The social determinants of this decision are compatible with the psychological ones I am suggesting by analogy with psychoanalytic character. Richardson has moved from the generic rake (not the comical squire that has been suggested) to the generic profligate husband capable of penitent behavior. Thus Lady Davers writes to Pamela in the sequel: it is "the case of all rakes, that though they indulge in all manner of libertinism themselves, there is no class of

3. "The Masochistic Contract," *International Journal of Psycho-analysis,* 50 (1969), 669, 666.

men who exact greater delicacy from the persons they marry, though they care not how bad they make the wives, the sisters, and daughters of others" (II, 28). Though Richardson is describing a familiar social phenomenon, the statement has special psychological meaning. For as long as B. thinks Pamela may become his mistress, he is willing that she endure degradation at the hands of his servants; however, once he decides to marry her, precisely the reverse happens. Pamela becomes the embodiment of all virtues – as over-estimated a love-object as she has been degraded.

Freud's famous analysis of "degradation in erotic life" suggests that the underlying motivation is incestuous.[4] In some men, Freud states, the Oedipus complex is not overcome; feeling remains fixated to incestuous objects or fantasies, with resulting total impotence at the genital stage or a less severe psychical impotence that allows a sexual outlet in reality, but at the price of feelings of tenderness. These feelings are reserved for incestuous objects. Psychical impotence is avoided by degrading the sexual object and, at the same time, overestimating the incestuous object and substitute figures. Freud adds: "It is possible, too, that the tendency so often observed in men of the highest classes of society to choose a woman of a lower class as a permanent mistress or even as a wife is nothing but a consequence of their need for a debased sexual object, to whom, psychologically, the possibility of complete satisfaction is linked" ("Contributions to the Psychology of Love," S.E., XI, 185).

Freud's theory suggests why Pamela ceases to be an object of lust, once she is wholly identified with the incestuous object, and why Richardson devotes much of the remainder of the novel and the sequel to a definition of love in marriage (a chief theme of *Sir Charles Grandison* also). Degraded, she can be sought as a sexual object; "you are *most* beautiful in your tears," B. tells her. Exalted, she can be more easily identified with the earlier incestuous object. Waning lust and feelings of tenderness supervene after the marriage. B. has come to love her with a "purer flame" than he had known in

4. Simon O. Lesser notes that B. is in part father-figure because he reminds Pamela of his mother: "Nor does the incest thread lead only in one direction: it may be conjectured that Mr. B. was attracted to Pamela in part because of her relationship to his mother and that in his unconscious she was in part a daughter or younger sister." "A Note on *Pamela*," *College English*, 14 (October, 1952), 15.

his earlier tumultuous love. Only her "unseasonable doubts" blighted his early feeling of love, he insists, for he cannot bear "slight and negligence" (I, 236). But these tender feelings are unsubstantial, and indeed give way later to new tumults aroused by events that suggest a reactivation of motifs in the earlier incestuous fantasy.

That B. sees in Pamela a resemblance to his mother, or at least wishes to establish a resemblance, is suggested by his concern over Pamela's clothing. On two occasions B.'s mother gave Pamela clothing before her death, and B. gives her more afterwards, telling her to wear it for his mother's sake (I, 7). Later, when she dresses in the clothes she has made preparatory to returning to her parents (clothes proper to her parent's lower station, in contrast to those she wore in service), he is enraged and accuses her of hypocrisy. When she defends her honesty – she has been "in disguise" since his mother took her from her parents and brought her into the household (I, 44) – B. shows his confused feelings by first taking her in his arms, and then pushing her away:

> "Mrs. Jervis," said he, "take the little witch from me; I can neither bear nor forbear her! " – Strange words these! – "But stay; you shan't go! – Yet begone! – No, come back again."
>
> I thought he was mad; for he knew not what he would have. I was going, however, but he stept after me, and took hold of my arm, and brought me in again: I am sure he made my arm black and blue, for the marks are upon it still. "Sir, Sir," said I, "pray have mercy; I will, I will come in! " (I, 44)

Following her abduction, he has the two bundles containing the mother's clothing sent to Lincolnshire in a portmanteau; later, immediately before his arrival, Mrs. Jewkes (presumably acting for him) orders Pamela to dress from the bundles, for she is to appear for the first time before the ladies of the neighborhood. In the articles submitted to her, B. offers to give her pieces of his mother's jewelry if she agrees to become his mistress (I, 166).

Following the attempted rape, Pamela indicates that she continued to wear her own clothes, though B. wished her to dress otherwise (I, 216). The issue of clothing arises more than once subsequently; before the wedding, B. tells her to dress as she "used to do," presumably as she dressed in his mother's service; "for now, at least, you may call your *two other bundles* your own" (I, 269-70). When Pamela does dress from the bundles, she is told by Mrs. Jewkes (restored to the role of servant) that she "now looked like her lady indeed" (I, 271). On seeing her, B. seems to relent: "Dress as you will, Pamela, you're a charming girl" (I, 271).

B. perhaps wishes to protect her from criticism, yet the underlying motive is more complex. Not surprisingly, the first of his many "facetious hints" on her conduct as his wife has to do with dress; for example, Pamela is not to become careless in dress and is to be fully dressed by the dinner hour. He intends to tell her his likes and dislikes, and she is to do the same, "that nothing may lie upon either of our minds, that may occasion the least reservedness" (I, 330).

These details suggest not only "the masochistic contract" but also its special meaning in the novel. For Smirnoff suggests that clothes determine the role the woman plays in the fantasies of the masochist, whether as angel or evil woman.[5] In general, the purpose of "rules" is to limit or prevent any display of passion in Pamela, though his own humors are to be tolerated. Pamela listens with amusement to his seemingly facetious but inwardly serious and inordinate demands: "if you see a gloom arising, or arisen, banish it instantly; smoothe your dear countenance; resume your former composure; and then my dearest, whose heart must always be seen in her face, and cannot be a hypocrite, will find this a means to smoothe her passions also; and if the occasion be too strong for so sudden a conquest, she will know how to do it more effectually, by repairing to her closet, and begging that gracious assistance which has never yet failed her" (I, 332).

B. is perhaps hinting that Pamela is to set him an example. Feeling must never exceed the limits he establishes for it – in himself, too. Once observing a footman break a dish at the house of a noble lady, he went home and dreamed that his coachman had broken the fore-glass of the carriage: "I was so solicitous, methought, to keep the good lady in countenance for *her* anger, that I broke his head in revenge, and stabbed one of my coach-horses" (I, 334).

Pamela is thus to play the role of wife-mother, doing nothing to remind him of the degradation he had subjected her to, or of the cunning and hypocrisy he continually inveighs against. Pamela accepts this role willingly, as her statements to B. about how she will conduct herself show. She will be the good Samaritan, in visiting the poor and the sick of the neighborhood and ministering to them,

5. "The Masochistic Contract," 666.

without however overdrawing on her husband's means. She will assist in household duties that are not beneath her new station, and will entertain the gentry, if they choose to accept her company. She proposes to relieve her husband of the household accounts and charities – which she had managed for his mother (I, 234-35). Even before the wedding, she begins to play her new role, carving at the table, as she used to do for her mistress (I, 186).

In light of the need to purify Pamela of her earlier role in fantasy, a number of later scenes have special meaning. The inordinately long one between Pamela and Lady Davers, shortly after the wedding ceremony, arouses and immediately allays fears much like those Pamela experienced during her confinement. She is again forcibly prevented from leaving the house when Lady Davers blocks her way, but this time she succeeds in escaping through a window. Another significant displacement occurs here. For Lady Davers reveals certain stubborn qualities of Pamela earlier. The displacement allows Pamela to assume a new character, suggested earlier but not represented with consistency. The worthy mother, who embodied the best qualities of womanhood according to her son (I, 331), is reborn in Pamela, whose gentle manners are a sharp contrast to those of B.'s rude sister. Pamela's former "romantic turn for virtue" is now characterized by B. as "the pious impulses of your own amiable mind" (I, 296).

It should be noted that Richardson found nothing contradictory or repellent about a passionless marriage. He explains his view on passion and friendship in marriage, in a letter to Hester Mulso:

> And is it not selfishness to propose to make all the world but two persons, and then these two but one; and, intending to become the same flesh as well as spirit, know no public, no other private?

He returns to this idea later in the same letter:

> Those will be found to be the most noble friendships which either flame between persons of the same sex; or where the dross of the passion is thrown out, and the ore purified by the union of minds in matrimony. And I am of opinion that love is but the harbinger to such a friendship; and that friendship therefore is the perfection of love, and superior to love; it is love purified, exalted, proved by experience and a consent of minds. . . . Love is a blazing, crackling, green-wood flame, as much smoke as flame; friendship, married friendship particularly, is a steady, intense, comfortable fire.[6]

The marked alteration of sexual themes, once the marriage is per-

6. *Selected Letters,* pp. 191, 193.

formed, suggests that the wish to identify Pamela with the mother leads to compensatory overestimation and simultaneously the exploitation of domestic and religious pieties, in the remainder of the novel and the sequel.

If Richardson's letter to Aaron Hill can be believed, he began writing with the intention of ending with a marriage; for he was writing about an actual nobleman and his low-born wife who had been his mother's maid-servant. He characterizes the woman in these words: "That she behaved herself with so much dignity, sweetness, and humility, that she made herself beloved of every body, and even by his relations, who, at first despised her; and now had the blessings both of rich and poor, and the love of her husband."[7] In the process of writing, his imagining of the relationship between B. and Pamela led him undoubtedly to unexpected themes, producing the riddling conflicts that he could work out only through a radical change in the characterization and details of plot halfway through the novel.

The result is that Pamela's confinement and torment are deliberately rationalized (as they will be in *Clarissa*) as "the trials of her virtue" (I, 242), as if putting Pamela through a test of her virtue had been B.'s intention from the beginning. Richardson's ability to skim over the moral complexities is most apparent in these later scenes, as in Pamela's statement to Mrs. Jewkes on reconciling with her: "I consider what you have done, was in obedience to a will I must also submit to; and so, if the *effects* of our obedience may be different, yet, as they proceed from *one* cause, *that* must be always reverenced by me" (I, 244).

Karen Horney, in her discussion of masochism, offers help in explaining why the displacement in Pamela cannot be a permanent solution to the tensions engendered by the earlier fantasy – that is, cannot be a solution psychoanalytically. The masochist, she states, depends on love for assurance; he needs constant attention because his anxiety is never alleviated:

> He is . . . very emotional in his relations to people; easily attached because he expects them to give him the necessary reassurance; easily disappointed because he never gets, and never can get, what he expects. The expectation or illusion of the "great love" often plays an important role. Sexuality being one of the most common ways of getting affection, he also tends to overvalue it and clings to the illusion that it holds the solution of all life's problems. How far this is conscious, or how easily he has actual sexual relations depends on

7. Ibid., p. 40.

> his inhibitions on this score. Where he has had sexual relations, or attempts at such, his history shows a frequency of "unhappy loves": he has been deserted, disappointed, humiliated, badly treated.[8]

Horney's description fits B.'s situation exactly, with the qualifications we have indicated. But badly treated by whom? The early scenes suggest the denying mother at the level of fantasy (though the real mother was indulgent of her son), a residue perhaps of the child's "family romance" (distinguished by Freud in the essay by this name) – in which the mother is fantasized as unfaithful and promiscuous. (S.E., IX, 239-40) In the novel we are told merely that B. seduced Sally Godfrey because her mother was trying to trick him into marriage (I, 435). We noted earlier the complex meaning of Pamela's clothing in the earlier fantasy, and also the conflicting incestuous trends that eventually give way to new themes. Perhaps the decisive and constant quality in Richardson's characterization is the ambivalence toward the mother-figure and her substitutes. With her lowly origins presumably erased, and with her attainment of gentility in the eyes of B.'s friends and neighbors, the marriage will be publicly acknowledged and Pamela will put on new clothing. In these circumstances only can she become B.'s "great love." The constant need of attention in the masochist is consistent with B.'s erratic behavior and recurring "tumults" – and most of all, his ambivalence – toward the end of the sequel.

These psychological patterns are in accord with the unconscious hostility and defiance sometimes associated with masochism.[9] Though the mother's clothing serves to identify Pamela with the virtuous mother, it also arouses hostilities that remain latent. Only a clear separation of the wife from the mother imago sustains erotic feeling: the joining of these roles leads to the virtual disappearance of sexual interest. Pamela cannot be wife and mistress both. The erotic interest is neutralized precisely at the point that the identification of roles is enforced – tenuously, however, because as the incestuous love-object in marriage Pamela is a reminder of both the virtuous mother, for whom tenderness is felt, and her opposite, who remains a source of anxiety. "This is where the use of dresses, uniforms and

8. "The Problem of Feminine Masochism," *Psychoanalytic Review,* 22 (1935), 252-53.

9. *Masochism in Modern Man,* pp. 156-73; Bernhard Berliner, "Libido and Reality in Masochism," *Psychoanalytic Quarterly*, 9 (1940), 332.

accessories is of utmost importance," Smirnoff suggests. "They are the indispensable means of maintaining these two images apart (from each other), lest their coalescence might nullify the ego defences and give place to delusion."[10]

The split in moral masochism, to which this divided image may be related, is discussed by Fritz Wittels, who was interested in the acting out of unconscious fantasies:

> What appears to be masochism belongs to the unreal person. The real person derives pleasure from the pain which is inflicted upon the unreal figure. . . . [Moral masochism] presupposes a split: two incarnations of which one is rejected and consequently harassed or even killed. The rejected incarnation is not always the one which has no real existence . . . . Often, it is the real one. Then we may find an unconscious princess (a prince or an eternal child) who must be carefully sheltered against the storms of reality. It is then part of this defense, that all kinds of predicaments and defeats must be arranged for the real person in order to annihilate him, to devaluate him as much as possible. What we call masochism in these cases is their enjoyment in the debasement of some undesired reality.[11]

The two images, however, do not remain apart, for Pamela becomes dominant in the marriage – a dominance originating in her acknowledged moral superiority. This dominance gains strength as her story gradually becomes known and, later, when she easily persuades B. to allow her to bring his illegitimate daughter, Miss Goodwin, into the family. As we shall see, Richardson locates the only conflict occurring between husband and wife in the sequel, in issues relating to child-rearing; his surrender to her wishes and views, anticipated in his acquiescence in her wish to raise Miss Goodwin, follows a quarrel over nursing their first son and his consequent involvement with a noble lady.

His humiliation in this affair is merely one of a series that begins when his treatment of Pamela is punished through the public circulation of the journal she kept during her captivity, in his confession of his part in her trials and Pamela's occasional references to them, in Miss Goodwin's presence in the household, and in Mrs. Jewkes's final repentance and death – this latter event belated and clearly improvised.

Masochistic trends, then, strengthen as the novel progresses. In the

10. "The Masochistic Contract," 669.
11. "The Mystery of Masochism," *Psychoanalytic Review,* 24 (1937), 140-41.

Bedfordshire scenes, B. is depicted as the aggressive lover, but is perhaps imagined differently –as masochistic and inwardly uncertain. This is perhaps why he is absent from the novel in the most sadistic scenes in Lincolnshire, reappearing in his previous role only briefly before his sudden reformation, and why he is so entirely a figure of fantasy during the attempted rape and immediately before. Richardson's unease with the characterization in these scenes is apparent in his effort to darken it – to invest B. with the sadistic qualities explored in Mrs. Jewkes and suggested in Colbrand, and to play on fear of "tumults" which in fact are nearly at an end. If Pamela's willingness to forgive him is credible, the reason is that the impression he makes is too indefinite to fix our response. Richardson also keeps our attention focused on Pamela's suffering.

Given these discrepancies, a rhetoric that conceals them becomes necessary; Richardson has the problem of making the reversal of character credible, having heightened new qualities. This concealment is managed through the contrast with Mrs. Jewkes and through the views of normative characters who stress B.'s capability for moral reforms. Pamela wishes to believe in his good qualities, as we have seen; Mrs. Jervis tells her that, despite his noble birth and Pamela's lower station, he loves her, and that his bad temper arises from his pride and inability to manage his feelings toward her (I, 29-30). This view (presented more than once) is not a sufficient explanation of his behavior in the Lincolnshire scenes. To cite one additional example, pride and frustrated love cannot explain his letter to Mrs. Jewkes concerning a legal action instituted against Parson Williams: "I think I now hate her perfectly; and, though I will do nothing to her *myself,* yet I can bear, for the sake of my revenge, *injured honour,* and *slighted love,* to see any thing, even what *she most fears,* be *done to her*; and then she may be turned loose to her evil destiny, and echo to the woods and groves her piteous lamentations for the loss of her fantastical innocence, which the romantic idiot makes such a work about" (I, 141).

Directly contradicting B.'s later statement on his instructions to Mrs. Jewkes, the letter shows the extent to which Richardson was able to heighten suspense over Pamela's fate without wholly sacrificing the reader's sympathy for B.; it also shows the difficulty of making him a consistent figure of reality. So long as he is absent from these scenes, his hostility and incestuous longing – components of the masochistic character – can be expressed in a series of improvised scenes, laden with fantasy and strongly masochistic in their unexpected turns, dilated action, and frequent delays. Once he appears at the house in Lincolnshire, Pamela's "trial" ends, and interest shifts to the impending marriage, modifications in the character must occur.

4

We have noted Richardson's statement to Hester Mulso that the noblest friendships exist "where the dross of the passion is thrown out, and the ore purified by the union of minds in matrimony."[12] This, precisely, is what Richardson wishes to show in the sequel. The analysis we have offered suggests this explanation for the marked alteration of sexual themes: B.'s wish to identify Pamela with the mother of fantasy leads imaginatively to compensatory overestimation and simultaneously the exploitation of domestic and religious pieties. We have reached this conclusion mainly through analogy with actual masochistic behavior as observed psychoanalytically, and we have carried our interpretation of B. and Pamela to the full limits of this and other kinds of behavior in order to test the consistency of characters and actions from a new point of view – a consistency usually denied by those who judge *Pamela* and the sequel to be failures.

The single crisis of the marriage occurs when B. and Pamela quarrel over whether she should suckle their first child. He writes that he does not wish to look for her in the nursery; the child may have her complete attention when he is absent, "but when I am at home, even a son and heir, so jealous am I of your affections, shall not be my rival in them." Nor will he permit their rest to be disturbed. And he further warns her "not to weaken, or, to speak in a phrase proper to the present subject, *wean* me from that love *to* you, and admiration *of* you, which hitherto has been rather increasing than otherwise, as your merit, and regard for me have increased" (II, 229-30). Pamela writes her parents that this is the first "will not" she has had from her husband (II, 228). The child of fantasy refuses to be displaced by a real one; any display of passionate regard is not to occur in his presence.

12. *Selected Letters*, p. 193.

The tensions of this episode materialize in B.'s affair with the Countess Dowager, whom he meets at a masquerade. Before their relationship can proceed to adultery, Pamela intervenes – by asking B. to proceed with her "trial" and pronounce "sentence" on her, as if she is to blame for what has happened. Her choice of words and indeed the whole of their confrontation reanimates the B. of Lincolnshire, for the scene is strongly erotic:

> "Dear charmer of my heart," said he, and clasped me to his bosom, "what a *new* PAMELA have I in my arms! A mysterious charmer! Let us instantly go to my closet, or yours, and come upon our mutual trial; for you have fired my soul with impatience! "

Pamela's tears intensify his ardor:

> He took me again into his arms: – "My dearest Pamela, if you love me, distract not my soul thus, by your dark and mysterious speeches. You are displeased with *me,* and I thought I had reason, of late, to take something amiss in *your* conduct; but, instead of your suffering by my anger, you have words and an air that penetrate my very soul." (II, 304-05)

Though the trial is actually his, Pamela insists on standing before him in her closet; three chairs have been arranged to form a bar. Her implied profession of guilt, superficially, is an instance of her customary subservience; but the more profound implication of this detail is to be discovered in her characteristic moral masochism. For as the patient sufferer who endures the unprovoked blows of fate, she serves as the instrument of mortification, embodying pious recrimination, and it is in this role that she excites her husband, as earlier he took pleasure in her journal.

In *Clarissa*, the sadism of the superego which strengthens Clarissa's even more pronounced moral masochism operates also in the guise of pious recrimination. To use Reik's description of the masochist's impatience and need of immediate gratification, Lovelace's "flight forward" is to rape rather than to desexualized marriage – to a series of events ending in his identification with Clarissa's death wish and symbolic castration (death) at the hands of her cousin Morden. Moral masochism operates in *Pamela*, too in the guise of pious sentimentality.

Pamela has revealed her masochism in her willingness to submit to B. during the "trial" in Lincolnshire and afterwards, including the "trial" of the sequel. The hypocrisy with which she has been charged has its explanation at the deeper level of fantasy. So intense are B.'s early threats of dreadful reckoning that her thoughts of suicide are wholly credible. In the opening pages she asks B., as he forcibly kisses her, "May I, Lucretia-like, justify myself with my death, if I am used barbarously? " (I, 20) But her own enactment of fantasy is in no way altered by these real fears. She has sought the situation that entraps her, which is why her efforts to escape have the quality of ineffectual nightmare flight. She is prepared to endure suffering because she unconsciously identifies it as a component of her erotic experience.

It is in the context of moral masochism that pious sentimentality and ideas are eroticized. Ernst Kris points to the explanation in this comment on the sexualization or eroticizing of thinking, which sentimentalism often represents: "We believe that in the process of becoming conscious the preconsciously prepared thought is sexualized, which accounts for the experiences accompanying revelation. Id energies suddenly combine with ego energies, mobile with bound and neutralized cathexes, to produce the unique experience of inspiration which is felt to reach consciousness from the outside."[13] To cite one example, before Pamela leaves the house in Bedfordshire B. urges her to remain another fortnight: "O how my heart throbbed! and I begun (for I did not know what I did) to say the Lord's Prayer. 'None of your beads to me, Pamela! ' said he; 'thou art a perfect nun.' But I said aloud, with my eyes lifted up to Heaven, *'Lead me not into temptation, but deliver me from evil,* O my good God! ' He hugged me in his arms, and said, 'Well, my dear girl, then you stay this fortnight, and you shall see what I will do for you" (I, 70)

More than once in the novel Richardson stresses that the "trial" in Lincolnshire has religious import, as Kinkead Weekes suggests.[14] We have a foreshadowing of *Clarissa* at one point when Pamela rationalizes her injuries as possibly deserved:

> "How do I know but *these bruises* and *maims* that I have received, while I pursued the escape I had meditated, may not have furnished myself with the opportunity to precipitate myself, and of surrendering up myself, spotless and unguilty, to that Merciful Being who gave it. Then," thought I, "who gave

13. *Psychoanalytic Explorations in Art* (New York: Schocken Books, 1964), p. 317.

14. In his introduction to the Everyman edition. "Behind all her faults there lies a stubborn pride and self-reliance, and to be like this, for Richardson, is to court despair when one's human fallibility is inevitably exposed. Pamela's battles against despair, her struggles to regain true faith not only in God but in Man, lie at the very centre of the novel's meaning" (I, ix).

> thee, presumptuous as thou art, a power over thy life? Who authorized thee to put an end to it, when the weakness of thy mind suggests not to thee a way to preserve it with honour? How knowest thou what purpose God may have to serve, by the trials with which thou art now exercised? (I, 151)

B.'s realistic comment on her "pretty turn for virtue" has unexpected pertinence. It is significant, Freud states, that "the sadism of the superego becomes for the most part glaringly conscious, whereas the masochistic trend of the ego remains as a rule concealed from the subject and has to be inferred from his behavior" (S.E., XIC, 169).

If the sentimentality of *Pamela* does serve as a channel for both the sadism of the superego and the masochism of the ego, this aspect of the novel is difficult to explain in light of the usual conception of sentimentalism as an affirmation of human goodness. Golden concludes that by this definition Richardson cannot be considered a sentimentalist.[15] Alan D. McKillop suggests that Richardson's approach to questions of conduct was conscientious rather than spontaneous. Richardson approved, McKillop states, "a polite benevolence, a favourable view of human nature, the conception of the feelings as materials to be arranged in order, an approval of that order which is at once aesthetic and rational. When feeling is thus put in its place, it often seems to be factitious, wrought up, gratuitous, or even supplanted by a doctrine that one ought to feel."[16] And he comments in an essay on *Grandison*: "This may be called sentimentalism if we mean by that term a harmonizing of the true, the good, and the beautiful, which is at the same time a harmonizing of self-love or self-approval with benevolence; but it is not sentimentalism in the sense that it exalts a mere release of feeling which carries with it the guarantee of its own virtue."[17]

Pamela suggests that the intensive involvement in inner emotional experiences introduces more serious psychological problems for writer and reader than critical theory usually allows for. Watt states that the novel allows for unrestricted identification, permitting the widest range of experiences possible and "the peculiar triumphs and

15. *Richardson's Characters*, p. 42.

16. *Samuel Richardson: Printer and Novelist* (Chapel Hill: University of North Carolina Press, 1936), p. 208.

17. "On *Sir Charles Grandison*," in *Samuel Richardson: A Collection of Critical Essays*, p. 130.

degradations of the novel form in general."[18] The guilt attendant on the exploration of sexual conflict complicates the presentation of character considerably. If the reader were only to pity the victim of sexual intrigue, there would be no need for Richardson to make his heroines feel that their degradation is somehow deserved and later deny the imputed cause. His effort to redefine the experience of *Pamela,* in the concluding pages of the novel and in the preface to the sequel, suggest that he was fully aware of the problem that his exploration of erotic experience created: Richardson hopes "the Letters which compose this Part will be found equally written to NATURE, avoiding all romantic flights, improbable surprises, and irrational machinery; and the passions are touched, where requisite; and rules, equally *new* and *practicable*, inculcated throughout the whole, for the *general conduct of life* . . ." (II, v).

Lacking the impulsion and psychological coherence of *Clarissa, Pamela* nevertheless exhibits enormous imaginative power, perhaps deriving from Richardson's imagining of sexual experience as aggression and rape. The rhetorical strategies he employs – including displacement and the virtual absence of inside views of B. – "defend" against this attitude as well as disguise those discrepancies of character that we have analyzed. Richardson need only have represented a young man in love, and indeed he gives us an attractive portrayal in the early scenes, in contrast to the gross and unsubtle portrayal in the Lincolnshire scenes – in which B. is almost wholly a figure of fantasy. It remained for *Clarissa* to show the uses of sentimentality in partially neutralizing guilt in the reader following the depiction of a successful assault.

18. *The Rise of the Novel,* p. 202.

Chapter Three

LOVELACE'S DREAM

Published in 1747-48, six years after the appearance of *Pamela* and its sequel (1740-41), *Clarissa* shows remarkable advances in the treatment of character and in the management of a complex plot that builds slowly and carefully to a series of powerful confrontations between Clarissa and Lovelace and to inevitable catastrophe, without the diversion of subplots and conflicting interests. Discussion of character is complicated, however, by Richardson's afterthoughts about the reception of hero and heroine and his wish to darken the character of Lovelace and exonerate Clarissa entirely of complicity in her downfall. Kinkead-Weekes has analyzed these changes in considerable detail in his authoritative study of the novels. In the account of the events leading up to the rape of Clarissa, I have followed the lead of Kinkead-Weekes in stressing Lovelace's gradual change of feeling toward Clarissa, though I shall suggest another explanation later for certain inconsistencies in Richardson's characterization of him.

In the opening scenes of the novel, Clarissa receives the attentions of the aristocratic Robert Lovelace, who briefly had paid suit to her older sister, Arabella, and had been rejected by the confused girl, much to his relief. Clarissa's Uncle Antony had arranged the interview by a mistake, as Lovelace later explains in a letter to his friend, John Belford: "My visit to Arabella, owing to a mistake of the sisters, into which . . . I was led by the blundering uncle; who was to introduce *me* (but lately come from abroad) to the *divinity* as I thought; but, instead of her, carried me to a *mere mortal*" (I, 145). Jealous of Clarissa who will inherit her grandfather's estate instead of him, and bearing Lovelace a previous grudge, James works with Bella to frustrate Lovelace's suit; and he succeeds in turning the family against Lovelace after being bested in a duel. "My brother was disarmed, as you have heard," Clarissa writes her friend, Anna Howe;

"and on being brought home, and giving us ground to suppose he was much worse hurt than he really was, and a fever ensuing, every one flamed out; and all was laid at my door" (I, 19).

Fearing the economic loss he will suffer if his sister marries Lovelace, but acting mainly out of hatred for her, James puts forward other possible suitors, and finally settles on the contemptible and miserly Solmes. Pushed to the limits of endurance by her importunate brother and sister, cut off from her weak mother and increasingly enraged father, and finding herself increasingly a prisoner in her own house, Clarissa begins an imprudent correspondence with Lovelace – who presses her to see him, and keeps the screw turning on the Harlowe family, hoping to revenge himself and lure Clarissa from her father's house. Clarissa responds with a mixture of fear and interest. "I am come back dissatisfied with myself," she writes Miss Howe, after depositing a letter in the garden wall. "But I think, my dear, there can be no harm in meeting him. If I do *not*, he may take some violent measures" (I, 317). Finally pressed beyond endurance, she does agree to a secret meeting, and through an elaborate ruse is lured out of the garden into a waiting carriage.

Though his motive has been one of revenge, Lovelace is genuinely attracted to Clarissa, and wishes to live with her unmarried – averse to marriage because of his cynical view that women are incapable of sustained loyalty or virtue. To this end he finds lodging for Clarissa in what seems a respectable London establishment but is in fact a brothel, run by a Mrs. Sinclair and occupied by women he previously seduced. Clarissa realizes that she has acted rashly in entering a correspondence with Lovelace: "O the vile encroacher! how my indignation, at times, rises at him! Thus to lead a young creature (too much indeed relying upon her own strength) from evil to evil! " (I, 486) Lovelace watches his prey with interest, attracted by her modesty and pride, and finding himself increasingly unable to reconcile her behavior with his view that women are natural rogues. "This lady says serious things in so agreeable a manner (and then her voice is all harmony when she touches a subject she is pleased with), that I could have listened to her for half a day together. But yet I am afraid if she *falls,* as they call it, she will lose a good deal of that *pathos,* of that noble self-confidence, which gives a good person, as I now see, a visible superiority over one *not* so good" (II, 69). His complex feeling for Clarissa – in particular, his ambivalent feeling which matches her own – is perfectly revealed in this remarkable statement.

For her part, Clarissa allows herself to be deceived by Lovelace's various new ruses which increasingly compromise her. Gradually recognizing that he will gain her only by meeting her demands of propriety, he moves toward proposing marriage. When finally he brings himself to as open a declaration as he can make, Clarissa seems to rebuff him by setting conditions. Lovelace seeks to discover her real feelings; he does so by arranging for the women of the house to copy the letters of her confidante, Anna Howe, while Clarissa is out of the house with him. In these letters, Lovelace discovers attitudes and feelings similar to his own – a scorn for men that matches his own scorn for women, whom he believes are hypocrites at heart – and he mistakenly assumes that Miss Howe is echoing Clarissa's own disguised and scornful feelings toward him:

> O this little fury Miss Howe! Well might her saucy friend (who has been equally free with me, or the occasion could not have been given) be so violent as she lately was, at my endeavouring to come at one of these letters.
>
> I was sure that this fair one, at so early an age, with a constitution so firm, health so blooming, eyes so sparkling, expectations therefore so lively, and hopes so predominating, could not be absolutely, and from her own vigilance, so guarded, and so apprehensive, as I have found her to be.
>
> Sparkling eyes, Jack, when the poetical tribe have said all they can for them, are an infallible sign of a rogue, or room for a rogue, in the heart. (II, 362)

Now bent on revenge against Clarissa, and anxious to prove the truth of the libertine view of women, "That once subdued, is always subdued! " – a view that inspired his many previous seductions – Lovelace plots with the women of the house to subvert Clarissa. Pressing his attentions upon the bewildered girl, he takes enjoyment in her recriminations and claims of moral superiority:

> I cast myself at her feet. Begone, Mr. Lovelace, said she, with a rejecting motion, her fan in her hand; for your own sake leave me! My soul is above thee, man! with both her hands pushing me from her! Urge me not to tell thee, how sincerely I think my soul above thee! Thou hast in mine, a proud, a too proud heart to contend with! Leave me, and leave me for ever! Thou hast a proud heart to contend with!
>
> Her air, her manner, her voice, were bewitchingly noble, though her words were so severe.

Lovelace's feelings are now more complex than they had been earlier.

Sadism, revenge, and love seem to be mixed in what now follows in this scene:

> Let me worship an angel, said I, no woman. Forgive me, dearest creature! Creature if you be forgive me! Forgive my inadvertencies! Forgive my inequalities! Pity my infirmities! Who is equal to my Clarissa?
>
> I trembled between admiration and love; and wrapped my arms about her knees, as she sat. She tried to rise at the moment; but my clasping round her thus ardently, drew her down again; and never was woman more frightened. But free as my clasping emotion might appear to her apprehensive heart, I had not, at the instant, any thought but what reverence inspired. (II, 382-83)

For her part, Clarissa feels love for him, though her suspicions about his real nature have begun to deepen. Lovelace reports that, believing that a feigned illness is real, "Tears were in her eyes more than once for me. She suffered me to take her hand, and kiss it as often as I pleased" (II, 436). In a letter to Miss Howe, Clarissa admits her confused feelings: "How lately did I think I hated him! But hatred and anger, I see, are but temporary passions with me. One cannot, my dear, hate people in danger of death, or who are in distress or affliction. My heart, I find, is not proof against kindness, and acknowledgement of errors committed! " (II, 437) She adds in this same letter, " 'Tis true I have owned more than once, that I could have liked Mr. Lovelace above all men. . . . But, O my dearest friend, am I not guilty of a punishable fault, were I to love this man of errors? And has not my own heart deceived me, when I thought I did not? " (II, 438)

These events reach their climax when Lovelace gains entry into her bedroom on pretext of saving her from a fire, and shows Clarissa his real intentions by taking advantage of her almost nude state. When she attempts to protect herself with a pair of sharp scissors, Lovelace seizes and throws them into the chimney. Inflamed by her beauty and her helplessness, he begins kissing the protesting girl:

> Wicked wretch! Insolent villain! – Yes, she called me insolent villain, although so much in my power! And for what? – only for kissing (*with passion indeed*) her inimitable neck, her lips, her cheeks, her forehead, and her streaming eyes, as this assemblage of beauties offered itself at once to my ravished sight; she continued kneeling at my feet as I sat.
>
> If I *am* a wretch, madam – And then my grasping, but trembling hand – I hope I did not hurt the tenderest and loveliest of all her beauties – If I *am* a villain, madam –
>
> She tore my ruffle, shrunk from my happy hand with amazing force and agility, as with my other arm I would have encircled her waist. (II, 503)

The "grasping" hand has touched her breast, and this violation is not only a prologue or preparation for the later act of rape, but actually a representation of it – as complete a representation as Richardson will allow. Clarissa's response is to clasp her bosom and beg Lovelace to kill her, or to give her the means to kill herself. His own response shows that the act is one of rape in his own mind: "I sat suspended for a moment. By my soul, thought I, thou art, upon full proof, an angel and no woman! " (II, 504) The "full proof" would be the rape itself.

So inflamed is Lovelace that he spies on the stricken girl through the keyhole of her bedroom door, observing her on her knees, "her arms extended," and sobbing. His feelings are now even more confused: "Recollection is my enemy! Divine excellence! Happy with her for so many days together; now so unhappy! And for what? But she is purity itself. And why, after all, should I thus torment – but I must not trust myself with myself, in the humour I am in" (II, 514). Clarissa almost immediately escapes from the house, and makes her way to Hampstead, where Lovelace soon finds her. Through imposters and a series of new ruses, he attempts to revive the prospect of marriage, out of conflicting motives (genuine love, pride, a wish to subjugate) that he realizes he cannot sort out. When she firmly rejects his offer, arguing the superiority of her mind to his, he is both enchanted and angry: "How great, how sublimely great, this creature! By my soul, I cannot forgive her for her virtues! There is no bearing the consciousness of the infinite inferiority she charged me with. But why will she break from me, when good resolutions are taking place? The red-hot iron she refuses to strike – Oh, why will she suffer the yielding wax to harden? " (III, 153-54)

Though he continues to express such conflicting feelings, Lovelace is now bent on rape: "And now what thinkest thou must become of the lady, whom LOVE itself gives up, and CONSCIENCE cannot plead for? " (III, 157) The suspense over what he will do really ends when he intercepts a letter from Miss Howe informing Clarissa of the extent of his character and actions. Given the deceptions he has practiced and the impossibility of an untroubled marriage, rape is now his only recourse to union – and this he effects by luring Clarissa back to the London house, having her drugged both in the carriage and in the house, and that same night performing the act on the half-conscious girl, in the presence of Mrs. Sinclair and two of the other women.

Afterwards Clarissa passes through madness and then recrimination and self-accusation – in a series of papers that bare her feelings. "I was too secure in the knowledge I thought I had of my own heart," she writes in one paper. "My supposed advantages became a snare to me." In the next she realizes that "prospects of a happy life" are now over: "Who now shall provide the nuptial ornaments which soften and divert the apprehensions of the fearful virgin? No court now to be paid to my smiles! No encouraging compliments to inspire thee with hope of a laying a mind not unworthy of thee under obligation! " Lovelace, she states in another paper, is the "pernicious caterpillar," a "fell blight," and "eating canker-worm, that preyest upon the opening bud, and turnest the damask rose into livid yellowness! " (III, 207). In her last paper, written to Lovelace, she tells him that he is "Satan himself," and begs him to protect him from Mrs. Sinclair – "a frightful woman! If she *be* a woman! " – and not "let me be made a show of, for my *family's* sake; nay, for your *own sake*" (III, 210-12).

These events complete the main course of action in the novel. Escaping from Lovelace and the women of the house a second time, having resisted a second assault by threatening to kill herself with a penknife, Clarissa finds temporary refuge in London, is arrested for debt on a warrant of Mrs. Sinclair and imprisoned in a sponging house, grows increasingly ill, is released and succeeds in evading Lovelace who has renewed his pursuit, and after a long period of self-examination and spiritual restoration dies. She remains unreconciled with her family, but gains a new family in the kind people who care for her in her final illness. Driven by pride and other feelings he can neither understand nor control, Lovelace courts death, finally dying at the hands of Clarissa's cousin, Morden.

2

This account of the surface action reveals a rising dramatic action that would be impossible if Lovelace were shown to be wholly sadistic and bent on rape from the beginning. As Kinkead-Weekes shows, Richardson (in the first edition at least) displays a gradual hardening of feeling and purpose. Nevertheless, dislocations in the characterization exist, and are sometimes at odds with the surface representation we have analyzed. We shall examine now this deeper representation and its implications.

Shortly after the rape, Lovelace plans a second attempt upon Clarissa, as we noted. He is urged by the women of the house, who wish the act performed while Clarissa is fully conscious: only such a performance will satisfy the "test" of virtue. Failing, Lovelace leaves the house and goes down to Berkshire to visit his sick uncle. Before leaving, he describes to Belford, in elaborate detail, a "fortunate dream" in which Clarissa runs from the house and gains the protection of a "grave matronly lady" to whom Clarissa's maid, Dorcas, "that subtle traitress," has appealed for help. Lovelace describes this part of the dream:

> Methought the old lady, moved with Dorcas's story, answered and said, "Hasten, O damsel, who in a happy moment art come to put it in my power to serve the innocent and the virtuous, which it has always been my delight to do: hasten to this young lady, and bid her hie hither to me with all speed; and tell her that my chariot shall be her asylum: and if I find all that thou sayest true, my house shall be her sanctuary, and I will protect her from all her oppressors."

As the dream continues, the old lady takes Clarissa home, and after listening to her tearful story, and weeping herself and complaining "against the arts of wicked men," persuades the girl to share her bed. During the night, Lovelace goes on, the old lady suffers an attack of colic and leaves the bed to find a cordial:

> Having thus risen and stepped to her closet, methought she let fall the wax taper in her return; and then [O metamorphosis still stranger than the former! What unaccountable things are dreams!] coming to bed again in the dark, the young lady, to her infinite astonishment, grief, and surprise, found Mother H. turned into a young person of the other sex; and although Lovelace was the *abhorred of her soul,* yet, fearing it was some *other* person, it was matter of some consolation to her, when she found it was no other than himself, and that she had been still the bedfellow of but *one* and the *same* man. (III, 249-50)

Lovelace concludes the dream with an erotic fantasy strongly voyeuristic in its motifs:

> A strange promiscuous huddle of adventures followed; scenes perpetually shifting; now nothing heard from the lady but sighs, groans, exclamations, faintings, dyings – from the gentleman but vows. promises, protestations, *disclaimers of purposes pursued,* and all the gentle and ungentle pressures of the lover's warfare.
>
> Then, as quick as thought (for dreams, thou knowest, confine not themselves to the rules of the drama) ensued recoveries, lyings-in, christenings, the smiling boy, amply, even in *her own* opinion, rewarding the suffering mother. (III, 250)

Clarissa is reconciled to friends and family, and so is Lovelace – all enjoying his "estate." He concludes his narrative: "I awoke, as thou mayest believe, in great disorder, and rejoiced to find my charmer in the next room, and Dorcas honest" (III, 251).

The dream fulfills an earlier wish of Lovelace to have Clarissa share her bed with Miss Partington; his plan is to substitute himself (III, 149). A few pages after he relates his dream, we discover that he has indeed arranged an abduction: "I can have no manner of doubt of succeeding in Mother H.'s part of the scheme; for will the lady (who resolves to throw herself into the *first house she can enter,* or to bespeak the protection of the *first person she meets*; and who thinks there can be no danger *out* of this house, equal to what she apprehends from me *in* it) scruple to accept of the chariot of a dowager, accidentally offering? And the lady's protection engaged by her faithful Dorcas, so highly bribed to promote her escape? And then Mrs. H. has the air and appearance of a venerable matron, and is not such a forbidding devil as Mrs. Sinclair" (III, 251-52). The ruse fails because Clarissa, at the crucial moment, refuses to go down to the coach. Shortly afterwards she confronts one last time a kneeling and suppliant Lovelace:

> She flew from me. The angel, as soon as she found her wings, flew from me. I, the reptile kneeler, the despicable slave, no more the proud victor, arose; and, retiring, tried to comfort myself that, circumstanced as she is, destitute of friends and fortune; her uncle moreover, who is to reconcile all so soon (as, I thank my stars, she still believes), expected.
>
> Oh, that she would forgive me! Would she but generously forgive me, and receive my vows at the altar, at the *instant* of her forgiving me, that I might not have time to relapse into my old prejudices! By my soul, Belford, this dear girl gives the lie to all our rakish maxims. There must be something more than a *name* in virtue! I now see that there is! *Once subdued, always subdued* – 'tis an egregious falsehood! (III, 261)

Clarissa soon escapes from the house by her own devices. She is never to see Lovelace again.

The episode is notable in that Lovelace for once does not state either that his dream has ended or that he has begun to make the waking dream a reality: "Who says, that, sleeping and waking, I have not fine helps from some *body,* some *spirit* rather, as thou'lt be apt to say? But no wonder that a Beelzebub has his devilkins to attend his call" (III, 251). The dream is more than one of the richly elaborated fantasies he develops in her letters – written, Belford indicates, with the "wit and spirit" typical of the libertine: "and then such an air of levity runs through thy most serious letters; such a false bravery, endeavouring to carry off ludicrously the subjects that most affect thee; that those letters are generally the least fit to be seen, which ought to be most to thy credit" (III, 461-62). His dream of Mother H. is significant, too, not only because Lovelace imagines the feminine emotions of one of his agents (indeed impersonates her), but also because he momentarily identifies with the "mother" and associates her with "Mother Sinclair."

The meaning of the displacement seems to be that he is both seducer and the cruel mother who collaborates in rape. More obviously than the role of B., whose infantile fantasies and behavior he shares, his imagined role is a feminine one. In fantasy he is a sadistic figure from the beginning of the novel, but sadistic in the special way of the masochist who shares the sadistic enjoyment of his tormentor, – to forget he is the victim. Lovelace pursues rape precisely because women are his potential tormentors.

3

Fantasy in *Clarissa* has received attention from numerous critics: Dorothy Van Ghent analyzes the novel as "a construct of irrationals similar to a dream," and notes the prevalence of death wishes that substitute for genuine sensual gratification.[1] Ian Watt suggests that Clarissa is the masochistic, asexual female who complements the sadistic male and unconsciously seeks rape and death as a realization of masochistic fantasy. A component of her death wish is that she cannot admit her part in the rape; Lovelace enacts the disguised sadism which the eighteenth century view of the male demanded, but he exhibits throughout the novel a frustrated goodness and by the end has come to love Clarissa completely. The two complement each other in morbidity and pathos.[2] Earlier we cited Fiedler's view that Clarissa and Lovelace are ego and id, "the Protestant virgin, proper to a society that has destroyed the splendid images of the Mother of God"; Lovelace is the cavalier temper, necessary to her drama.[3] Golden goes beyond these typical views in concluding that Lovelace

1. *The English Novel* (New York: Harper Torchbooks, 1961), p. 61.
2. *The Rise of the Novel,* pp. 232, 235-36.
3. *Love and Death in the American Novel,* pp. 41, 34-35.

exhibits masochism, particularly in his worship of Clarissa, and represents "the androgynous male-female urges in everyman."[4]

By contrast with these psychological views, Doody approaches the characters historically and generically, stating that Lovelace joins the "sexual genius" of Restoration comedy with the "hubris" of the "tyrant-lover" of Restoration and eighteenth century heroic tragedy. Clarissa is his innocent victim, and his victor finally. Neither character can be identified with a single historical mode or type.[5]

I shall go one step further in my analysis of Lovelace and suggest that his pursuit of Clarissa is masochistic in a way we encountered in *Pamela.* More specifically, his dream of changing from Mrs. H. into his own person is a disguised expression of feminine masochism, though he seeks to play the active role and guide his own fortunes, and his admitted intentions are frequently sadistic. There is in Lovelace, in the scenes immediately preceding and following the rape, a reflexive second self moving between active and passive attitudes; not merely an indeterminateness of motive, but a watchfulness – of himself, and of Clarissa, with whom he identifies as his tormentor. For Clarissa satisfies the requirements of his fantasy in becoming the punishing mother.

What appears to resemble castration anxiety comes to the surface after the rape, and strengthens this interpretation. The usual stress on Satanic and anarchic personality misses Richardson's representation of intense, genuine surprise over Clarissa's effect on him. We saw evidence of this in his statement to Belford about subduing women. Earlier he complains to Belford that love of Clarissa has weakened his independence and self-esteem: "How does this damned love unman me! " he writes after Clarissa makes her first escape from Mrs. Sinclair's house. "But nobody ever loved as I love! It is even increased by her unworthy flight, and my disappointment" (II, 526). After the rape he compares himself to a "tottering paralytic" whose nerves have been convulsed by "tumults" Clarissa has excited (III, 475). He dreams that she is united with her heavenly father: "And then (horrid to relate!) the floor sinking under *me,* as the firmament had opened for *her,* I dropped into a hole more frightful than that of Elden, and, tumbling over and over down it, without view of a bottom, I awaked in a panic; and was as effectually disordered for

4. *Richardson's Characters,* pp. 23, 25.
5. *A Natural Passion,* pp. 108-09, 114-15, 122.

half an hour, as if my dream had been a reality" (IV, 136). His courting of death grows increasingly intense, finally making this late dream a reality.

Earlier in the novel Richardson exhibits in Lovelace this strange interplay of sadistic and masochistic traits. Thus he fantasizes the kidnapping of Clarissa's friend Miss Howe, and her mother, and the drowning of their protector, the captain of a vessel, whom Lovelace pushes overboard: "Dost not see him, Jack? I do – popping up and down, his wig and hat floating by him; and paddling, pawing, and dashing, like a frightened mongrel – I am afraid he never ventured to learn to swim" (II, 421). Thereupon he rapes the women and their maid, and afterwards – in a long, remarkably detailed passage – imagines his trial:

> I know I shall get off for one – were it but for family sake: and being a handsome fellow, I shall have a dozen or two of young maidens, all dressed in white, go to court to beg my life. And what a pretty show they will make, with their white hoods, white gowns, white petticoats, white scarves, white gloves, kneeling for me, with their white handkerchiefs at their eyes, in two pretty rows, as his majesty walks through them, and nods my pardon for their sakes! And, if once pardoned, all is over: for, Jack, in a crime of this nature, there lies no appeal, as in a murder. (II, 424)

The fantasy, he understands, reflects his true character: he improvises each action, then suddenly leaps into it: "Thou knowest that I never absolutely conclude upon a project, till 'tis time for execution; and then lightning strikes not quicker than I" (II, 425).

Freud's characterization of moral masochism has bearing on Lovelace's behavior, late in the novel, as we suggested earlier: "An individual may . . . have preserved the whole or some measure of ethical sense alongside of his masochism; but, alternatively, a large part of his conscience may have vanished into his masochism. Again, masochism, creates a temptation to perform 'sinful' actions, which must then be expiated by the reproaches of the sadistic conscience . . . or by chastisement from the great parental power of Destiny" (S.E., XIX, 169). It is Clarissa, however, who exhibits the unconscious resexualization of morality that we analyzed in *Pamela.* Freud distinguishes, in "The Economic Problem of Masochism," the "ultra-morality" of "an especially sensitive conscience," in which the ego is subjected to "the heightened sadism of the super-ego," from moral masochism, in which the masochism of the ego itself, "seeks punishment, whether from the super-ego, or from the parental powers outside" (S.E., XIX, 169).

Dorothy Van Ghent shows that Clarissa acquiesces in her parents' wishes and values and returns symbolically "to her Father's house" where she tells Lovelace she will meet him.[6] In other words, she is able to identify with those parental values that she challenged in considering flight, and that Lovelace rejects as long as he can identify them with the Harlowe family. What he cannot reject is a threat that Clarissa increasingly presents to him – to be discovered in his complex and ambivalent view of her and in his fantasies.

4

We discover in his letters a sustained conflict between his realistic view of Clarissa and his desire to see her as she wishes to see herself. His frequent ingenuousness and humor – qualities that Richardson presumably introduces to make Clarissa's attraction realistic, but are nevertheless fully imagined and therefore credible[7] – must be taken into account in his alternately rapturous and, as his frustration increases, infuriated comments. He is described by Belford, whose views become normative as the novel progresses, as "a good-natured man with all his faults" (IV, 433), and also "ingenuous" (IV, 76), echoing Lovelace's estimate of his own character: "I must assure thee that I have a prodigious high opinion of virtue; as I have of all those graces and excellences, which I have not been able to attain myself. Every free-liver would not *say* this nor *think* thus; every argument he uses, condemnatory of his own actions, as some would think. But ingenuousness was ever a signal part of my character" (II, 40). His comment to Hickman, Miss Howe's fiance, reiterates this quality: "I cannot be grave six minutes together, for the blood of me. I am a descendant of old Chancellor More, I believe, and should not forbear to cut a joke, were I upon a scaffold" (III, 495). The Lovelace of Richardson's social and moral parable is thus different from the Lovelace who displays a variety of feelings and motives.

Richardson's intention was to exhibit in Lovelace an "honourable Love" until Clarissa is in his power, in order to strengthen the moral of the novel that one should avoid the first evil at hand.[8] But the

6. *The English Novel*, p. 61.

7. McKillop, *Samuel Richardson*, pp. 131-32; *The Rise of the Novel*, p. 236.

8. "I must still say, that I would not have Clarissa in Love, at setting out: And that I intended the Passion should be inspired and grow, unknown to

Lovelace that Richardson creates is much less in control of the affair than his letters to Belford suggest; for he is alternately willing to pursue his revenge against the Harlowe family for scorning him, to prove Clarissa's virtue through subversion and attempted seduction (the virtuous woman, he assumes, will manage to withstand assault), and to marry his "angel" when his love for her overpowers his other inclinations. Richardson thus suggests as compatible motives love, revenge, ambition and the "desire of conquest" (II, 495). Up to the moment of the rape, it is Clarissa who determines which of these motives is dominant.

As Richardson portrays Lovelace in the most intense pages of the novel, his anger and bewilderment grow as he increasingly senses how Clarissa uses the situation to her advantage, and these feelings reach their peak after the rape. He states to Miss Howe, when they meet after Clarissa's second escape, that she "obtained such a glorious triumph over me the last time I had the honour to see her, as, with my penitence, ought to have qualified her former resentments" (IV, 25). One of her letters to his relatives, he comments to Belford, is "so written as to make *herself* more admired, *me* more detested" (IV, 69). He feels that she takes pleasure in looking down on him from her moral height: "And now to be able to look down upon me, while her exalted head is hid from me among the stars, sometimes with scorn, at other times with pity, I cannot bear it" (IV, 89). He takes notice, too, of qualities that seem to him perverse and vain. The following statement (reminiscent of B.'s letter to Mrs. Jewkes quoted earlier) is typical of his view when his frustration is most intense: "Some one passion predominating, in every human breast, breaks through principle, and controls us all. Mine is *love* and *revenge* taking turns. Hers is *hatred.* But this is my consolation, that *hatred appeased is love begun*; or *love renewed* I may rather say, if love ever had footing here" (III, 244).

Like B. in his early pursuit of Pamela, he senses in Clarissa an erotic nature equal to his own. He comments to Miss Howe presum-

herself, and be more obvious, for a good while, to every-body than to herself; and when it became glowing, that it should be owing more to unreasonable Opposition, than to the Merits of the Man: And yet that her chief Objections to him should be rather from *Hearsay* bad Fame than *personal Detection.* . . . And in his first Letter to his Friend, he acknowledges honourable Love; and has no Intention of other, till he find her in his Power." *Selected Letters,* p. 81.

ably with Clarissa in mind: "Sweet creatures and true Christians these young girls! They love their enemies. But rakes in their hearts all of them" (II, 371).

Statements like this are clearly intended to illustrate the libertine philosophy that Richardson is criticizing. Lovelace writes Belford in the course of luring Clarissa back to Mrs. Sinclair's: "All women are born to intrigue, Jack; and practice it more or less, as fathers, guardians, governesses, from dear experience, can tell; and in love affairs are naturally expert, and quicker in their wits by half than men" (III, 161). Women are never what they profess to be, and the true man seeks eternally to expose their pretense. This at least is his professed motive. Richardson also shows, however, that underlying his pride and frequent disgust are attitudes in which fear and hatred combine – that is, so long as the libertine stands unreformed.

Lovelace exhibits here many of the attributes of the Don Juan figure. Psychoanalytic writers who have studied this figure agree that he is only apparently free to act as he wishes. Angel Garma, in a recent discussion, suggests that Don Juan is in flight from pleasure and all love-objects, driven by the mania of continual conquest and wishing to make the woman suffer for seeking sexual fulfillment; his powerful superego reinforces the attitude that women will suffer dire consequences in trying to escape the dictates of their own.[9] Fenichel suggests that the Don Juan figure is not only narcissistic but becomes increasingly sadistic when his self-esteem is threatened.[10] A prevalent view of psychoanalytic writers is that libertinism is a phenomenon of the "masculine protest," which Freud, disagreeing with Adler, considered narcissistic, a derivative of the castration complex, that is, of an unresolved Oedipus complex ("On Narcissism," S.E., XIV, 92-93).

Narcissism is undoubtedly the basis, in Richardson's characters, of mutual identifications at the levels of fantasy and reality, and is the basis also of marked ambivalence. The general emphasis on castration anxiety in the views noted further explains why, in the libertine's view, the woman must prove herself capable of degradation. She is

9. "The Deceiving Superego and the Masochistic Ego in Mania," *Psychoanalytic Quarterly,* 37 (1968), 75.

10. The Oedipus complex of the Don Juan figure is "dominated by the pregenital aim of incorporation, pervaded by narcissistic needs and tinged with sadistic impulses," *Psychoanalytic Theory of Neurosis,* p. 243.

sexually desirable under this condition only, no matter what may be said about the desirability of her being virtuous. Thus Lovelace insists that Clarissa is to undergo a trial (a repeated motif in *Pamela,* as we have seen) to determine whether "her frost be frost indeed? Whether her virtue be principle? " (III, 190) He is almost certain that it is not – at least this is his feeling when, after demonstrating her feeling for him as she weeps on his shoulder, she refuses marriage or any "state of probation" or trial engagement (II, 28), at least until she is certain that her flight is not condemned by his uncle and kinswomen or by Miss Howe, and that she has done all in her power to effect a reconciliation with her family, which would imply their approval of Lovelace (II, 28, 141). When Lovelace follows her to Mrs. Moore's at Hampstead, and she tells him again that she cannot marry him, he is certain that her motive is the counterpart of his own: "Don't tell me that virtue and principle are her guides on this occasion! 'Tis *pride,* a greater pride than my own, that governs her. Love, she has none, thou seest; nor ever had, at least not in a superior degree. Love, that deserves the name, never was under the dominion of *prudence,* or of any *reasoning* power. She cannot bear to be thought a *woman,* I warrant! And if, in the last attempt, I find her *not* one, what will she be the worse for the trial? No one is to blame for suffering an evil he cannot shun or avoid" (III, 175-76). Despite conflicting motives cited earlier, he remains determined to prove that his judgment is right. As we noted earlier, even after the rape, having failed to subvert her character and prove her "a woman," Lovelace plans a second trial and rationalizes it in the same terms. Clarissa was in a drugged state and therefore not free to resist him: "And for what should her heart be broken? Her will is unviolated: – at *present,* however, her will is unviolated. The destroying of good habits, and the introducing of bad, to the corrupting of the whole heart, is the violation. That her will is not to be corrupted, that her mind is not to be debased, she has hitherto unquestionably proved" (III, 242). "Hitherto," because almost to the end the issue remains whether Clarissa can be brought to accommodation with the evil suffered, as the women of the brothel have been.

Richardson seems at times to subscribe to the familiar double moral standard; that is, he tends to judge Clarissa on narrower moral grounds than he judges Lovelace, or other men in the novel. He seems even to accept that women wish to be degraded; as Pamela suggests, all women are under the curse of Eve. Thus Belford and Morden both assume that a seduced woman probably has consented, or at least encouraged her seducer, and therefore deserves to marry a man she despises (IV, 458-59). Indeed, Morden is willing to consider Clarissa's marriage to Lovelace as long as she thinks she has given encouragement; his opinion changes only when he discovers that Lovelace has confined her at Mrs. Sinclair's. Yet Richardson also shows that Lovelace's attitude has deeper roots. His quest of "love" is unending because his narcissistic needs are insatiable; no "trial" can ever entirely relieve his conflict. He can never, like Belford, be brought to "reason" by the sight of exhausted libertines, their once "erect necks then denying support to their aching heads" (III, 484). Richardson's psychological insight is never more evident than in Miss Howe's statement to Belford toward the end of the novel: "Well do your sex contrive to bring us up fools and idiots, in order to make us bear the yoke you lay upon our shoulders; and that we may not despise you from our hearts (as we certainly should if we were brought up as you are) for your *ignorance*, as much as you often make us do (as it is) for your insolence" (IV, 477). Whatever prejudices of his age Richardson may have shared, in his psychology he judges the motives of men and women objectively and dispassionately.

5

Had Richardson commented less about his characters and his art, his reputation as a moralist might not have obscured for so long his penetrating psychological and social realism. His extraordinary insight into masochistic men and women emerges in his exploration of Clarissa's tragedy, in comments like Miss Howe's. As we shall see, *Grandison* offers equally remarkable insights, chiefly through Miss Howe's counterpart – Charlotte Grandison. Often, however, Richardson wrote at moral cross-purposes.

In stating his purpose in writing *Clarissa,* he stresses moral and rhetorical concerns, mainly because he was compelled to answer critics of the novel; thus he stresses that "moral equity" cannot be achieved without "future reward" and insists that moral considerations were paramount in drawing Lovelace's character. He wrote Aaron Hill in 1746: "Lovelace's Character I *intend* to be unamiable, as I hinted: I once read to a young Lady Part of his Character, and then his End; and upon her pitying him, and wishing he had been rather made a Penitent, than to be killed, I made him still more and more odious, by his heighten'd Arrogance and Triumph, as well as by vile Actions, leaving only some Qualities in him, laudable enough to justify her first Liking."[11] Had he restricted inside views to Clarissa, as he largely restricted them to Pamela, his plan to make Lovelace "more and more odious" could have been accomplished easily; but the circumstances of the rape and its aftermath made an inside view of him necessary. The clear-eyed Lovelace on the night of the rape can view Clarissa as the drugged girl obviously cannot view herself. This necessity gives Richardson the opportunity to imagine conflicting emotional states fully. He had done so in Pamela, never in B., though the potentialities for development exist in the character. Indeed Richardson suggests that Lovelace and B. were drawn from the same man: "Yet I must own, that I am a good deal warped by the Character of a Gentleman I had in my Eye when I drew both him, and Mr. B. in Pamela. The best of that Gentleman, for the latter; the worst of him for Lovelace, made still worse by mingling the worst of two other Characters, that were as well known to me, of that Gentleman's Acquaintance."[12]

The range of psychological exploration, within these norms of character, indeed, is even broader than this and other comments on Lovelace in Richardson's letters suggest. Spurred by responses such as he quotes to Hill, he extended the range of characterization; yet he need not have shown Lovelace to be so genuinely and ardently in love. Nor does his professed wish to show that his good qualities could be as dangerous to women as his despicable ones account for the wide-ranging exploration of his feelings. Sustained inside views created more sympathy for Lovelace than Richardson had intended, with the result that he found it necessary to darken his character, to the extent also of darkening the character of his accomplices (precisely the situation in *Pamela*). Nevertheless, Lovelace is a complex figure in Richardson's imagination from the beginning – capable of loving, in mysterious ways.

Ultimately for Richardson Lovelace becomes a figure of fantasy, and so powerful is the fantasy that the "dream" with which we began this consideration of *Clarissa* is defended against by its nega-

11. *Selected Letters*, pp. 73-74.
12. *Ibid.*, p. 79.

tion through action; that is, we discover that the dream of Clarissa's abduction through the agency of Mother H. may be a narration of what Lovelace actually has arranged. It is, in fact, being presented to Belford as a waking fantasy, like the rapes of Miss Howe, her mother and their maid-servant. The turn to action is therefore a displacement from a rendering of character that proved threatening to Richardson. He permits Lovelace to act once the darker qualities of character and the attendant fantasy become so strong that supervening action (the rape) relieves anxiety by turning the reader away from its source. In attending to action, we attend least to motive – to "trends" of character that are indefinite and indeterminate in the fully imagined fantasy.

Probably Richardson imagined a character resembling B., overtly sadistic and voyeuristic, particularly as Bergler describes the type. Perverse voyeurs, he suggests, are basically masochistic; each woman secretly observed is identified unconsciously with the denying mother infancy of her substitute.[13] We noted the voyeuristic behavior of B., behavior that suggests in real people the reactivation of repressions of the genital stage. Consistent with these trends, Lovelace's ambivalence toward Clarissa, who as love-object is simultaneously desired and feared, increases as she takes on qualities that generate anxiety and must be defended against. At this point Lovelace doubtless exceeded the needs of Richardson's moral parable, and he seems to have sensed it.

In darkening Lovelace's character, Richardson intensifies a sadism he associated with the free-living – but not free-thinking – libertine. It is a peculiarity of *Clarissa* that he felt it necessary to explain in the postscript why this is so: "Had he been an infidel, there would have been no room at all for hope of him" (IV, 560). Clarissa's tentative hope that Lovelace may become a better man is based on this "consolation." The psychological interpretation we have been developing suggests a reason that brings Lovelace to her view: he must believe in the same God to share her belief, once the rape has occurred, that he is a fallen man. Basic to the role that becomes dominant in later episodes is that he imagines his fate as Clarissa does. Increasingly his apparent sadism becomes the counterpart of her masochism, or

13. Edmund Bergler, *"Voyeurism," Archives of Criminal Psychodynamics*, 2 (1957), 216.

rather is a version of it; for at times protagonist and antagonist seem to constitute a single mind.

On the night of the rape, he can identify with Clarissa's feelings totally. Other passages confirm this quality. Thus, after intercepting a letter of Miss Howe, he imagines the revenge he will take upon the two women: "How sweetly pretty to see the two lovely friends, when humbled and tame, both sitting in the darkest corner of a room, arm in arm, weeping and sobbing for each other! And I their emperor, their then *acknowledged* emperor, reclined at my ease in the same room, uncertain to which I should first, Grand Signor-like, throw out my handkerchief! " (II, 369) His imaginativeness in passages like this supply images and feelings associated with the conventional sentimental heroine. Neither Clarissa nor Miss Howe is of this type or exhibits these imagined qualities.

The play on masochistic feelings generates the basic rhythm of the novel: the dilation of episodes leading to the rape and the sudden masochistic "flight forward" to it, almost as soon as Lovelace tricks Clarissa into returning to the city from Hampstead. It also explains the impetus towards death, once the rape has been effected. In the course of the transition from sadism to masochism, Freud states in the essay "Instincts and Their Vicissitudes," "The active voice is changed, not into the passive, but into the reflexive, middle voice" (S.E., XIV, 128). We used this idea previously to characterize Lovelace's alternation between active and passive attitudes. Ultimately the "middle voice" heard in the scenes leading to the rape – in Lovelace's account and later in Clarissa's parallel account to Miss Howe – represents a dual consciousness that unites the characters in the underlying masochistic fantasy.

Masochism in the two characters is mutually reinforcing. Though Clarissa is drawn to Lovelace by his strength and courage – qualities sorely lacking in her father, as Wolff points out – her feelings from the beginning are deeper and complex, shown in her fantasies of burial even before she has reason to fear Lovelace.[14] In an early dream he stabs her, buries her body, and tramples on her grave. She says to her Uncle Antony, in the presence of Solmes: "I will even consent to enter into the awful vault of my ancestors, and to have that bricked up upon me, rather than consent to be miserable for

14. *Samuel Richardson and the Eighteenth-Century Puritan Character,* p. 98.

life" (I, 380). After the rape she urges Lovelace to "dig a hole deep enough to cram in and conceal this unhappy body" (III, 235), and later fantasizes that his accomplices could have avoided ruin perhaps by "murdering her, and burying her in their garden or cellar, too deep for detection" (III, 308). Toward the end of the novel, she writes Belford that she wishes Lovelace "good," though (referring to herself) "*he hath overwhelmed the fatherless, and digged a pit for his friend*" (IV, 78). These fantasies join Lovelace to her father, both of whom confine or imprison her. One psychoanalytic writer notes the fear of one's own body and of sexual experience expressed in the fear of being buried alive.[15]

Sensing that she is stubborn enough to realize her wish for death, Lovelace writes to Belford: "Set before her the sin of her preparation, as if she thought she could depart when she pleased. She'll persuade herself, at this rate, that she has nothing to do, when all is ready, but to lie down and go to sleep: and such a lively fancy as hers will make a reality of a jest at any time." He adds: "Tell, therefore, the dear creature that she must not be wicked in her piety. There is a *too much,* as well as a *too little,* even in righteousness" (IV, 260-61). Shortly before she dies, she shows that he is still unwilling to accept her professed motives: "But I'll have none of her forgiveness! My own heart tells me I do not deserve it; and I cannot bear it! And what is it but a mere *verbal* forgiveness, as ostentatiously as cruelly given, with a view to magnify herself and wound me deeper? A little, dear, specious – but let me stop, lest I blaspheme! " (IV, 326). In brief, if at first he thinks that her opposition to him is a challenge to his libertinism, he comes to recognize it as a morbid wish for nothing less than the sacrifice of his erotic life. The "wretch" she prefers to him, he tells Hickman, has estates in England and out of it: "Ay sir, we have all heard of him – but none of us care to be intimate with him – except this lady – and that as I told you, in spite to me. His name, in short, is DEATH! DEATH! sir . . ." (III, 495).

The usual discussions of the Lovelace of these final pages do not explain this extreme compulsiveness. The psychological view does: Clarissa has become in his imagination a punishing mother who he thinks has charmed him, and now seeks to destroy him.

This masochistic trait emerges most strikingly in his statements

15. Sandor Feldmann, "On the Fear of Being Buried Alive," *Psychiatric Quarterly,* 16 (1942).

following the rape. These contain images parallel to Clarissa's. Thus he finds that he cannot sleep: "See the difference in our cases, thought I! She, the charming injured, can sweetly sleep, while the varlet injurer cannot close his eyes; and has been trying to no purpose the whole night to divert his melancholy, and to fly from himself! " (III, 226). Despite his contrivances, he finds himself "near tumbling into the pit which it was the end of all my plots to shun! " (III, 236) Hell is a kind of burial alive. Upon discovering that Clarissa has escaped a second time, he imagines his future punishment in Hell: ". . . it must be none of the smallest mortifications, that a *new* devil shall be punished by a worse *old one.* And, *take that*! And, *take that*! to have the old satyr cry to the screaming sufferer, laying on with a cat-o'-nine-tails, with a star of burning brass at the end of each: and *for what*! *for what*! Why, if the truth might be fairly told, for not being so bad a devil as myself" (III, 315). Though he banters about Clarissa's "pretty employment in *new dismals,* when she had hardly worn round her *blazing joyfuls*! ", and suggests that Belford may have to send him a coffin and shroud (IV, 113), he has come to identify with her dying. In his uncle's house, appearing to lie delirious, he is prayed over by a parson who reads from Clarissa's meditation: "It is as suitable to my case as to the lady's, as thou'lt observe if thou readest it again. At the passage where it is said, that *when a man is chastened for sin, his beauty consumes away,* I stepped to the glass: A poor figure, by Jupiter! cried I" (IV, 114). Clarissa will live to "bury me," he writes Belford, and soon he falls in with her wish. His masochism takes on the coloration of hers to the extent that by the end of the novel he has wholly identified with her view of him.

6

Richardson makes few references to Lovelace's mother. His uncle Lord M. mentions only "her indulgent folly to this favourite boy of hers" (III, 406), and Lovelace late in the novel writes that she was cruel in not teaching him to endure disappointment. Lovelace adds: "What a punishment, to have my first great disappointment touch my intellect! " (IV, 442-43) His reference is to a disappointing early love, mentioned in an earlier letter: "I have boasted that I was once in love before: and indeed I thought I was. It was in my early manhood – with that quality-jilt, whose infidelity I have vowed to revenge upon as many of the sex as shall come into my power. I believe, in different climes, I have already sacrificed an hecatomb to my Nemesis, in pursuance of this vow. But upon recollecting what I was *then,* and comparing it with what I find in myself *now,* I cannot say that I was ever in love before" (I, 145).

This early love is presented by Lovelace as an explanation for his attitude to women, early in the novel; its importance to Richardson is suggested not only by the similarity to B.'s disappointment over Sally Godfrey, but by the circumstances of the rape – which suggest the motifs of Oedipal fantasy familiar in psychoanalytic writings. Dominating the scene of the rape is Mrs. Sinclair, who, with other women of the brothel, urges Lovelace to proceed. As in *Pamela,* Richardson concentrates on events leading to the rape rather than on the actual assault, as we have noted. He could have not have shown more than he does; but the requirements of literary decorum are not a sufficient explanation, given the physical violation of Clarissa during the fire scene analyzed earlier. The explanation is perhaps that Mrs. Sinclair is, in Lovelace's description of Clarissa's terror of her following the rape, "the mother, the hitherto *dreaded* mother" (III, 287). In the penknife scene, in which this reference is made, Lovelace imagines that Mrs. Sinclair has almost called him "son" (III, 286). His increasingly fierce description of the woman expresses perhaps his own disgust and hidden terror, as we noted in our discussion of Mrs. Jewkes. The terrified Clarissa who "lives" despite the rape is much like the Oedipal mother of fantasy, whose violation the Dark Mother consents to and collaborates in, first by drugging her, then by hovering over the half-conscious girl during the assault.

The rape is thus more an event in the underlying fantasy than in the represented action, as Richardson's unwillingness to dramatize Clarissa's feelings immediately upon awakening show. In the depiction of events leading to the rape Richardson focuses on the women of the house rather than on the drugged girl. Her impressions are chiefly of rising terror as the realization grows that the women she has taken for Lady Betty and Charlotte Montague will not return that night. In short, the anxieties of these moments must be defended against in the actual representation. At no point in the novel is Lovelace's identification with Clarissa greater. His letter to Belford presumably written immediately after the event, is brief and telling: "And now, Belford, I can go no farther. The affair is over. Clarissa lives" (III, 196). And at no point is his behavior more manic, exhibiting "the tinge of the violent, the overdone, the exaggerated," to quote Reik's characterization of masochism at its most depressed, and exhibiting also the characteristics cited by Garma, "elation, hyperactivity, search for objects, flight of thoughts, increased self-esteem, feelings of omnipotence."[16]

To repeat a previous qualification, I am referring in what follows to the "trends" of psychoanalytic character, whatever may have been the cultural and personal influences that shaped the character for Richardson. Lovelace's professed need to prove the virtue of his "beloved" is, psychoanalytically, a disguised wish to prove the virtue of the mother – in fantasy to free her of the father. The house in which he imprisons Clarissa, Miss Lardner tells Miss Howe, consists of two houses, "the one *in which all decent appearances were preserved, and guests rarely admitted*; the other, the receptacle of those who were absolutely engaged, and broken to the vile yoke" (III, 5). Interpreted in the language of infantile fantasy, the house is the parental home, maintaining a decent appearance yet serving as a place of lust. Lovelace is the Oedipal child whom Clarissa suckles; before the rape he thinks of her as the mother of his children and writes of "the pleasure of seeing a twin Lovelace at each charming breast, drawing from it his first sustenance" (II, 477). His later dreams in the novel center on male children; he will laugh at Belford if "all her grievous distresses shall end in a man-child: which I shall love better than all the cherubims and seraphims that may come after; though there were to be as many of them as I beheld in my dream; in which a vast expanse of firmament was stuck as full of them as it could hold" (IV, 164).

The conflicting trends of character we analyzed in B. are also evident in Lovelace: the pattern is nearly the same. The two currents of feeling – the tender and the erotic – cannot unite; the sexual object must be degraded, the rape justified as a means of "proving" her virtue. We discover, too, the masochistic "flight forward." The "prolonged tension and indecision," to quote McKillop's characterization of Richardson's art, suddenly gives way under

16. *Masochism in Modern Man,* p. 132; Garma, "The Deceiving Ego," 63. Compare Freud's discussion of hysterical symptoms, "Hysterical Phantasies and Their Relationship to Bisexuality," S.E., IX, 159-66.

unmanageable anxiety.[17] The enjoyment of seduction is in the "progress" rather than in the "crowning act: for that's a vapour, a bubble! " (II, 337), Lovelace writes. A later statement of Belford shows that Richardson was fully aware of the psychological implications of this view. "With regard to the passion itself, the less of soul in either man or woman, the more sensual are they. Thou, Lovelace, hast a soul, though a corrupted one; and art more intent . . . upon the preparative stratagem, than upon the end of conquering" (II, 487). The wife-mother in Lovelace's fantasies is simultaneously degraded and proved an angel – a contradiction that Clarissa keeps before him.

The child she is breeding, Lovelace realizes, is death – though he continues to hope it will be the contrary (IV, 41), and, indeed, earlier in the same letter expresses hope that "the dear creature is in the way to be a mama" (IV, 38). His realization grows that Clarissa's fate is inextricably bound with his and is pointed toward death. This may be the partial significance of his dream that Morden (death) leaps through a window, a sword in hand, and is prevented by Clarissa from killing him. He dreams also that his uncle, Morden's accomplice in the dream, has thrown his mantle over his face. He imagines Clarissa welcomed to Heaven by "golden cherubs and glittering seraphs" and Lovelace is left with her robe, "all stuck thick with stars of embossed silver" (IV, 136). His dream of falling into "a hole more frightful than that of Elden," discussed earlier, follows.

As he tries to interpret the dream to his own advantage, Lovelace again implicitly associates cherubs with the children Clarissa will bear him, in his fantasy. In these statements death is the implied avenue to erotic fulfillment: "The opening cloud is the reconciliation in view. The bright form, lifting up my charmer through it to a firmament stuck round with golden cherubims and seraphims, indicates the charming little boys and girls that will be the fruits of this happy reconciliation" (IV, 158). The fall into the "frightful hole" is an allusion to marriage, he suggests – "a bottomless pit," a gulf. He ends by suggesting that, had he not awakened from the dream in terror, he would have been carried to Clarissa, rid of his faults. Commenting later on Belford's statement that Clarissa was sent to rescue him from the "miry gulf" (IV, 214), he is reminded of a statue of Lady Elizabeth Carteret in Westminster Abbey, her hand

17. *Samuel Richardson,* p. 127.

in the grip of a "Cupid," who will not ascend to Heaven with her; for one foot is "riveted to its native earth, bemired . . . beyond the possibility of unsticking itself" (IV, 252-53).

These motifs indicate that the aborted fantasy of *Pamela*, ending in desexualization of the marriage and B.'s increasing subordination to his wife, is revived and perfected in *Clarissa.* Though Lovelace changes as the novel progresses, the fantasy he enacts later in the novel is imagined from the beginning. Later fantasies – Clarissa's robe "stuck thick with stars," his whipping in Hell, "with a cat-o'-nine-tails, with a star of burning brass at the end of each" – are prefigured in his exultation early in the novel over having taken Clarissa from her parents: "I am taller by half a yard in my imagination than I was. I look *down* upon everybody now. Last night I was still more extravagant. I took off my hat as I walked, to see if the lace were not scorched, supposing it had brushed down a star. and, before I put it on again, in mere wantonness, and heart's ease, I was for buffeting the moon" (I, 515).

Pointed objects recur; numerous episodes and incidental images suggest punishment and castration. Clarissa tries to protect herself with a sharp pair of scissors in the fire scene analyzed, when Lovelace forces his way into her bedroom (II, 502), and much later, after the rape, threatens to kill herself with a penknife if she is molested again. Earlier, as we have seen, Lovelace imagines his being condemned to hanging for raping Miss Howe, her mother and their servant. After Clarissa's second escape, he is seized with remorse on hearing that she has been arrested on a charge by Mrs. Sinclair, and shut up in a sponging-house: "already I can fancy that, to pink by body like my mind, I need only to be put into a hogshead stuck full of steel-pointed spikes, and rolled down a hill three times as high as the Monument" (III, 451). The horrible amputation Mrs. Sinclair suffers before her death is described at considerable length by Belford, and given Lovelace's earlier identification with the woman has the implication of castration. Indeed, Richardson concentrates his detail on the horrors of the amputation: "All the time that the surgeons run on with their anatomical process the wretched woman most frightfully roared and bellowed; which the gentleman (who showed themselves to be of the class of those who are not affected with the evils they do not *feel*) took no other notice of than by raising *their* voices to be *heard,* as she raised *hers* . . ." (IV, 386).

Lovelace struggles to the end between his realistic view of Clarissa and irreconcilable fantasy. Rape of the mother demands castration, thus his question to his uncle after her death, "is death the *natural* consequence of a rape? " (IV, 453) Though he wishes to believe that he can return to his previous life, the growing fatalism that we have analyzed characterizes his thoughts. In his dream he is "muffled" in the mantle of his uncle, his substitute father. The "great parental authority Destiny" dominates the final pages.

In an early letter Lovelace considers that rape of Clarissa would be "a rape worthy of a Jupiter! " (I, 175) Toward the end of the novel he reflects on her intimation, in her last letter to him, that he is no longer a god:

> "Your golden dream cannot last long." – Divine prophetess! my golden dream is *already* over. "Thought and reflection *are* no longer to be kept off." No *longer continues* that "hardened insensibility" thou chargest upon me. "Remorse *has* broken in upon me." "Dreadful *is* my condition! " "It *is* all reproach and horror with me! " – A thousand vultures in turn are preying upon my heart! (IV, 440)

His conviction that he loves her – joined with his growing conviction that he is Satanic, in contrast to Clarissa, who has exhibited the virtues of Job and rejects wicked counsel that she marry her seducer – increases as he comes to accept death. He writes to Belford that Fate "spins threads for tragedies" (IV, 450), and speaks of fate in his dying words to Morden: "There is a fate in it! . . . a cursed fate! – or this could not have been! But be ye all witnesses that I have provoked my destiny, and acknowledge that I fall by a man of honour" (IV, 529). His early intimation of doom – "Fate is weaving a whimsical web for thy friend, and I see not but I shall be inevitably manacled" (II, 182) – has become a reality.

His ambivalence remains to the end. One purpose of the masochistic fantasy, according to Fenichel, is the preservation of sexuality: ". . . all active sexuality becomes so intimately connected with castration anxiety, that the sole remaining available sexual aim seems to be the wish to be castrated. A number of masochistic practices therefore represent a symbolic castration. Here may be seen clearly that the so-called wish to be castrated in no way allays castration anxiety but enhances it instead." Fenichel then makes an important qualification that helps explain why the preparation for events that promise disaster is so prolonged: the final catastrophe is not really believed in. "The symbols of castration used by the masochist are, after all, merely symbols, and as Freud has pointed out, most masochists will endure pain of all kinds and will desire to be hurt in many ways, – but they always protect the genital from injury."[18]

Trends of character which seem incompatible or unresolved can be joined in psychoanalytic theory. The need to preserve his sexual freedom and protect himself from injury is, psychoanalytically, the explanation for Lovelace's spirited actions and pretense of gaiety before Clarissa's death and afterwards, even as his anxiety noticeably increases. As Richardson imagines the end of their relationship, it is his misfortune that she is relentless in her destruction of his sexuality. Lovelace does not miss veiled hints that she wishes him to follow her (IV, 217, 251), for these hints realize the conditions he has been seeking. Ironically, the obstacle that in his mind keeps him apart from his "beloved" – her wish for death – is the means of erotic fulfillment, as the passages previously quoted show. Under other circumstances, both might have continued living their fantasies; Lovelace is destroyed because these prove unexpectedly compatible.

The longer the masochistic fantasy lasts, Reik states in his analysis of men more bridled than Lovelace, the more assured is the transfer from the hero's triumphs (based on good qualities) to his iniquities, ending with mysterious and unearned suffering. These iniquities and difficulties, Reik states, "now occupy the greater and more important part of the daydreamer's imaginations and the subsequent rehabilitation appears as a kind of accessory. It looks as if the pleasure has been displaced from the phantasy of the enforcement of one's own will to the punishment and sufferings preceding and conditioning it. Finally this originally essential climax occurs, like a feeble concession, in the background only, whereas the mysterious and apparently unjustified suffering of the hero attracts all attention and all excitement."[19] Lovelace's "triumph" is based on more ambiguous qualities than Richardson indicates, yet the pattern is remarkably similar. We have noted the progress in his characterization from good qualities to their opposite and eventually his surrender to an increasingly intense sense of fatality.

The following passage suggests how the shift is managed stylisti-

18. *Outline of Clinical Psychoanalysis* (New York: Psychoanalytic Quarterly Press and W. W. Norton, 1934), p. 274.

19. *Masochism in Modern Man,* p. 317.

cally. Lovelace writes in the first half of the novel: "Nor had I at another time any mercy upon the daughter of an old epicure, who had taught the girl, without the least remorse, to roast lobsters alive; to cause a poor pig to be whipped to death; to scrape carp the contrary way of the scales, making them leap in the stew-pan, and dressing them in their own blood for sauce. And this for luxury sake, and to provoke an appetite; which I had without stimulation, in my way, and that I can tell thee a very ravenous one" (II, 248). The opening sentences suggest revulsion; the concluding sentences, similar pleasures that do not require "stimulation." At this point in the novel the dominant impression of Lovelace has the accent of sadism, yet the underlying fantasy is here already masochistic. Richardson in this way prepares for the later change in characterization.

We see the change also in Lovelace's identification with his victims and consequently with their sexual qualities, as passages previously quoted show. Early in the novel he playfully fantasizes about creating separate churches for men and women – suggesting that "were it so, and life to be the forfeiture of being found at the female churches, I believe that I, like a second Clodius, should change my dress, to come at my Portia or Pompeia, though one the daughter of a Cato, the other the wife of a Caesar" (II, 24). Clodius was unsuccessfully prosecuted for disguising himself as a woman harpist in Caesar's house, at the ceremony of Bona Dea.

To summarize, he begins as a figure moving between fantasy and reality and ends a wholly fantastic one. Richardson rationalizes the portrayal feebly in his letters: he added "some deeper Shades" into Lovelace to prevent his inducing pity in the reader.[20] But he goes further than this in explaining his behavior at the end: "What a Goddess does he makes of the exalted Clarissa! – Yet how deplorably impious, hardly thinks of invoking the highest assistance and mercy! " His final "Let this expiate! " is a further exhibition of his "wonted haughtiness of spirit." Richardson concludes the letter: "Have I not then given rather a dreadful than a hopeful Exit, with respect to Futurity, to the unhappy Lovelace! – I protest I have been unable to reperuse the acct: of his Death *with this great Circumstance* in my Head, and to think of the triumphant one of my divine

20. *Selected Letters,* p. 113.

Clarissa, without pity – and I did hope that the contrast if attentively considered would be very striking."[21]

The guiding difficulty is that the rape occurs, unlike the situation in *Pamela.* There can be no forgiveness or alteration of qualities in the direction of goodness, as in B., if the event is given as real. By contrast, Belford, whose exploits are merely referred to, is permitted to learn from Clarissa that women are capable of natural virtue, to reform his life, and to marry Charlotte Montague and presumably make a good husband (contrary to Richardson's belief that former rakes make bad husbands). The importance of represented attitudes is seen in Lovelace's modern counterpart, the handsome rake of films of the 'thirties and 'forties, who is permitted every liberty short of rape and yet remains sympathetic so long as he is not *shown* to succeed. Coincidentally, a means of seduction in comedies is the performance of effeminate behavior or the pretense of sexual impotence, in the style of Wycherley's Horner in *The Country Wife.*

An example is the 1962 film *Lover Come Back*: the rakish hero pretends shyness to the point of sexual impotence as a means of seduction; the confused woman, at first hostile, takes on the job of building his confidence. At the moment of seduction she accidentally discovers the truth and realizes her danger. The increasingly aggressive style of women in films of the 'sixties and early 'seventies departs from earlier styles, for example, the Hepburn-Tracy films in which the woman's superiority in one field or activity is the *comic* issue. The recent *Diary of a Mad Housewife* – a portrayal of reinforcing masochism in a contemporary marriage – suggests that the absence of aggressiveness is becoming the comic norm. Being forced into aggressive behavior, as in Shakespeare's middle comedies, is not the same as being naturally aggressive; Helena, in *Midsummer's Night's Dream,* is comic because she is.

7

The ease with which Richardson lightens or darkens his characters as the need arises shows that in the sentimental tragedy he was perfecting character is a normative construction, a sum of implied qualities, latent possibilities, whose unpredictableness arouses intense anxiety in the reader. No single motive can be ascribed

21. Ibid., pp. 121-22.

permanently: only trends can be established, discarded, revived if needed, and finally reconciled. Indeed our interest in the character may depend on our freedom to imagine motives that are never directly stated. To quote Freud again, "Laws of poetic economy necessitate this way of presenting the situation, for this deeper motive could not be explicitly enunciated. It had to remain concealed, kept from the easy perception of the spectator or the reader; otherwise serious resistances, based on the most distressing emotions, would have arisen, which might have imperilled the effect of the drama" (S.E., XIV, 329). The philosopher Schelling states the idea in a different way: "The emotions are glorious when they stay in the depths, but not when they come forth into the day and wish to become of the essence and to rule."

In Clarissa's dream of being stabbed and buried, it is precisely the absence of a clear motive for her fear that arouses anxiety and dread – emotions that are particularly strong whenever Clarissa is faced with the prospect of dealing with cruelty in clearly immoral ways. Thus the interest of the first quarter of the novel centers on whether she will take flight from her family, whose intransigence and cruelty are stressed; the later revelation that the family was on the verge of relenting in their demands reinforces the impression that her act is blameable.

Later, to preserve her reputation, she is forced to consider marriage to Lovelace; to keep her "will inviolate," she is forced to threaten suicide. Despite her independent mind and wit, she is beaten down so completely that her only weapon is spiritual aggression – realized finally in her death. At every point, even as the situation grows increasingly desperate, she is obliged to rationalize her situation in the same terms as before: modesty, generosity, duty. Anxiety and dread depend on the awareness that the moral code to which she alone remains faithful is irrelevant to each of the worlds she inhabits; the values by which her family and Lovelace and his circle live are materialistic and pragmatic, never Christian. Richardson is plain about this view of the world in his postscript: "It will be seen by this time that the author had a great end in view. He has lived to see scepticism and infidelity openly avowed, and even endeavoured to be propagated from the press: the great doctrines of the gospel brought into question: those of self-denial and mortification blotted out of the catalogue of Christian virtues: and a taste even to wantonness for outdoor pleasure and luxury, to the general exclusion of domestic as well as public virtue, industriously promoted among all ranks and degrees of people" (IV, 553).

I have suggested that underlying this kind of represented action and character are the energies of moral masochism, arising in the culture and perhaps Richardson himself. One defense of the moral masochist, Charles Socarides suggests, is the impression of "docility, self-effacement, and excessive gentleness."[22] It is these "Pollyanna-ish" qualities, to use Margaret Brenman's phrase, that are often associated with sentimentality.[23] Yet even the gentlest masochist, Reik suggests, enjoys triumph over another.[24] Clarissa's characteristic gentleness, as we have seen, combines with searing realism and a deepening self-understanding.

This is the meaning of her pride, examined psychoanalytically rather than from the Christian perspective. From the beginning she imagines herself as the punisher of her family, whose pride she identifies with her own: "I was the pride of all my friends, proud *myself* of *their* pride, and glorying in my standing. Who knows what the justice of Heaven may inflict, in order to convince us that we are not out of the reach of misfortune, and to reduce us to a better reliance, than that we have hitherto presumptuously made?" (I, 419) Toward the end of the novel, she imagines their sufferings that her death will occasion. She sees her mother robbed of peace of mind and pitied by visitors, "condoling where they used to congratulate: the affected silence wounding: the compassionating look reminding: the half-suppressed sigh in *them* calling up deeper sighs from her; and their averted eyes, while they endeavour to restrain the rising tear, provoking tears from *her,* that will not be restrained" (IV, 60). Clarissa writes to Mrs. Norton, who helped to

22. "The Function of Moral Masochism," *International Journal of Psycho-analysis*, 39 (1958), 592.

23. "In a more complex fashion, the projective mechanism in a masochistic formation may be used as the vehicle for what one might call a benevolent paranoid attitude, where the usual *denials* of and *reaction formations* against, hostile impulses are projected wholesale and people are seen as essentially good and without malice, the Pollyanna-ism so familiar in the masochist." "On Teasing and Being Teased and the Problem of 'Moral Masochism,'" in *Psychoanalytic Psychiatry and Psychology* (New York: International Universities Press, 1954), p. 328.

24. *Masochism in Modern Man,* p. 328.

educate her: "But when I am no more, get over, I charge you, as soon as you can, the smarting pangs of grief that will attend a recent loss; and let all be early turned into that sweetly melancholy regard to MEMORY which, engaging us to forget all faults, and to remember nothing but what was thought amiable, gives more pleasure than pain to survivors – especially if they can comfort themselves with the humble hope that the Divine mercy have taken the dear departed to itself" (IV, 112).

In the same way, the inscription on her coffin – "HERE the wicked cease from troubling: and HERE the weary be at rest" (IV, 257) – is hardly intended to comfort the grieving, nor does it. Clarissa's parents die a few years following her death, and her brother and sister, unrelenting in their hatred of her, suffer unhappy marriages. Reik's statement that the masochist in his fantasies experiences the pleasure of "posthumous revenge and rehabilitation" is confirmed in these details.[25]

The distinctive sentimental experience of *Clarissa* is this most sublime of pleasures. Richardson's perception of this pleasure is probably defended against in his showing that Clarissa makes an effort to live. To the end of the novel cruelty and affection are joined even where masochistic trends are dominant: Lovelace can express his love as a sublime emotion even as he is planning to be cruel and simultaneously feels remorse. Love and death, grief and joy, are inseparable experiences. He writes to Belford: "Grief mollifies and enervates. The grieved mind looks round it, silently implores consolation, and loves the soother. Grief is ever an inmate of joy. Though they won't show themselves at the same window at *one* time, yet have they the whole house in common between them" (II, 188). He is here referring to Clarissa's grief after her abduction.

Clarissa shows clearly that sentimentality as a distinctive literary experience is inseparable from the enjoyment of suffering. Eighteenth century writers were sensitive to this connection: thus Burke suggest that the feeling of the sublime and pain are closely related: ". . . if the pain and terror are so modified as not to be actually noxious; if the pain is not carried to violence, and the terror is not conversant about the present destruction of the person, as these emotions clear the parts, whether fine, or gross, of a dangerous

25. Ibid., p. 328.

and troublesome incumbrance, they are capable of producing delight: not pleasure, but a sort of delightful horror, a sort of tranquility tinged with terror; which as it belongs to self-preservation is one of the strongest of all the passions."[26]

For Richardson cruelty and affection are closely allied: this is one essential feature of sentimental tragedy. Lovelace can express his love as a sublime emotion even as he is planning to be cruel. His compulsiveness, expressed as a fatality which brings the libertine and his "angel" into collision, as we have seen, is projected outward. In *Beyond the Pleasure Principle* Freud makes this comment on the meaning of fate in the lives of neurotic and certain normal people:

> The impression they give is of being pursued by a malignant fate or possessed by some 'daemonic' power; but psychoanalysis has always taken the view that their fate is for the most part arranged by themselves and determined by early infantile influences. The compulsion which is here in evidence differs in no way from the compulsion to repeat which we have found in neurotics, even though the people we are now considering have never shown any signs of dealing with a neurotic conflict by producing symptoms. Thus we have come across people all of whose human relationships have the same outcome . . . .

The last of these people cited is "the lover each of whose love affairs with a woman passes through the same phases and reaches the same conclusion" (S.E., XVIII, 21-22). And Freud adds in the same passage: "We are much more impressed by cases where the subject appears to have a *passive* experience, over which he has no influence, but in which he meets with a repetition of the same fatality."

The Oedipal dream, whose representation is complicated by the feminine displacements in Lovelace's characterization, remains the source of unresolved tensions because of the compulsion to repeat in a general sense (Freud is referring to the compulsion that he identified with the death instinct in his later reformulation of instinctual theory). So, too, the reader's enjoyment is necessarily complicated by attendant guilt; the pieties dominating the falling action disguise the reinforcing masochism of the final scenes but also serve to allay guilt, though the tensions that have been brought into play are only half relieved.

26. *A Philosophical Enquiry into the Origin of Our Ideas of the Sublime and the Beautiful* (London: Routledge and Kegan Paul, 1958), p. 136. Other ideas and depictions of painful experience in eighteenth century literature are discussed by Praz, *The Romantic Agony*, Chapter 3.

Chapter Four

THE "FAMILY ROMANCE" OF *SIR CHARLES GRANDISON*

1

Morris Golden finds in Richardson's fourth and last novel the fantasy of dominance and "physical mastery." Although arrogance and impetuosity characterize Harriet Byron's suitors, even the gentle, well-mannered Sir Charles seeks to dominate those around him. The essence of the fantasy centering on him is polygamy, the subordination of a series of languishing women who share Grandison as "sisters."[1] I shall follow this insight, and further show that the fantasy in *Sir Charles Grandison* may be analyzed as a variant of the common childhood "family romance" described by Freud. More than this, we shall see that the particular elaboration Richardson gives to it has striking connections with patterns noted in the previous novels.

Grandison departs from the earlier novels in that Richardson begins not with the rake whose reformation is possible if he stops short of rape, or if the rake is not represented (B., Belford), or whose damnation is possible if rape is shown – but rather with the virtuous gentleman. Richardson's continuing concern with the rake centers in Harriet's aggressive suitors Greville and Sir Hargrave Pollexfen, and he gives frequent reminders that rakes overawe their wives and, like Grandison's father, make bad husbands and fathers (Part 1, Volume II, 299). Grandison's view of the reformed rake is the same Richardson develops in *Pamela* and *Clarissa*: "A *Rake* in Passion is not a Rake in *love.* Such a one can seldom be in Love: From a laudable passion he cannot. He has no delicacy" (1, II, 429-30).[2]

With the representation of the father (a representation missing in the previous novels, in which the dead fathers are virtually unmen-

1. *Richardson's Characters,* pp. 15, 21.
2. See also Part 2, Volume III, 103, 110.

tioned), a new element is introduced into the novels: the rakish father looks to his virtuous son for his salvation. Thus, Sir Thomas calls on Grandison, as he lies dying: "Sometimes, when the unhappy man was quietest, he would call upon his son, in words generally of kindness and love; Once in particular, crying out – O save me! my Grandison, by thy presence! I shall be consumed by the fire that is already lighted up in my boiling blood" (1, II, 356). In brief, the virtuous son is looked upon as a substitute father; after Sir Thomas's death, Grandison plays this role as brother, guardian, friend, and husband-protector.

Since this event occurs before the novel begins, we see Grandison in this role past and present: we see no developing feeling or insight, only a fixed character in action. The novel throughout has the tone of parable. Paradoxically, however, he is far more a figure of fantasy than B. or Lovelace, and rich as *Grandison* is in social details and the exploration of serious social issues, it conveys the impression of a dream in which threatened assaults are almost at once aborted. The epistolary form here presents most such events through later narrative: with a few exceptions, it does not immerse the readers in actions felt and experienced at the moment of their occurrence – as in Lovelace's intense, interrupted communications to Belford at the height of his attempt upon Clarissa.

2

The main events of the novel may be summarized briefly. Following his mother's death, Grandison is sent abroad by his father to be educated. In Italy he has occasion to save the life of Jeronymo della Porretta, the youngest son of a noble family, who in gratitude welcome Grandison as a "fourth son." Their daughter, Lady Clementina, falls in love with Grandison, who has agreed to tutor her. When he proposes marriage, after considerable anguish she rejects him; she gives the reason that Grandison has refused conversion to Roman Catholicism, though consenting to arrangements that will guarantee her freedom of worship in England. Her sacrifice leads to a state of derangement.

Upon his father's death, Grandison returns to England; nine years have passed. The events of these years are presented in retrospect. The novel begins with his return, very soon after which he rescues Harriet Byron from Sir Hargrave, who has abducted her after her rejection of his aggressive advances and refusal of marriage – an event parallel to Grandison's own courtship of Clementina. Though Grandison falls in love with Harriet, he does not propose marriage until, at the request of the Porretta family, he returns to Italy, aids in Clementina's mental recovery, and is refused a second time. On returning to England, he marries Harriet. Urged by her family to marry Count Belvedere and discouraged by them from entering a convent, Clementina flees to England, where she seeks Grandison's counsel. Her parents and brother follow her to England, and they are quickly reconciled with Clementina, who promises to reconsider marriage to the Count in a year's time.

To describe Grandison as the virtuous gentleman is to understate his character considerably; for he is almost without fault: chivalrous, generous, prudent, pious, good-natured, serene in temper, yet spirited when the occasion warrants. He says about himself to Mr. Jordan, during his confrontation with Sir Hargrave: "I have always considered Spirit as the distinction of a man. My father was a man of spirit. I never fear'd man, since I could write man. As I never sought danger, or went out of my way to meet it, I looked upon it when it came, as an unavoidable evil, and as a call upon me for fortitude. And hence I hardly ever wanted that presence of mind in it, which a man ought to shew; and which sometimes, indeed, was the means of extricating me from it" (1, II, 256-57).

Though a young man, he exceeds the wisdom of older men. Throughout the novel, he is engaged in rescuing or rehabilitating the unfortunate and morally infirm. After his father's death he is able to remedy the mistreatment of his sister Caroline by arranging her marriage to Lord L. In the course of the novel he rescues his gouty uncle, Lord W., from his tyrannous mistress, Mrs. Giffard; when he arranges to pension her according to her wishes, she is stricken with remorse (2, III, 52). He arranges a marriage between his uncle and the much younger Miss Mansfield, as a way of helping to recoup the fortunes of her family. Acting as executor for his dead friend Danby, he arranges the careers and marriages of Danby's nephews and niece. He also pensions his father's mistress, Mrs. Oldham, provides for his father's illegitimate children, and redeems his honor in an abortive affair with Miss Obrien, whom he had been inveigled into promising marriage. He reconciles the divided Beauchamp family and his ward, Emily Jervois, with her once-wicked mother and new stepfather. He brings his high-spirited and sometimes selfish and proud sister Charlotte into accord with her good-natured but long-suffering husband. He tries to persuade the lovesick Lady Olivia, who follows him to England from Italy, to give up hope of marrying him; when she attacks him with a dagger, he offers forgiveness: "He only said, when he had got it from her, Unhappy violent woman, I return not this instrument of mischief! You will have no use for it in England – And would not let her have it again" (2, IV, 380). Failing to effect a reformation of character in a person, he can at least bestow grave looks. But he is almost never unsuccessful.

Doody points out that, wishing to display a Christian gentleman acting in several spheres of life, and to show that women could be as much attracted to exemplary qualities as to those of the unbridled individual or rake (Fielding's Tom Jones, as Richardson perceived the character), he stresses the moral code by which Grandison guides his actions. His chivalric and benevolent acts are those dictated by a Christian moral code so perfect that, when impulse is guided by reason as it must be in the Christian gentleman, good for the individual and the community must result.[3] Wolff states: "Grandison's moral behavior is always seen as an exercise of *duty*; there is no sense that it flows from a spontaneous, innate impulse toward good."[4] Yet this is not all Richardson shows. The letters show that he was aware of the problems created in such a representation: "I would not make him guilty of too great refinements: I would draw him as a mortal. He should have all the human passions to struggle with; and those he cannot conquer he shall endeavour to make subservient to the cause of virtue."[5]

Unhappy families rather than unhappy individuals are Grandison's chief concern. The fantasy that pervades the novel is not mainly or solely personal and sexual as we find it in Clarissa and Lovelace: the substitute-father in the many subplots noted is the dominant figure in an encompassing family romance, and the dominant fantasy is energized here. The establishment of a steadily enlarging family circle is the chief concern of the novel, as numerous critics have noted; the virtues of family life are explored at length; Harriet's approval of her grandfather's statement that families are "little communities" and

3. *A Natural Passion,* pp. 253-55, 270.
4. *Samuel Richardson and the Eighteenth-Century Puritan Character,* p. 180.
5. *Selected Letters,* p. 186.

that few enduring friendships can be formed outside them represents Richardson's normative view (1, I, 25). No sooner is Harriet rescued from Sir Hargrave than she joins the family circle of her rescuer. Grandison asks, "Was she not stolen from us in her cradle? " (1, I, 148) Throughout the novel marriage is seen as a widening of friendship: passion is the enemy of marital and familial accord.

The essence of the "family romance," in its first stage, Freud states in his essay of 1909, is that the child fantasizes that he is adopted or a stepchild; for his real parents he substitutes ones of higher birth, as in earlier childhood fantasies provoked by feelings or slight or neglect. This first feeling of estrangement – the idea that the parents are not the child's own – occurs in early childhood, and reinforces these later fantasies of substitution that gain strength before puberty. So long as the child remains ignorant of the facts of sexuality, he is able to make substitutions for both parents; but the onset of puberty changes the situation. Once the facts are known, substitution for the mother is impossible, for she is the real mother. The child knows that his father's identity cannot be certain and so can continue to exalt him through substitutions as before; but retaliation against the mother must now take a different form. Where his former fantasies were asexual, his mother is now fantasied in erotic situations – as being unfaithful and engaged in secret affairs. The previous motives of hostility and revenge thus are sustained. Freud also distinguishes a related fantasy in which the child returns to legitimize himself and bastardize his brothers and sisters. "So too if there are any other particular interests at work they can direct the course to be taken by the family romance; for its many-sidedness and its great range of applicability enable it to meet every sort of requirement" (S.E., IX, 240). Toward the end of the essay, Freud makes an important qualification: the new parents who replace the imposters actually are conceived as and invested with the qualities of the child's parents as he knew them in early childhood – his father noble and brave, his mother the most beautiful of women. The overvaluation of the parents, in early childhood, thus survives in the fantasies of normal grown people.

Freud makes a similar point in a later essay, "A Special Type of Choice of Object Made by Men," which discusses a fantasy related to the "family romance" – the rescue fantasy. Here the child rescues his parents from dangerous situations. In the rescue fantasy affectionate feelings combine with egoistic impulses. Thus the child feels gratitude to those who gave him life and nurture; still the rescue of the father from danger and death does express hidden defiance – the rescue representing a squaring of accounts. By contrast, the rescue of the mother expresses wholly affectionate feelings, the fantasy having developed independently of those dominating the grown man's experiences of love. More than this, the son expresses his affection by wishing to take the role of his father and with his mother produce a son who resembles himself: "All his instincts, those of tenderness, gratitude, lustfulness, defiance and independence, find satisfaction in the single wish *to be his own father*" (S.E., XI, 172-73). The rescue fantasy is a way of making a total identification with the father.

Other psychoanalytic writers interpret these fantasies somewhat differently: Fenichel discusses various motives in the family romance, including narcissistic gratification;[6] others give greater stress to defiance and aggression in the rescue fantasy. Thus Karl Abraham discovered in fantasies of his patients strong Oedipal wishes and unconscious defiance toward the father. Carriages, bolting horses, chance encounters recur, with complex and shifting meanings; dueling is frequent between son and father or his representative, In one fantasy significant for *Grandison,* the king (the masculine ideal) is endangered when the horse drawing his carriage bolts; the bolting horse and carriage symbolize the mother's wish to endanger the father and usher him to the son. Neurotic guilt is allayed if the son tries to save the father's life. Abraham concludes that rescue fantasies are aggressive in intent – a conclusion reached by other investigators.[7]

In the numerous rescue fantasies that comprise the family romance of *Grandison* (including Grandison's rescue of his father from Mrs. Oldham and Miss Obrien through financial settlements), we dis-

6. *Psychoanalytic Theory of Neurosis,* pp. 96, 346. Discussing the family romance, John Frosch suggests that threats to the child's sense of omnipotence lead him to project this same quality on to the parents; however his need to desexualize them during the Oedipal phase leads him to seek substitutes. "Transference Derivatives of the Family Romance," *American Psychoanalytic Association Journal,* 7 (1959), 508, 518.

7. Karl Abraham, "Rescue and Murder of the Father in Neurotic Phantasies," *International Journal of Psycho-analysis,* 3 (1922), 470-71. For a confirming view that rescue fantasies are aggressive in nature, see Richard Sterba, "Aggression in the Rescue Fantasy," *Psychoanalytic Quarterly,* 9 (1940), 505-08.

cover underlying tensions similar to those identified by Fenichel and Abraham. As we might expect, these are strongly defended against in the surface representation – mainly through the conscientiousness and decorum of Grandison and Harriet Byron. The various plots may, in fact, be defensive strategies that permit a disguised exploration of erotic themes, particularly where these conflict with other interests in the novel.

One such strategy is the effort to invest Grandison with certain traits of his strong-tempered father. Impulse and reason in Grandison are not always shown in perfect accord; or at least Grandison reports that they are not. He refers more than once to his "tumults," and on occasion finds it necessary to leave a room to bring his feelings under control. "I am naturally passionate," he tells Mr. Reeves. "You know not the pains it has cost me, to keep my passion under: But I have suffered too much in my after-regret, when I have been hurried away by it, not to endeavour to restrain its first sallies" (1, I, 206). Richardson also has Harriet refer to him as the "free, gay, Raillier of Lady Beauchamp," particularly of female foibles (2, IV, 293). His sister Charlotte describes him as "so lively, that he has all *the young man* in his behaviour, whenever occasions call for relaxation" (3, VI, 241). Indeed, Grandison calls attention to his lively dress, and compares himself to his father in this preference: "In my own dress, I am generally a conformist to the fashion. Singularity is usually the indication of something wrong in judgment. I rather perhaps dress too shewy, tho' a young man, for one who builds nothing on outward appearance: But my father loved to be dressed" (3, VI, 124).

These references are infrequent, however, and this aspect of the characterization unsuccessful because these attributed qualities are both inconstant and in conflict with other qualities of Grandison. Harriet catches the meaning of his railliery when she identifies his target. On these occasions he is a faintly sadistic figure, in one instance able to threaten Charlotte with a cutting off of their relationship if she continues to mistreat her husband. But these episodes are few in the seven long volumes of the novel. Much more in evidence are Grandison's personal restraint, conscientiousness and decorous behavior – qualities that rather suggest masochistic trends. These give the novel its peculiar moral coloration – a moralizing tone similar to the last quarter of *Clarissa.*

Freud shows that castration anxiety arising from the Oedipal wish is defended against through desexualization of the Oedipus complex; masochism becomes especially strong when the complex is unmastered. In *Grandison,* fantasies are enacted at the price of erotic interests; but instead of exploring these and then defending against them, as he did in *Pamela* and *Clarissa,* Richardson restricts them severely – the result being the extremely decorous characterization of Grandison and the two heroines, Harriet and Clementina, as well as the exploitation of domestic and religious pieties voiced chiefly through Grandison.

3

The displacement of the rakish father by the virtuous son is accomplished through the neutralization of aggressive suitors and similar figures, and the continuous formation of a family circle that encompasses the various smaller family groups that Grandison reconciles or aids. As in the Oedipus legend, the threatening son is sent away – but after the death of his mother and not at the time of birth. The details of these early years and Grandison's exile prepare for his substitution in what is an all encompassing family romance.

As in his depiction of several other rakish men in the novel, Richardson concentrates on wounds that fail to heal, or heal very slowly. The mother's death is indirectly the result of the father's profligacy; for her health fails following a serious wound that Sir Thomas sustains in a duel. Though he does recover, he has to be carried to her deathbed when a wound that has been healing opens (1, II, 316). Before she dies, Lady Grandison tells her daughters that they will have to look to their brother for protection; for their father is typical in regarding daughters as "encumbrances" and in giving all thought to the son. Though he loves them, he means to restrict their dowry and personal fortune: "Your brother loves you: He loves me. It will be in *his* power, should he survive your father, to be a good friend to you. – Love your brother" (1, II, 315) Her prophecy is borne out, for after her death Sir Thomas refuses to consider Caroline's marriage to Lord L. and the question of dowry, and he also forbids her and Charlotte from corresponding with his son, from whom he wishes to conceal the facts of his dissolute life. After Sir Thomas's death, Grandison does prove the worthy father: he arranges Caroline's marriage to Lord L., and later, Charlotte's to Lord G.

These couples form the nucleus of the enlarging family circle. There is further enlargement in the restoration of the wife-mother in Harriet after her rescue from Sir Hargrave. For this is how Harriet is imagined: from the beginning of the novel we hear the sentiments and ideas that will fit her for her chief domestic role. The details of her rescue are consistent with the fantasy as Freud and Abraham analyze it. As the substitute-mother she is saved from a symbolic aggressing father, as Grandison in real life could not save his mother. Dueling is a recurrent element in rescue fantasies, Abraham points out; in *Grandison* sword-duels or their possibility dominate the subplots.[8] Though Grandison expresses no overt hostility and is remarkably uncritical of his father's prodigality with the estate he is to inherit, there is symbolic defiance in his righting wrongs his father has inflicted on others, and less directly in the several episodes where Grandison stands against aggressive suitors.[9]

The first of these is Greville, a singularly "oral" lover who believes that women wish to be devoured and who leaves his teeth marks on Harriet's hand: "And *Oh*! said he, mimicking (and snatching my other hand, as I would have run from him) and patting it, speaking thro' his closed teeth, You may be glad you have an hand left. By my soul, I could eat you" (1, I, 101). His defeat in love late in the novel probably is a kind of emasculation, his effort to attack Grandison with his sword in order to prevent his marriage to Harriet proving ineffectual. For Grandison is a master of disarming his opponents and afterwards treating them with extreme courtesy: "Mr. Greville, had he been disposed for mischief, had no use of his right-arm. It was sprained by the twisting of his sword from it, and in a sling" (3, VI, 72). The second aggressive suitor, Sir Hargrave, suffers injuries during the abduction of Harriet that also suggest emasculation – a limp caused by a fall and possibly from the crushing of his foot under the carriage wheel (1, I, 140-41), an unspecified "hurt," the loss of three front teeth, and a disfigured mouth and lip. After the abduction, he tries to provoke Grandison into a duel, and when Grandison finally consents to go with him into the garden, is almost immediately

8. "Rescue and Murder of the Father," 469.

9. Prodded by criticism, Richardson in a later edition of the novel added a comment suggesting that Grandison would not have sacrified his fortune to his father's "unreasonable desires." See R. C. Pierson, "The Revisions of *Sir Charles Grandison*," *Studies in Bibliography*, 21 (1968), 168.

disarmed: "Sir Hargrave seemed still to insist upon his drawing, and put himself into a fencing attitude. Sir Charles then calmly stepping towards him, put down Sir Hargrave's sword with his hand, and put his left-arm under Sir Hargrave's sword-arm. Sir Hargrave lifted up the other arm passionately: But Sir Charles, who was on his guard, immediately laid hold of the other arm, and seemed to say something mildly to him; and letting go his left-hand, led him towards the house; his drawn sword still in his hand. Sir Hargrave seemed to expostulate, and to resist being led, tho' but faintly, and as a man overcome with Sir Charles's behavior" (1, I, 253). Later in France, after assisting his friend Bagenhall in an attempted seduction, he is beaten with a whip butt – like a third confederate Merceda, who is stabbed in the thigh as well as beaten, and eventually dies of the unhealing wound (2, IV, 443).

Stabbing images like those associated with Lovelace occur in Sir Hargrave's talk (1, I, 82); Greville threatens to cut throats (1, I, 94). Other characters suffer mysterious injuries. During the abduction, while struggling to escape, Harriet strikes her nose on a door (1, I, 158); earlier she injures her finger in a lock (1, I, 114). These random details (like similar ones in *Clarissa*) contribute to an emerging pattern similar to ones we noted in the earlier novels. We have already noted that in Sir Hargrave's remorseful letter, written just before his death, he gives evidence of the fatality we saw in Lovelace: "I am on the very brink of the grave. It appears to me as ready dug: It yawns for me: I am neither fit to die, nor to live" (3, VI, 143).

Yet neither Greville nor Sir Hargrave wishes to seduce or rape Harriet: they are mere violent lovers. Both have presumably ruined other women; however, their previous history is not the basis for their condemnation. For, as *Pamela* and *Clarissa* show, Richardson condemns only what is fully represented in the novel. Still, *any* display of erotic feeling is excessive since it may lead to sexual assault; it is of little importance whether the initial motive is innocent or blameworthy. This is one reason perhaps that sexual experience is virtually absent in the marriage scenes (as in *Pamela*); Grandison's uncertainty over whether a longer engagement is required before the wedding ceremony is, in fact, the chief interest of the brief courtship scenes. The ceremony follows quickly, probably because of the imminent and necessary reintroduction of Clementina, whose appearance in England would revive for a second time the question of her marriage to Grandison.

The similarity of *Grandison* to the earlier novels is most obvious here. The various subplots summarized earlier explored the dangers of erotic feeling, at the same time stressing Grandison's paternal qualities. The women in these episodes frequently resemble the headstrong or sinister women encountered in earlier novels: they are wicked or jealous mothers or stepmothers whose reformation depends on their reconciliation with estranged children. They are reminders of that stage of the family romance in which the child, in full knowledge of the facts of sexuality, imagines the mother in illicit love affairs.

Thus in a subplot paralleling the main plot in several ways, Grandison's friend Beauchamp is sent abroad by his father to pacify his new wife, who has a grievance against the son (he has rejected the overtures of a friend of hers) and is jealous of the elder Beauchamp's affection. Later, Grandison helps to effect his friend's return to England and his reconciliation with his stepmother. The father's death soon afterwards (a common theme in rescue fantasie) strengthens the tie between stepmother and stepson.

Mrs. Jervois, from whom Grandison seeks to protect her daughter, Emily, is more demonstrably wicked; her first husband's forgiveness of an "atrocious crime" only hardens her toward him (2, III, 73). Grandison is challenged to a duel by her second husband, O'Hara, and his brother-in-law, Salmonet, both of whom he quickly disarms. The episode concludes with a familiar motif: "O'Hara, skipping about, as if he watched for an opportunity to make a push with safety to himself, lost his sword, by the usual trick whereby a man, anything skilled in his weapons, knows how sometimes to disarm a *less* skilful adversary" (2, III, 67). He pushes them somewhat roughly into the square outside: "They limped into the coach they came in." Emily's reconciliation with her mother and stepfather depends on her achieving dominance over them through her competence to keep them in funds – another recurring motif of the family romance, parallel to Grandison's control of people like Mrs. Giffard through his largesse.

These themes are most fully treated in the Italian plot. Jeronymo, the libertine son whom Grandison rescues from assassins hired by a rival in love, is only indirectly involved in his sister Clementina's plight. His role suggests, however, that the nuclear fantasy energizing the main and subplots is Oedipal; not surprisingly, like his brothers he is a more dominant figure than the dim and ineffectual Marchese.

His unhealing wound – a motif in the pattern distinguished earlier – weakens him to the extent that, though he partially recovers when Grandison brings a physician to Italy to promote his cure, on following his sister to England he remains to complete his recovery. In effect, he joins the marriage circle as son to Grandison, a true and wise father who knows (better than the Marchese) how to restore disrupted family relations and bring peace of mind to the passionate brother and sister.

The ostensible basis for Clementina's rejection of Grandison is religious, she refuses marriage because he is a Protestant and she fears being influenced into conversion. That the religious issue is not a real concern becomes clear when, in the scenes following Grandison's return to Italy, Richardson keeps alive the possibility that Clementina may change her mind. The suspense of the novel arises, in short, not from issues on which Richardson grounds the intellectual interest, but from tensions of character in the women which the plot is constructed to explore. Clementina's appearance after the marriage intensifies the exploration of masochistic traits in the dual heroines, the issue of religion having been easily disposed of.

4

The role of women in the family romance in *Grandison* is complex and ambivalent. Clementina and Harriet, behaving to each other and regarded by Grandison as "sister-excellencies" (3, VII, 354), resemble Grandison's mother in patience and purity of mind; both are capable of performing the role of wife-mother generated in the nuclear fantasy. This role is conceived as masochistic, the reason probably for the occasionally sadistic impression that Grandison conveys. Similar trends of character in *Pamela* suggest that the two women are being preserved for exalted roles, unstained by sexual feeling – at least in the surface representation.

Beneath the surface we discover the play of familiar motifs. As in *Pamela* and *Clarissa,* Richardson demonstrates his acute understanding that the social disabilities of women are in part to blame for their being victimized (we may recall Miss Howe's statement that women are raised to be fools and idiots). The aggressiveness of men like Sir Hargrave and Greville depends on women's presumed weakness and social inferiority. Thus Harriet writes to Lucy Selby on Greville's pretense to "violent love":

> O these dissemblers! The hyaena, my dear, was a *male* devourer. The men in malice, and to extenuate their own guilt, made the creature a *female.* And yet there may be male and female of this species of monsters. But as women have more to lose with regard to reputation than men, the male hyaena must be infinitely the more dangerous creature of the two; since he will come to us, even into our very houses, fawning, cringing, weeping, licking our hands; while the den of the female is by the highway-side, and wretched youths must enter into it, to put it in her power to devour them. (1, I, 24)

And she adds:

> It is not difficult, my dear, to find out these men, were we earnest to detect them. Their chief strength lies in our weakness. But however weak we are, I think we should not add to the triumph of those who make our weakness the general subject of their satire. We should not prove the justice of their ridicule by our own indiscretions. But the traitor is within us. If we guard against ourselves, we may bid defiance to all the arts of man.

At the same time, the many strong-willed and sometimes unbalanced women show that feeling in women – including Harriet, as we shall see – easily becomes anarchic. Harriet is alone among the younger women of the novel in recognizing the danger of the passions: "Good sense, and solid judgment, a natural complacency of temper, a desire of obliging, and an easiness to be obliged," she writes Lucy concerning Lord L., "procure the silent, the serene happiness, to which the fluttering, tumultous, impetuous, fervors of passions can never contribute. Nothing violent can be lasting" (2, III, 98). This is in part why Richardson's women are able to assume increasingly dominant roles, whether as wife-mothers like Pamela or as punishing figures like Clarissa, and even voice their realism about men. Their voices, even when their views are in accord with Grandison, seem tentative. They stand subject to correction; even the most high-spirited of Richardson's women, unless a termagent like Lady Olivia, is capable of control.

In *Grandison,* the tendency toward anarchic feeling is most apparent in Charlotte, who, after her engagement to the disreputable Captain Anderson is terminated by her brother without dishonor to her, marries lord G. at his urging. Almost immediately she begins to tease him mercilessly. Her objection is to what she regards as an effeminate liking for china, butterflies, and fancy clothes. Thus, when he comes to her for his "reward" after arranging a set of dishes, she cannot refrain from laughter: "And when he had done, taking the *liberty*, as he phrased it, half fearful, half resolute, to salute his bride for his reward; and then pacing backwards several steps, with such a strut and a crow – I see him yet! – Indulge me, Harriet! – I burst into a hearty laugh; I could not help it: And he, reddening, looked round himself, and round himself, to see if anything was amiss in his garb. The man, the man! honest friend, I could have said, but had too much reverence for my husband, is the oddity! Nothing amiss in the garb" (2, IV, 418). Grandison says to her before the marriage, in the course of a long exchange over her behavior to her future husband: "But if *you* cannot be *more* than civil; and if *he* is to be very observant; you'll make it your agreement with him, before you meet him at the altar, that he shall subscribe to the woman's part of the vow; and that you shall answer to the man's" (2, III, 101).

Considerable discussion is given to the need of women to subdue their selfish passions and will in the interest of a happy marriage and social order. Grandison lectures Mrs. Giffard on woman's proper role: "Chastity is the crown and glory of a woman. The most profligate of men love modesty in sex, at the very time they are forming plots to destroy it in a particular object." And he adds to Dr. Bartlett, to whom he is describing the scene: "Nothing can be weaker, in the eye of an observer, who himself disdains artifice, than a woman who makes artifice her study. In such a departure from honest nature, there will be such curvings, that the eyes, the countenance, must ever betray the heart; while the lips, either breaking out into apologies, or aiming at reserve, confirm the suspicion, that all is not right in the mind" (2, III, 52-53). "Why, my good Dr. Bartlett," he asks in an earlier scene, "are these women ashamed of owning a laudable passion? Surely there is nothing shameful in *discreet* Love" (1, II, 453). He is referring here to Miss Danby, whose marriage he is trying to arrange. He states his belief more than once that marriage should be the humbler of the spirit. Given the general view taken by women of marriage – even Charlotte – we should expect it would be. They faint or weep when "yoked"; Harriet drops the pen in signing the marriage contract, just as Pamela had to be helped down the stairs by Mrs. Jewkes on the day of her wedding and that night awaits the dreaded "guest." Charlotte speaks for all of Richardson's women in one passage: "we women, dressed out in ribbands, and gaudy trappings, and in Virgin-white, on our Wedding days, seem but like milk-white heifers led to sacrifice. We ought to be indulged, if we are not shameless things, and very wrong indeed, in our choice of the man we *can* love" (3, VI, 236).

If they are soon in control of their husbands (unless married to paragons like Lord L. and Grandison), the reason is not that initial fears have been overcome. Weakness and compensatory aggression in marriage point to deeper sources of conflict. Like Pamela, whom B. instructs to control her passions at all times, and lose all "pretty tricks and artifices" (I, 268), Harriet is instructed by Grandison to show the same face in marriage she had shown before. B. had given the same instruction: "my dearest, whose heart must always be seen in her face, and cannot be a hypocrite, will find this a means to smoothe her passions also" (I, 332). A serene composure is a sign that erotic feeling is under control. Richardson's specific view is clear in his response to Hester Mulso's criticism that he represents love as a "little selfish passion": "Now, Madam, if that passion is not little and selfish that makes two vehement souls prefer the gratification of each other, often to a sense of duty, and always to the whole world without them, be pleased to tell me what is? And pray be so good as to define to me, what the noble passion is, of which so few of either sex are capable?"[10]

Social duty is not the decisive issue for Richardson, however. When Lord G. in one episode throws his arms about Charlotte in the presence of a servant, she asks whether their recent marriage is license for "want of breeding." His response is total astonishment:

> Want of breeding, madam! – And he did so stare! Leave me, this instant – I looked good-natured, I suppose, in my anger; for he declared he would not; and again throwing his arms about me as I sat, joined his sharp face to mine, and presumed to kiss me; Jenny still in the room.
>
> Now Harriet, you never will desert me in a point of delicacy, I am sure. You cannot defend these odious freedoms in a matrimony so young, unless you would be willing to be served so yourself. (2, IV, 392)[11]

Her subsequent comment on her husband's artifice shows that the real issue is sexual feeling itself, not social decorum:

> I told him, Miss Byron, There he stands, let him deny it, if he can; that I married a man with another face. Would not any other man have taken this

10. *Selected Letters,* p. 188.

11. Charlotte probably speaks for Richardson here, as his statement to Lady Bradshaigh suggests: "But when we are giving Examples to Lovers, I think we should not indulge purer Characters, [in Kissing], in *downright* Kissing, as your Ladyship phrases it." *Selected Letters,* p. 269.

for a compliment to his natural undistorted face, and instantly have pulled off the ugly mask of passion, and shewn his own? – (2, IV, 398)

Outspoken and capable of insight, Charlotte seems a far more complex character than Harriet or Clementina because she represents diverse attitudes that Richardson ultimately fails to reconcile; only her voiced fear of sexual experience saves her from seeming as monstrous as the women of the subplots. The series of rescue fantasies that dominate these, as well as the main plot, confirm what we saw earlier: Richardson's women tend to be idealized or debased (the dark Mother conceived as the embodiment of lust). It is true at the same time that differences of sex are far less important to Richardson than potentialities for erotic experience; the mutual identifications we discover in *Clarissa* are possible because of this unacknowledged view. If these are absent in Grandison and other respectable men in the novel, the reason is that they do not cross the bounds of sexual decorum. The women, by contrast, do approach them.

The source of this complex view lies deeper than the social view of Richardson's age; yet individual psychology and social attitudes are mutually reinforcing. Arnold Kamiat states that masochistic men often attribute dominance to a wife or mistress who in reality enjoys an equal or even subordinate status.[12] Smirnoff states that the tendency to view women in a double way is a phenomenon of individual as well as of cultural masochism: the "dual feminine ideal of the masochist" results when he turns from an unavailable ideal woman to her opposite: "Two figures which can never be perceived simultaneously, but who coexist on two sides of the coin."[13] This view is consistent with Freud's comment that "what, in the conscious, is found split into a pair of opposites often occurs in the unconscious as a unity" (S.E., XI, 170). In *Grandison,* this double view is apparent in the remarkable outbursts of Grandison against the wickedness of mothers like Mrs. Jervois and against artifice generally, as in his amazing statement to Charlotte: "Men and Women are Devils to one another. They need no other temper" (1, II, 439).

The dual feminine ideal explains further why Richardson's women are capable of such caustic realism and irony. Lady Olivia's statement to Grandison, in reference to herself, is one remarkable example: "But you, Grandison, were too *delicate* to be taken with her *sin-*

12. "Male Masochism and Culture," *Psychoanalytic Review*, 23 (1936), 89.
13. "The Masochistic Contract," 669.

cerity. If you had penetration to distinguish between reserve and openness of heart, you had not greatness of mind enough to break thro' the low restraints of custom; and to reward the latter in preference to the former. Yet who, better than you, knows, that women in Love are actuated by *one* view, and differ only in outward appearance? Will bars, bolts, walls, rivers, seas, any more with-hold the supercilious, than the less reserved? " (2, V, 646)[14] The statement stands condemned by the force of its expression, yet it has unexpected bearing on qualities of Grandison that even Harriet notices. Her remarkable comment that, in the Garden, Grandison would not have fallen before his temptress is clearly not meant to be ironic, yet has the effect of being so: "No; it is my opinion, that your brother would have had gallantry enough to his fallen spouse, to have made him extremely regret her lapse; but that he would have done *his own duty,* were it but for the sake of posterity, and left it to the Almighty, if such had been his pleasure, to have annihilated his first Eve, and given him a second" (2, V, 609). And so does Charlotte's estimate of her brother, in a discussion of religious enthusiasts: "These *overdoers,* my dear, are wicked wretches. What do they, but make religion look unlovely, and put *underdoers* out of heart? My brother is *The Man.* . . . Since it is always the way of those who intend not to mend, to set their hearts against their correctors – My brother professes not the one half of what he practices. He uses the fashion, without abusing it, or himself, by following it. Some such words in a sacred book rumble in my mad head; but I known I have not them right" (2, V, 498).

The qualification that concludes the statement shows Richardson's own unease with what Charlotte has shown. More so than Olivia, whose views are malicious and therefore unreliable, Charlotte resembles Lovelace and Miss Howe in her unadorned views of human nature. "I believe we women are all rogues in our hearts," she says to Harriet early in the novel. And much later: "We can be very generous for others, Harriet, when we apprehend that one day we may want the same pity ourselves. Our best passions, my dear, have their mixtures of self-love" (2, IV, 308). When Harriet responds that she

14. Olivia bears striking resemblance to Rosa Dartle in *David Copperfield.* Her 'darting" eyes match the dagger she carries on her person. There seem to be traces of Charlotte Grandison in Mercy Pecksniff, in *Martin Chuzzlewit*, who marries Jonas Chuzzlewit to "hate and tease him" (Chapter 20).

has presented an unpleasant view of human nature, Charlotte replies, "It *is* a likeness for all that." Despite Richardson's espousal of optimistic views in *Grandison,* and his attack in the concluding note on writers who portray human nature in a vicious light, these views of Charlotte stand uncorrected – indeed are echoed by Grandison himself.

The dual feminine ideal also explains why Harriet and Clementina are imagined as women in need of rescue, guilt-ridden or conscious of their inferiority to Grandison – in the terms of our earlier analysis, as moral masochists who are saved by Grandison from unspecified faults of character. Clementina's sacrifice of Grandison and her subsequent madness are conceived masochistically, the representation intensified by details of her mistreatment by her cousin Laurana, who puts her in a strait jacket, and particularly of her fear of being beaten. Her belief that she will shortly die is a constant refrain. Thinking of Grandison, she relates a dream of stumbling over a dead man in an orange grove (2, III, 241). It is in dreams only that ambivalence or hostility toward Grandison can be expressed fully.

Harriet's complementary masochism is most evident in her dreams before her marriage. In the first of these "contradictory vagaries," she is married and then not marriet to Grandison: "I was rejected with scorn, as a presumptuous creature. I sought to hide myself in holes and corners. I was dragged out of a subterraneous cavern, which the sea had made when it once broke bounds, and seemed the dwelling of howling and conflicting winds; and when I expected to be punished for my audaciousness, and for repining at my lot, I was turned into an Angel of light; stars of diamonds, like a glory, encompassing my head: a dear little baby was put into my arms. Once it was Lucy's; another time it was Emily's; and at another time Lady Clementina's! – I was fond of it, beyond expression" (3, VI, 148). Harriet's audacity in loving Grandison is rewarded by his scorn but also with a baby that symbolizes, perhaps, the one creature admired or loved by these women simultaneously – Grandison himself. Harriet dreams again that she is married to Grandison, who does not love her; her grandmother and her aunt plead with him to love her. In a continuation of this dream, Grandison upbraids her for preventing him from marrying Clementina: "I fell down at his feet. I called it my misfortune, that he could not love me: I would not say it was his fault. It might, perhaps, be his misfortune too! – And then I said,

Love and Hatred are not always in one's power. If you cannot love the poor creature who kneels before you, *that* shall be a cause sufficient with me for a divorce: I desire not to fasten myself on the man who cannot love me" (3, VI, 148).

In another part of this "reverie" Grandison loves her intensely, but as he approaches he becomes a ghost and flits away. The scene alternates between England and Italy, the countries confused in Harriet's mind: Jeronymo's wounds are healed but soon reopen. Harriet dreams also that a "fourth brother" (Grandison) joins with Laurana in a plot, presumably against Clementina, and is killed by another brother, the general. The series of dreams ends with Grandison's assassination at the hands of Greville, who "fled his country for it, and became a vagabond, a Cain, the Accursed, I thought, of God and Man – I, your poor Harriet, a widow; left in the most calamitous circumstance that a woman can be in – Good Heaven! – But, avaunt, recollection! – Painful, *most* painful recollection of ideas so terrible! none of your intrusions –" (3, VI, 149).

In these dreams the rakish brother and those who threaten Harriet or injure Grandison are associated with the rakish father who sent his son into exile; for Jeronymo's unhealing wound resembles the "hurts" suffered not only by Sir Thomas, Sir Hargrave and Merceda but more remotely by Greville. Grandison plays a double role – that of the Oedipal son of fantasy who wins the mother and is torn by conflicting emotions until he is finally punished by Greville, and that of the punishing lover who collaborates in the maltreatment of Clementina and turns angrily upon Harriet. Richardson does not suggest an interpretation; Harriet refers to her dreams as "illusions of the working mind, fettered and debased as it is by the organs through which it conveys its confined powers to the grosser matter, body, then sleeping, inactive, as in the shades of death" (3, VI, 149). The dreams suggest that the effort to resolve tensions through Grandison's substitution for the father in the family romance and related rescue fantasies is unsuccessful and indeed promotes even greater anxiety.

5

The meaning of these trends may be summarized. The sentimentalization of character in the surface plot – a purification of feeling, promoted by guilt inherent in moral masochism – at one level is intended to preserve the wife-mother from sexual degradation, perhaps as a way of defending against the threat of the Oedipal father whom Grandison displaced. Regardless of the forms and pieties that ennoble it, sexuality remains the dreaded "guest" – a desecration of the virginal heart whose passions are best left unawakened.

Another reason the passions must be overcome is epitomized in Charlotte's statement, "And *who* of us, after all, have our first Love? " (2, V, 552) This theme is a recurring one: Emily Jervois will presumably overcome her infatuation for her guardian and marry Beauchamp, a man much like him; Lucy Selby, in Harriet's words to her, "nobly conquered a first Love, on the discovered unworthiness of the man" (3, VII, 437), and marries a good-natured nobleman; Mrs. Shirley, Harriet's grandmother, toward the end of the novel relates how she overcame an early passion and found love and friendship in her marriage (3, VII, 399-400). Charlotte discovers the need of self-control and begins to develop better relations with her husband, though the reconciliation of interests almost certainly is to be on her terms.

The energies of moral masochism pass ultimately into stoicism, with increasing reference to the ideal of moderate happiness – this in spite of Richardson's effort to show that Grandison is not a stoic. "A susceptibility of the passion called *Love*, I condemn not as a fault," he tells Charlotte in the matter of Captain Anderson; "but the contrary. Your *brother* . . . is no Stoic" (1, II, 414). The chief speaker for the stoic ideal is Mrs. Shirley, who insists that happiness is relative and is to be found in resignation to present realities: "As for that kind of Love, which in its very beginning is contrary to Duty, to suppose *that* unconquerable, is making ourselves wretched indeed: And for first-sight impressions, and *beginning* inclinations, though always dangerous, and often guilty to indulge, they are absolutely trifles to overcome and suppress, to a person of prudence of virtue" (3, VII, 401). Moral masochism in *Grandison* is an instrument for controlling the passions, though the novel shows how much a freer play of fantasy is possible when the sexual content is transformed from the beginning in sentimentalized character and plot.

In *Grandison,* sentimentality operates through moral masochism in the guise of an aggressive piety. But moral masochism is usually identified by guilt which lacks a specified cause – guilt originating in the need of the ego for punishment from the superego or from external parental figures. We may hypothesize that where moral masochism energizes the literary work, character and plot are likely to be generic rather than individualized or highly original.

A comment of Lady Davers suggests that, in the intensive presentation of emotional experience, "telling" is the bound to aroused fears: knowing what Pamela endured at the hands of B. puts "a bound, as it were, to one's fears of what you suffered, which otherwise must have been injurious to your purity, though you could not help it" (II, 28). The need to set a bound to fears – to relieve imagination – is perhaps one basis of realistic detail. Action itself – the "flight forward" of the masochist, noted by Reik – is a similar defense, one increasingly important to Richardson in the exploration of emotional experience.

Concomitant with this "telling" is the presentation in certain characters of a general motive (the destructive urge of Sir Hargrave or Greville, the wickedness of fathers and mothers) rather than careful working out of specific motives in narration and action. The peculiar power of the representation lies, not in what is usually taken to be the individual psychological characterization, but in the type – given a "semblance of reality," in the words of E. E. Stoll, through a careful selection of detail. Stoll's comment on Shakespeare's characterization is pertinent to this discussion: "Two things above all else he sought – a striking situation and a vivid impression of personality; and perfection of structure and adequacy of motive were secondary. Indeed, it is when the spectators' minds are preoccupied with the hero's personality, as Mr. Bridges says above [in the essay "On the Influence of the Audience"], 'that the actions follow as unquestionable realities.' And this effect in turn is produced by the 'convincing verisimilitude and richness of Shakespeare's detail,' in part by the fact that the characters seem to 'live with a larger life than that of the action,' but above all else, I think, by the manner or quality of their speech. In the place of psychology, with its analysis and subtleties, the poet had an infinite tact, the artist's delicate, plastic, life-giving touch."[15]

The distinction between the "vivid impression of personality" and "psychology" seems to imply an absence of motivation; but the difficulty is removed somewhat if we restate the distinction in

15. *Shakespeare Studies* (New York: Macmillan, 1927), p. 115.

psychoanalytic language. Motivation inheres, as Holland suggests, in the interplay between the reader and the literary character. Basing his analysis on Freud's third type of identification (in *Group Psychology and the Analysis of the Ego*) – "identification unconnected to any object-relation, but rather [in Freud's words] 'based upon the possibility or desire of putting oneself in the same situation' " – Holland puts the stress on shared qualities.[16] He summarizes his conception as a "balance" or "management" of fantasy, having to do with the satisfaction of drives and simultaneously alleviation of anxiety. The greater the anxiety associated with the fantasy, the less control the fantasy is under; the greater the defense provided by the form of the literary work, the greater the gratifications provided.[17]

We noted that for Freud moral masochism represents a regression to the Oedipus complex and that the source of guilt in this kind of masochism remains indefinite. Anxiety similar to castration dread is precisely what so many of the episodes in *Grandison* play upon. Through the presentation of general, unrationalized feeling the sentimental novel reinforces guilt in the reader arising from intensive representations of vicious behavior as well as noble suffering. Aroused fears are only half allayed; paradoxically, anxiety is increased by the act of making the presentation of emotional experience morally constructive – in accordance with Richardson's declared wish of making the generous impulses the instrument of reformation (2, IV, 342), and showing that the basis of happiness is the cultivation of "innate good principles" (2, III, 61). Here perhaps is one explanation for the failure of melodrama and other derivatives of sentimental tragedy to achieve a tragic effect.

Sir Charles Grandison shows that plot, like character, may represent a compromise of conflicting trends. The traditional compromises offered Richardson by the literary conventions of his age were absorbed into the novels to the extent that they permitted him to achieve his double purpose of fostering the good heart and mortifying the guilty. Pamela's reward for preserving her virginity is "a triumph of triumphs" (II, 42); Clarissa's aggression is the means to her triumph over Lovelace. The notorious confusion of values in *Pamela* – but also in *Clarissa* and *Grandison* – is also the result of Richardson's effort to reconcile aggressive piety with notions of

16. *Dynamics of Literary Response*, p. 278.
17. Ibid., p. 213.

decorum. Censure in the form of aggressive piety is conceived as playing a constructive role; yet, though remaining within the bounds of decorum, it becomes increasingly intense in the actual representation of vicious behavior, creating the peculiar effect of sentimental tragedy and its related forms.

Chapter Five

RICHARDSON'S ART

1

Richardson states in a letter to Lady Bradshaigh in 1748 the Christian idea that shaped the plot of *Clarissa*: "A writer who follows Nature and pretends to keep the Christian system in his Eye, cannot make a Heaven in this world for his Favourites; or represent this Live otherwise than as a State of Probation. Clarissa I once more averr could not be rewarded in this World. To have given her her Reward here, as in a happy Marriage, would have been as if a Poet had placed his Catastrophe in the Third Act of his Play, when the Audience were *obliged* to expect two more."[1] Such statements were for Richardson afterthoughts – how much so we cannot be quite certain. Points of conduct and philosophy are not applied with equal rigor in the whole novel. Lovelace's belief that his death will expiate his crime and his calling upon Clarissa (his "goddess") instead of upon God shows he is unrepentant, Richardson states in another letter. But he had also been able to defend Lovelace's good qualities. In a letter to Edward Moore, written earlier in 1748, he mentions his generosity and ingenuousness: "Does he not on all Occasions exalt the Lady at his own Expence? – Has he not therefore many Sparks of Goodness in his Heart; tho', with regard to the Sex and to carry a favourable Point against them he sticks at nothing? "[2]

Though, as Frederick W. Hilles has shown, Richardson planned *Clarissa* as a whole, he also wrote "to the moment," as Sherburn has shown: "He wrote uneasily and at times did not clearly convey what he evidently saw. He had little interest in environmental detail or in objective description."[3] Fantasy and the defenses provided by a

1. *Selected Letters*, p. 108.
2. Ibid., p. 89.
3. " 'Writing to the Moment': One Aspect," *Samuel Richardson: A Collec-*

realistic plot – action itself, to which Lovelace makes his "flight forward" – demanded a framework which would allow an improvisation of character and feeling. Both were necessary to Richardson as an artist. We have seen that his stress on qualities that alternately lightened or darkened a character depended on the responses of his readers as well as on ideas that happened to capture his interest at the moment of composition. Much of the sequel to *Pamela* seems improvised in ideas: Pamela's extensive comments on the education of children are one example. Grandison's numerous comments on the need for reform of manners – the desirability of reviving Sumptuary Laws, for example – are even revealing of this improvisation.

The epistolary technique further permitted Richardson to show his characters considering possible views of their conduct – views to which they are uncommitted at the moment of discussion and to which Richardson can return in asides to the reader and in statements of characters as *evidence* of motives. The discovery of character for Richardson was what at each point in the novel Clarissa and Lovelace imagine themselves to be. No reader of *Clarissa* in particular can be unimpressed by his willingness to follow the turns of feeling wherever they might lead and indeed to provide opportunities for additional exploration in what seem improvised actions.

The famous penknife scene in *Clarissa,* following the rape, is one remarkable example. Before being given Clarissa's own account of the events leading up to it – in her letters following her final successful escape from Lovelace – we are given Lovelace's description of her resistance to further assault:

> Madam, said I, let me tell you; and was advancing towards her, with a fierce aspect, most cursedly vexed, and ashamed too.
>
> But she turned to me; "Stop where thou art, O vilest and most abandoned of men! Stop where thou art! Nor, with that determined face, offer to touch me, if thou wouldst not that I should be a corpse at thy feet! "
>
> To my astonishment, she held forth a penknife in her hand, the point to her own bosom, grasping resolutely the whole handle, so that there was no offering to take it from her.
>
> "I offer not mischief to anybody but myself. You, sir, and ye women, are safe from every violence of mine. The LAW shall be all my resource: the LAW," and she spoke the word with emphasis, that to such people carries natural terror with it, and now struck a panic into them.

tion of Critical Essays, p. 152. See also Kinkead-Weekes, *Samuel Richardson, Dramatist Novelist,* pp. 124-26.

> No wonder, since those who will damn themselves to procure ease and plenty in this world, will tremble at everything that seems to threaten their methods of obtaining that ease and plenty.
>
> "The LAW only shall be my refuge! " –
>
> The infamous mother whispered me that it were better to *make terms* and with this *strange* lady, and let her go. (III, 288-89)

The improbability of Lovelace's comment, his ability to judge Clarissa's character and read the mind of Mrs. Sinclair and the other women of the house probably does not occur to readers. "Innocence so triumphant: villainy so debased," he concludes later in his account (III, 290). Though the scene serves the purposes of revealing Clarissa's triumphant virtue despite the rape, giving the lie to the libertine view of the seduced woman, Richardson in fact is returning to prior themes and interests – chiefly to tensions generated in Lovelace's effort to seduce Clarissa during her first confinement. He is seeking to imagine feelings and sexual dangers that, once the rape has occurred, should give way to denouement. Like the masochist in Smirnoff's description, he rehearses the preparation for rape to guarantee that the act itself will not be improvised.

We cannot know the extent to which the mutual identifications of his characters became his own. The letters suggest that for Richardson character was an impersonation, to the extent that he was able to imagine the emotional consequences of behavior rather than its cause: "Clementina's Fate is not yet come to my Knowledge[he wrote William Duncombe]. I have hinder'd from enquiring after her; in other words, from pursuing her story. But I think she rises upon me. And as I know not what to offer next; being too irregular a scribbler to be able to write by a plan, I seem to be at a loss, to know what to do with her, or to fetch up Harriet, again, and make her the principal Female character."[4] The novels suggest that his acute understanding of the psychological forces underlying the moral type – chiefly related and often complementary masochistic traits and attitudes – led Richardson to favor plots that permitted the exploration of these qualities. It is, of course, difficult to square this understanding with the moralizing person we hear in the letters and in hundreds of pages of *Clarissa* and *Grandison* mainly; the statement of Eaves and Kimpel that "Richardson is one of the clearest cases in literature of the difference between the imaginative mind and the

4. *Selected Letters,* pp. 194-95.

speculative mind" expresses a mystery of character that probably will never be answered biographically.[5] A comment of Reik is, however, worth quoting with regard to this mystery: "I could just as well quote most, no, all the great men to whom mankind is indebted for progress and increased joy of life. In none of them is an intense, latent masochistic tendency lacking; in every single one we can detect a pain-addict feature despite all divergencies of character."[6] Reik is here stressing that not all forms of masochism are pathological. Edmund Bergler makes the same point in his discussion of the pervasive "psychic masochism" that he finds in great writers.[7]

The relation between fantasy and social and moral structure in a work of fiction is highly complex. Holland states that the intellectual meaning of the literary work is "an ego-syntonic transformation of the unacceptable fantasy content," the nuclear fantasy remaining unconscious.[8] The guilt or anxiety aroused by the fantasy is managed by the form of the work, as in "Dover Beach" despair is defended against in the reassuring seascape and the imagery which creates distance between several elements in the poem. The elements of fantasy, in turn, are split, isolated, undone, displaced, repressed, or (as in "Dover Beach") denied. The range of these possibilities is wide, because the audience is able to tolerate a wide range of fantasies and because, in Holland's words, "Almost any kind of coherent thought about the work will open up the paths of gratification, so long as it 'makes sense' of the text."[9] In instances where plot remains unfinished, the defense may not be strong enough to assuage the tensions aroused by the fantasy; indeed, "The very form of the poem, in acting out a denial, may gratify an aggressive wish to annihilate those guilty of the offending sight."[10] In many ways, then, a residue of guilt and anxiety may remain.

We have suggested a residue of guilt and anxiety in each of the novels resulting from the engagement of the reader in intensive inside views of the characters. Given the danger of increasing sympathy for characters whom the writer considers undeserving of it, it is signifi-

5. *Samuel Richardson,* p. 618.
6. *Masochism in Modern Man,* p. 393.
7. *The Writer and Psychoanalysis,* p. 239.
8. *Dynamics of Literary Response,* pp. 180-81.
9. Ibid., p. 185.
10. Ibid., p. 131.

cant that Richardson risks generating sympathy for Lovelace though he fails to provide inside views of Grandison, whose feelings are as central to his novel as Lovelace's are to *Clarissa.* The explanation is that Grandison does not exist as a character in the way Clarissa and Lovelace do. The moral type instead is rigorously exploited, perhaps because Grandison's qualities are consistent with the dominant fantasy realized in the surface plot. The evidence on which we base our discovery of the dominant fantasy is drawn from the plot itself, supported by details reported rather than felt as thoughts. It is perhaps not coincidental that the family romance is a fantasy existing close to consciousness and associated often with daydreams.

2

Our analysis of the three novels focused on a series of strategies through which Richardson defends against the nuclear fantasy. One of these is pious moralizing, generated by moral masochism and pleasurable in its own right. To state the idea in another way, the sentimental experience is grounded in heightened feeling that, consistent with eighteenth century ideas, is cultivated for its own sake (deep feeling is itself a good); but also may express a sadism inherent in the "aggressive wish to annihilate those guilty of the offending sight" (Holland). *Pamela* and *Clarissa* contain voyeuristic elements which might be explained through Bergler's theory that "the basic drive which underlies imagination is voyeurism; imagination is the 'purified' successor to infantile peeping."[11] There may be a more profound relation, for the novels suggest a close connection between voyeurism and moral masochism.

Richardson's letters reveal a highly defensive conception of form, dependent on the reader's conscious awareness of the moral structure. In other words, the reader is expected to attend to each feature of action as if the mode were allegorical. Richardson could and did discuss his characters with correspondents with concern for the pleasure in the moral representation. This way of experiencing the novel is consistent with the eighteenth century idea that the pleasure of tragedy arises from the artistry of the tragic writer rather than from the distinctively tragic element in the work, thus

11. *The Writer and Psychoanalysis,* pp. 90-91; cf. Watt, *The Rise of the Novel,* p. 199; Dorothy Van Ghent, *The English Novel* (New York: Harper Torchbooks, 1961), p. 49.

Addison's argument in *Spectator* 418 that tragedy offers the highest kind of pleasure because tragic experience is the hardest to imitate. Additional support is to be found in the Cartesian idea that vigorous passions like pity and fear are made pleasurable by the unreality of the drama, thus the statement of John Dennis: " 'tho' sometimes a vigorously lively Imitation of Creatures that are in their Natures noxious, may be capable of giving us Terror, yet Nature, by giving us a secret Intelligence that the Object is not real, can turn even that tormenting Passion to Pleasure."[12] Later in the century, Johnson states in the Preface on Shakespeare that "the delight of tragedy proceeds from our consciousness of fiction."[13] But later in the century, too, occurs the shift toward sentimentality, which stressed feeling and sensitivity as the central experience of living, and displaced the Aristotelian idea of conscious artistry and intellectual design.[14]

Richardson's identification with his audience as the judge of his own characters and plot, and his promotion of their moral views, explain the form of his novels and their complex effects. Ernst Kris's statement on the artist and his audience is pertinent: "To the artist the public is not necessarily, and not only, a distant and powerful judge, on whom he projects his own superego. He also puts himself into the place of the public and identifies in ego (and superego) with his audience. Once more it is a process of infinite complexity. While the artist creates, in the state of inspiration, he and his work are one; when he looks upon the product of his creative urge, he sees it from the outside, and as his own first audience he participates in 'what the voice has done.' "[15] In a novelist who for whatever reason disguises painful feelings and displaces them to moral ones, an esthetic stance that joins a demonstration of artistry to the depiction of heightened feeling is crucial – especially when he stresses the redemptive powers of feeling.

The penknife scene shows this stance well: the dramatic *scena*

12. Earl Wasserman, "The Pleasures of Tragedy," *ELH* 14 (1947), 289. On Dennis and Richardson's conception of tragedy, see Ira Konigsberg, *Samuel Richardson and the Dramatic Novel* (Lexington: University of Kentucky Press, 1968), p. 75.

13. Wasserman, 295.

14. Ibid., 296-97.

15. *Psychoanalytic Explorations in Art*, p. 61.

distances the characters from the reader, producing a static effect as in a tableau. Clarissa's repeated "The LAW shall be all my resource" (or words to this effect), and Lovelace's distanced comments that show his command of his feelings – these reduce anxiety over Clarissa's fate. More subtly, Clarissa herself seems to stand apart from the suffering she endures by moralizing and judging each act she performs and each feeling. In the whole novel she is pictorialized in acts of suffering, in a series of tableaux: being watched rather than watching. She is more the subject of intensive views than the constant viewer. Lovelace, by contrast, is the active figure, though in fantasy the reverse is the case.

Dickens shows in *Martin Chuzzlewit,* in characters like Pecksniff and Sarah Gamp – whose villainy is exemplary, yet who never for a moment cease to be comic – how divergent moral and esthetic interests (in the moral type and in grotesquely comic behavior) can produce characters richer in effect than such a single-minded hero and heroine as young Martin and Mary Graham.[16] The American comic characters – for example, Elijah Pogram, the Congressman, and Hannibal Chollop, the frontiersman – are less successful to the extent that they are more consistent as moral types that serve the ethical satire. As in Richardson, it is the rent in the moral surface that generates interest.

Despite the moral irregularities and occasional lurid episodes – lurid only in preparation for such sadistic acts as the penknife scene hints at only – Richardson could be taken as a moralist in his time and in the century following because of his joining of heightened feeling and suffering. In effect, readers could respond to his characters as moral types without a sacrifice of other interests. It is a measure of the great popular novelist (and dramatist, as Stoll makes clear) that he utilizes these interests rather than sacrificing them.

With the increasing emphasis on feeling, character in the tragic modes of fiction gradually ceases to be something known and definable. It must, however, remain consistent with the moral type re-

16. The opening description of the hypocritical Pecksniff is representative: "His very throat was moral. You saw a good deal of it. You looked over a very low fence of white cravat . . . and there it lay, a valley between two jutting heights of collar, serene and whiskerless before you. It seemed to say, on the part of Mr. Pecksniff, 'There is no deception, ladies and gentlemen, all is peace, a holy calm pervades me.' " (Chapter 2).

quired by the surface plot. The eighteenth century religious milieu fostered this view, with its stress on the mysterious roots of character: Bunyan's *Grace Abounding to the Chief of Sinners* (about 1666) is typical of seventeenth and eighteenth century works in which the writer searches for these roots and states his dilemma through complex and not easily defined feelings. Richardson's friend, Edward Young, writes in his *Night-Thoughts* of 1742:

> A Worm! a God – I tremble at myself,
> And in myself am lost! At home a Stranger,
> Thought wanders up and down, surpris'd, aghast,
> And wond'ring at her *own*: How Reason reels!
> O what a Miracle to Man is Man,
> Triumphantly distress'd! what Joy, what Dread!
> Alternately transported, and alarm'd!

The vogue of sentimentality exploited this sense of wonderment and discovery. Writers as different as Richardson and Goethe, and later Dickens, explore it in Lovelace and Werther and even Mr. Pickwick.

This view of emotional life promotes a different rhetoric from what we find in a work like *Samson Agonistes,* in which, to quote Kenneth Burke, "dramatic subterfuge" is used to "include what we would have had to exclude, if reduced to a conceptually analytic statement."[17] The premise of Milton's rhetoric is that feelings can be conceived and specified: at least their origin can be determined by their effects and so judged. The sentimental view of man by contrast implies that effects are not easily discoverable. The mind wonders at itself: "How Reason reels! "

The sentimental novelist thus is able to debate about his characters and their counterparts in real life, as if the qualities adduced were not quite proved. Richardson's assured tone in numerous passages quoted in this study should not be mistaken for an absolute and fixed view of motives or their proper names and the judgment to be made about them. This kind of rhetoric enforces norms of judgment, instead of merely declaring them: a sign of uncertainty or anxiety. In the sentimental novel the more absolute the moral feelings and judgments, the more a character becomes a figure of fantasy – like

17. *A Rhetoric of Motives* (Berkeley: University of California Press, 1969), p. 5.

Clarissa in the final quarter of her novel, and Grandison throughout his.

Where such a view of feeling prevails, fantasy becomes prominent. It is not coincidental that this kind of fantasy is masochistic; for, as Berliner suggests, masochistic trends in the individual can be projected into society under these circumstances: "This childhood pattern [of sadism] is reenacted not only by the masochistic adult but also by society. Adult society reflects on a large scale the conditions of childhood. There is a general need for love and there are the various hostile attitudes among all peoples. . . . Since the individual has to accept society, he has to accept those destructive tendencies too and turns against his own ego in a submissive self-destructive way. . . . The masochist dreams loving souls into those men who hate him and who wish that he harm and destroy himself, and he helps to fill the world with them."[18] Character is thus the agency of transformation from the level of fantasy to that of social and intellectual meaning. For this reason, style in Richardson can be discussed as the style of individualized thought and feeling. One critic relates these styles to theatrical and dramatic currents in Richardson's age: "Although [the theatrical, declamatory mode] functions somewhat differently from Lovelace's courtly rhetoric, it too follows the movement of the action and underlines the dramatic progress of the narrative. Just as Lovelace's plain, sober speech gives way to romantic rhapsodies in moments of triumph or desperation, so too Clarissa's language loses its conventional idiom to the pathetic accents of formal stage-rhetoric as she nears her tragic fate."[19]

The complex displacements and splitting of character that permitted Richardson to explore dream and fantasy are not peculiar to his work or his age. We will shortly examine the remarkably similar modes of characterization in Lawrence – particularly in *Sons and Lovers* and *Women in Love* in which characters reflect upon their feelings and interpret them, and in which plot functions as a series of events that explore recurrent states of consciousness.

Richardson would have found a model in the drama of his time. In Sir Richard Steele's *The Tender Husband* (1705), to which he refers to *Pamela,* is to be found a splitting of character types similar to his

18. "Libido and Reality in Masochism," 332.

19. William J. Farrell, "The Style and the Action in *Clarissa,*" in *Samuel Richardson: A Collection of Critical Essays,* p. 97.

own treatment of the libertine. One critic of Steele suggests that he modified the libertine comedy of the Restoration by dividing the typical qualities of the libertine between two characters in the play: his brutality is given to Clerimont Senior, who uses his mistress Fainlove (disguised as a man) to make love to his wife; his cunning and wit are given to Captain Clerimont, who, like Fainlove, also resorts to disguise – to prevent marriage between Biddy Tipkin and the gull of the play, Humphry Gubbin.[20] This splitting has the incidental effect of blurring social and moral norms; for Fainlove and Captain Clerimont use their wit to achieve their fortunes, not to expose social pretensions or moral hypocrisy. Issues of character (hypocrisy, self-deception) that earlier comic dramatists might have explored satirically through characters embodying wit and good sense are not defined clearly or are undeveloped and therefore remain unresolved.

Thus Captain Clerimont says to the impressionable Biddy, who has been reading Arcadian romances: "Fortune points out to us this only occasion of our happiness. Love's of celestial origin and needs no long acquaintance to be manifest. Lovers like angels speak of intuition, their souls are in their eyes."[21] We cannot be certain of the *implied* norm here. We are likely to consider Biddy pretentious; but it is not clear how Clerimont is to be judged – or whether he and Fainlove are themselves targets of satire. When moral and social norms are established by the least unattractive characters, these may be shifted with relative ease, giving a freer play to romantic feeling and fantasy – even when elements or fantasy seem the target of satirical criticism.

Early twentieth century satirical comedy depends on similar indistinctness of norms for its effect. We cannot say with assurance whether Shaw's Tanner and Ann Whitefield are being satirized – and if they are, how they are. Tanner, according to his own view, is the man to be depended on in the serious matters of living because he has no illusions about romantic love. The comic issue arises in the discovery that he is Ann's quarry. But is he the quarry, or has he indeed been the pursuer all along? From the beginning of *Man and Superman* he has enchanted Ann by seeming to be beyond reach.

20. Calhoun Winton, in his introduction to *The Tender Husband* (Lincoln: University of Nebraska Press, 1967), p. 10.

21. Ibid., p. 61.

"What a shocking flirt you are, Jack! " Ann tells him in the first act; in the fourth, he admits he is enchanted: "The Life Force enchants me: I have the whole world in my arms when I clasp you. But I am fighting for my freedom, for my honor, for my self, one and indivisible." Are both in the grip of forces neither understands? Are they, interchangeably, spider and fly?

A condition of the comic mode of *Man and Superman* is that no answer to this question is possible. The frequent nonsequiturs of characters like Ann, who should know what they are about, contribute to this effect. "You must be a sentimental old bachelor for my sake," she tells Octavius at the end of the play. "A broken heart is a very pleasant complaint for a man in London if he has a comfortable income." If an answer to questions raised is to be had, it is likely to be a sentimental one – that is, an affirmation of basic human goodness in the teeth of the facts. Improbable marriages will turn out well; quarreling parents and children, husband and wives will reconcile, as in the conclusion of several Dickens novels. Sentimental comedy joins with sentimental tragedy in this easy transfer of belief in the denouement: old Martin Chuzzlewit, the picture of irascibility and parental tyranny toward his grandson young Martin, in the final pages of the novel is transformed into a youthful, affectionate figure. In Richardson, the rake-hero turns out to be benign or his "fall" (like B.'s, in his affair with Sally Godfrey) is rationalized: he has been the victim of a deception engineered by women. His reformation is possible in these circumstances; but, less consistently, his potential worthiness as a husband is warrant that nothing has happened to anyone.

This is the reason that efforts at seduction are constantly interrupted. When successful, they are not in all writers a basis of irrevocable condemnation; rather the woman in literature up to our own time invariably suffers the blame. Not only may the rakish hero be virginal in spirit (he has not truly loved), he is also (like Tanner) a moralist for whom antifeminist views obviously have social or religious sanction. We have seen that Lovelace and his nemesis Morden meet in their heavily moralized view of women. The premise of the sentimental comedy we have been discussing is precisely that of sentimental tragedy: the hero, even if he is not an emotional castrate, can do no lasting harm. The underlying fantasy can be imaginatively enacted only through denial of it in the plot or in its denouement.

Inevitably displacements of character mean that identifications for the writer as well as the reader occur not on the basis of marked sexual or psychological differentiation at the level of surface plot, but on the basis of dislocations marked by conflicting trends of character. Characters with whom identification is most possible (B., Clarissa, Lovelace, Clementina – rather than Miss Howe, Lord G., even Harriet) are shown in such depth that consistency is not important to their "reality," even if consistency were possible. Instead they are unified by a stereotype that stands for "character" in the surface plot – Clarissa is the blameless victim, Lovelace the heartless rake – but is at odds with underlying realities that every reader intuits.

Stoll, who would not have liked being cited in a psychoanalytic discussion of character, in his analysis of Falstaff and other Shakespearean characters sheds light on the importance and operation of stereotypes, as we noted earlier. The rich detail of the characterization provides the extraordinary impression of personality, even though the character is built on a single impression that depends on traditional motifs – in Falstaff, the qualities of the braggart captain, with large belly, a dwarfish page, a fraudulent weapon, and the cowardly and unbridled qualities associated with the type. Tradition, however, is not the same thing as realism. The stereotype, indeed, is available precisely because it is rare or unreal: ". . . nothing is so rare as realism – nothing in itself so hateful to the public or by name so dear. The braggart captains, the valets who beat and bamboozle their masters, the nurses and chambermaids who scold them or thwart them in every wish, the women who put their husbands in bodily fear, and the timid and pureminded maidens who upon provocation make love, and in men's clothing seek the beloved through field and forest in lands remote, all please only by their rarity or unreality, being incompatible with conditions under which women and servants knew no liberty, and a soldier stood or fell by his personal prowess alone."[22] The awareness of stereotype contributes to the sense of "unreality." The characterization is entertaining precisely because it is not life and, more important for our analysis of Richardson's surface plots and underlying fantasies, may seem to deny the nuclear

22. *Shakespeare Studies,* pp. 430-31.

fantasy. The double or reflexive value to which W. K. Wimsatt refers in his analysis of Falstaff may originate in mutually denying qualities – youth and age, joyousness and gloom, sexual exuberance and impotence.[23]

In other words, a firmly conceived structure of social meanings and norms permits the descent into fantasy. This is one implication of Watt's observation that the novel confuses differences between reality and dream, flattering the reader's own dreams in the process.[24] The pattern of the sentimental tragedy perfected by Richardson derives from widely shared fantasies, transformed in the complex displacements we have noted. The guilt arising from the enacting of these fantasies is itself transformed into, and at the same time, controlled by the sentimentalism and piety of the surface plot. The pleasure generated by this defence intensifies the experience. Sentimentality, in the exploration of sexual experience ending in assault and rape, is sadomasochistic in its trend.

4

A chief concern of eighteenth century criticism is the "appetite after pain" which Lord Kames rationalized as a form of sympathetic, ethical self-development. His concern with "pathetic" tragedy shows how the sentimental tragedy might have been rationalized: pathetic tragedy depicts the suffering of the wholly good person and asks for our admiration as well as our imitation of the virtues exhibited – in psychoanalytic language, for a strong defense against the libidinal components of the experience. The sadism engendered in the libidinal fantasy and intensified by the defense is only partly allayed. Holland's statement on the management of fantasy is highly pertinent: "Weakly managed, we experience the affects of gratification. Strongly managed, we experience the affects appropriate to frustration. If the aggressive side of the drive is managed, we feel a general muting of affect. In the libidinal side is denied satisfaction . . . we feel the anger from the aggressive component."[25] In these terms, sentimental piety is strongly managed, with associated intensifications of style. As if to balance the "unreality" of these expressions, a

23. *The Verbal Icon* (Lexington: University of Kentucky Press, 1954), pp. 78-79.
24. *The Rise of the Novel*, p. 205.
25. *The Dynamics of Literary Response*, p. 300.

complementary realism is reserved to characters like Lovelace and Charlotte, who are permitted to speak the truth on condition that they stand condemned or censured. We find a similar situation in Dickens – in characters like Edith Dombey and Rosa Dartle, who have been victimized or neglected by unscrupulous or unfeeling men. We have here the counterpart of those dislocations in characterization (the actor often distanced from and judging his own action and previous statements) noted earlier.

So, too, in George Lillo's *The London Merchant* (1731) – one of the important sentimental tragedies of Richardson's time – the voice of realism is given to the sexually degraded woman. Specifically, Pamela's comment, in the sequel, that the sexual degradation of women is the result of their social inferiority is given to Millwood. She states that her "arts were such as my conversation with your sex had furnished me withal." And further: "Men of all degrees and all professions I have known, yet found no difference but in their several capacities; all were alike wicked to the utmost of their power. In pride, contention, avarice, cruelty and revenge, the revered priesthood were unerring guides" (Act IV, Scene 2). The willingness of readers and audiences to accept widely ranging normative views from unsympathetic characters suggests that the rhythm of the play or novel is experienced as a balancing of extreme emotional attitudes. In *The London Merchant,* such a stark admission and expression of motive in Millwood is in sharp contrast to the grossly motivated hero George Barnwell, whose unprovoked killing of his uncle demands understanding. But in place of motivation, we are given a moralized picture of what happens once a young man begins the descent from virtue.

Disconnections of motive and action are also evident in two later masterpieces of sentimental tragedy – Henry Mackenzie's *The Man of Feeling* (1771) and Goethe's *The Sorrows of Young Werther* (1774, 1787). More so than in Lillo and other plays of its type, the disconnections in Mackenzie's narrative promote an exploration of motives at the level of fantasy; the surface plot, depending on the sentimental traveller (a structure exploited in *Grandison* and other works of the period), is barely kept intact. What might have been the central interest of the work, Harley's relationship to Miss Walton, though scarcely explored, instead is permitted to dominate the final pages.

Thus Harley's jealousy of Sir Harry Benson's presumed engagement to Miss Walton provides occasion for this display of romantic melancholy: "His resolution failed; he slunk back, and, locking the gate as softly as he could, stood on tiptoe looking over the wall till they were gone. At that instant a shepherd blew his horn; the romantic melancholy of the sound quite overcame him! – it was the very note that wanted to be touched – he sighed! he dropped a tear! – and returned."[26] The cause of Harley's death is not specified: only his extreme sensitivity is stressed. His dying is an act of revenge against Miss Walton. He tells the narrator that the world is "a scene of dissimulation, of restraint, of disappointment. I leave it to enter on that state which I have learned to believe is replete with the genuine happiness attendant upon virtue."[27] The final words of Miss Walton stress an unnamed guilt:

> "Let me entreat you," said she, "to have better hopes – Let not life be so indifferent to you; if my wishes can put any value on it – I will not pretend to misunderstand you – I know your worth – I have known it long – I have esteemed it – What would you have me say? – I have loved it as it deserved." – He seized her hand – a languid colour reddened his cheek – a smile brightened faintly in his eye. As he gazed on her, it grew dim, it fixed, it closed – He sighed and fell back on his seat – Miss Walton screamed at the sight – His aunt and the servants rushed into the room – They found them lying motionless together.[28]

These are familiar motifs in the sentimental novel of the next century. *Pickwick Papers* employs the sentimental traveller who contemplates the suffering of the world but, unlike Harley, is unaffected by it until he finds himself imprisoned and forced to confront undeserved suffering. No novel of Dickens exhibits more clearly the dislocations of character and plot we have called attention to. The comic plot of a suit for breach of promise of marriage is the occasion for the contrasting prison scenes, in which sentimental themes rise to crescendo. The discrepancies in Pickwick's character are apparent to most readers without damaging the effect. Dickens himself, in the Preface, calls attention to the change in character: "It has been observed of Mr. Pickwick, that there is a decided change in his character . . . and that he becomes more good and more sensible. I do not think this change will appear forced or unnatural to my readers, if

26. Albert J. Kuhn, ed., *Three Sentimental Novels* (New York: Holt, Rinehart and Winston, 1970), p. 209.
27. Ibid., pp. 222-23.
28. Ibid., 224-25.

they will reflect that in real life the peculiarities and oddities of a man who has anything whimsical about him, generally impress us first, and that it is not until we are better acquainted with him that we usually begin to look below these superficial traits, and to know the better part of him." Pickwick does gain a deeper understanding of his world and the sufferings of the poor. Perhaps the change is credible because it so sudden, though the dislocation and alteration in feeling are prepared for in the famous sentimental tales of suffering that intersperse the novel. Pickwick shows again that moral masochism is central to the sentimental experience; for the sentimental tales are so plotted that the cause of suffering are superficially or barely developed. We must look instead to secret motives – evident in how we defend ourselves against them. We identify with the characters of these tales at this deeper level only.

In Dickens's later novels, as the devices that transform the nuclear fantasy (chiefly money relationships, property and other forms of "filth") are perfected through a maturation of the social commentary, the structure exhibits a greater integration than we find in *Pickwick.* Still, as in Esther Summerson in *Bleak House,* Dickens reserves certain characters for a development of moral masochism that considerably exceeds the needs of plot. Readers who attack the sentimentality of Esther Summerson do not respond in the same way to similar representations in other novels in which the cause of suffering (Uriah Heep, for example) is directly portrayed. Dickens, unlike Richardson, was able to introduce the masochistic fantasy virtually without transformation in many pages – *Bleak House* and the Steerforth and the Little Emily episodes in *David Copperfield* are supreme examples – one reason, perhaps, that he is often charged with being sentimental and melodramatic.

In its moral masochism *Pickwick* has important affinities with *The Man of Feeling.* As in *Grandison,* Harley's moral masochism is suggested in the contrast between his goodness and the world's selfishness; Mackenzie imagines his death as a fitting end to earthly "weaknesses" which may be regarded as virtues in Heaven: "I look back on the tenor of my life, with the consciousness of few great offences to account for. There are blemishes, I confess, which deform in some degree the picture. But I know the benignity of the Supreme Being, and rejoice at the thoughts of its exercises in my favour. My mind expands at the thought I shall enter into the society of the blessed, wise as angels, with the simplicity of children."[29] As in moral masochism, guilt is unspecified, that is, it is without content. Mackenzie like Richardson explores the tragedy of excessive feeling, and shows it to be defective in promoting earthly happiness and redemptive as Clarissa's tragedy is. We have, then, a tragedy centered on the failure of vital feeling in an imperfect world (spending itself in grief), rather than one of ethical failings, of flaws of character, whether or not these are suggested. This is the essence of sentimental tragedy from Richardson to Dickens and beyond. As does Richardson, Mackenzie stresses the cultivation of vital feeling in the whole book, most significantly in this statement of one character, Ben Silton: "There is at least . . . one advantage in the poetical inclination, that it is an incentive to philanthropy. There is a certain poetic ground, on which a man cannot tread without feelings that enlarge the heart: the causes of human depravity vanish before the romantic enthusiasm he professes, and many who are not able to reach the Parnassian heights, may yet approach so near as to be bettered by the air of the climate."[30]

5

Goethe's Charlotte and Werther reveal the role of moral masochism in the sentimental novel even more directly.[31] That pattern, as worked out in the novel, has much in common with *Grandison*, particularly in its exploitation of motifs associated with the family romance, chief among these family substitutes. Charlotte, with whom Werther falls in love, is introduced as the mother to six brothers and sisters, the real mother having died before the novel begins, and she is portrayed chiefly in this role. Though her father lives, he is a negligible figure in the Oedipal drama. Her husband, Albert, plays this role; it is Werther's momentary wish to murder Albert that pushes him to suicide. The pistols with which he kills himself seem instruments of symbolic castration: one of them shatters the thumb of a servant girl, for example.

Basic to *Werther* is the view that the incapacity to relieve passion is a "physical infirmity." This view is implied in Werther's descrip-

29. Ibid., p. 223.

30. Ibid., pp. 182-83.

31. K. R. Eissler discusses masochism in Goethe himself. *Goethe: A Psychoanalytic Study*, p. 453.

tion to Albert of the young girl who kills herself on being abandoned by her lover. Death is her only escape:

> All is darkness around her. No prospect, no hope, no consolation – forsaken by him in whom her existence was centered! She sees nothing of the world before her, thinks nothing of the many others who might fill the void in her heart; she feels herself deserted, forsaken by all the world; and, unseeing and impelled by the agony in her soul, she plunges into the deep, to end her sufferings in the broad embrace of death. You see, Albert, this is the story of thousands; and now tell me, is not this a case of physical infirmity? Nature can find no way out of the labyrinth of confusion and contradiction; and the poor creature must die.[32]

Suffering is the constant in human experience and, as in *Grandison*, is to be endured for its own sake. Romantic melancholy and despair are, not surprisingly, masochistic in their trends. These explain why nature to the Romantic is both plenitude and destruction:

> My heart is wasted by the thought of that destructive power which lies latent in every part of universal Nature. Nature has formed nothing that does not destroy itself, and everything near it. And so, surrounded by earth and air and all the active forces, I stagger on with anguished heart; the universe to me is an ever devouring, ever ruminating monster.[33]

In such a universe God is silent; in psychoanalytic language, the crime against the father earns no forgiveness:

> Father, Whom I know not – Who wert once wont to fill my soul, but Who now hidest Thy face from me – call me back to Thee; be silent no longer! Thy silence cannot sustain a soul which thirsts after Thee. What man, what father, could be angry with a son for returning to him unexpectedly, for falling on his neck, and exclaiming, "Here I am again, my father! Forgive me if I have shortened my journey to return before the appointed time! The world is everywhere the same – for labor and pain, pleasure and reward; but what does it all avail? I am happy only where thou art, and in thy presence I am content to suffer or enjoy." And Thou, Heavenly Father, wouldst Thou turn such a child from Thee?[34]

The motive of suffering is scarcely disguised. Werther's impulse to murder Albert, who has taken Charlotte from him, requires nothing less than his own death; yet it is the suffering itself that is important. His frustrated love for Charlotte, which we might expect is a central motive, is in effect a secondary concern. As the surrogate mother,

32. *The Sorrows of Young Werther,* trans. Victor Lange (New York: Holt, Rinehart and Winston, 1949), p. 46.
33. Ibid., p. 49.
34. Ibid., p. 93.

Charlotte cannot express her love openly – she can express only pity. Before his death Werther writes to her that "we shall see each other again; see your mother; I shall find her, and pour out my inmost heart to her. Your mother – your image! "[35]

Charlotte, in turn, realizes her love for Werther only at the moment she apprehends his "terrible plan." It is Charlotte who hands the pistols to the servant, at Albert's command: Werther experiences "transports of delight" when he is told this.[36]

Eissler has shown that Goethe was acutely aware of the close relationship between sadism and sentimental tragedy. "This passing feeling of the crushing effect of individuality," Eissler comments, "was, in my opinion, that expression of suffering at the hands of life that is encountered almost regularly in masochistic phases."[37] In five incomplete essays on the nature of drama, in *Wilhelm Meister,* "sadism is discovered as the infantile root of man's pleasure."[38] The complex role that moral masochism plays in esthetic experience, I have tried to show, is plumbed in Richardson's art and is one of his important legacies to Goethe and other later novelists. Richardson gave shape and content to the sentimental experience but, more importantly, showed how trends of character could mediate between the nuclear fantasy and surface plot without a sense of glaring inconsistency. Perhaps no better definition of this experience is to be found than Sade's: "if after twelve or fifteen volumes the immortal Richardson had *virtuously* ended by converting Lovelace and having him *peacefully* marry Clarissa, would you, in reading this novel taken in the opposite sense, have shed the delicious tears which it won from every feeling reader? It is, then, nature one must capture in working this genre, it is the heart of man, the strangest of its products, and not at all virtue, because virtue, however beautiful and necessary it may be, is still only one of the modes of this amazing heart, the profound style of which is so necessary to the novelist and which the novel, faithful mirror of this heart, must necessarily map out in all its windings."[39]

35. Ibid., p. 121.
36. Ibid., p. 124.
37. Eissler, p. 458.
38. Ibid., p. 726.
39. Eaves and Kimpel, *Samuel Richardson,* p. 604.

Chapter Six

RICHARDSON AND LAWRENCE: THE RHETORIC OF CONCEALMENT

1

Despite his doubts about the wisdom of writing "to the moment," Richardson's letters show that, at least in *Grandison,* he favored this procedure, perhaps intuiting that unexpected revelations into character arose in this way. Thus he wrote to Lady Bradshaigh: "The world is not enough used to this way of writing, to the moment. It knows not that in the minutiae lie often the unfoldings of the Story, as well as of the heart; and judges of an action undecided, as if it were absolutely decided. Nor will it easily part with its first impressions."[1] He states earlier in the same letter that he did not wish to anticipate what the process of composition would reveal: "We often cheat ourselves on the Entrance into a Character, by setting it down in our minds for such or such and when it rises or sinks upon us, are hardly able to reconcile it to our first hasty Impressions."[2] Lawrence, in his essay "Why the Novel Matters," expresses a similar idea. In the living novel, the characters "can do nothing but *live.*" The advantage of the novel is that only in it "are *all* things given full play, or at least, they may be given full play, when we realize that life itself, and not inert safety, is the reason for living. For out of the full play of all things emerges the only thing that is anything, the wholeness of a man, the wholeness of a woman, man alive, and live woman."[3]

I suggested earlier that Richardson and Lawrence share a conception of form that is one with their view of character: however plot is organized and developed, it must provide the basis for exploring

1. *Selected Letters,* p. 289.
2. Ibid., p. 287.
3. *Phoenix,* pp. 537-38.

recurrent states of consciousness. Characters grow in feeling and perception but they do not change as people. Clarissa grows in awareness of her character and situation as her misfortune increases, but she expresses nothing about herself or Lovelace or the world that she could not and did not know earlier. Lovelace, too, shows no obvious progression of character – rather a gradual increase in complexity on which the action depends and which reveals itself in action. Nor do any of the major characters in *Grandison.* Rather, the action tends toward reduplication.

Though Richardson's plots have been analyzed as plots of character – plots in which, according to R. S. Crane, action and thought lead to change of character in the protagonist – they are really plots of action, in which character and thought produce a change in fortune.[4] *Clarissa* perhaps is better classified with Norman Friedman's plots of "fortune," more specifically, the "pathetic" plot, in which "a sympathetic protagonist . . . undergoes misfortune through no particular fault of his own," joined to the "punitive," in which an unsympathetic protagonist, possibly "admirable for his strength of will and intellectual sophistication," receives his just deserts.[5] Friedman's example of the "pathetic" plot is Hardy's *Tess of the d'Urbervilles* and those naturalistic novels in which characters are directed by inscrutable forces. Our analysis has shown that, where a sense of fatality is strong, the action is likely to repeat itself. Lawrence's plots – at least in *Sons and Lovers, The Rainbow,* and *Women in Love* – are plots of action in the most general sense. The sense of fatality is as strong as in Richardson; the action of these novels tends toward reduplication.

Thus in *Women in Love,* Birkin's various statements and reflections on men and women in no way advance the action; they are instead individual events occasioned by his conflict with Ursula over the basis of their relationship, as well as by the emotional demands of Hermione. Though Ursula is suspicious of and indeed resists Birkin's idea of love as a balance or "equilibrium" rather than a fusion of personalities, she agrees to marry him. Her suspicion that Birkin wishes to dominate her in love is never directly contradicted,

4. "The Concept of Plot and the Plot of *Tom Jones,*" in *Critics and Criticism,* ed. R. S. Crane, (Chicago: University of Chicago Press, 1952), pp. 620-21.
5. "Forms of the Plot," in Philip Stevick, ed., *The Theory of the Novel* (New York: The Free Press, 1967), pp. 158-59.

nor does the subsequent action of the novel resolve this conflict in viewpoints. Lawrence instead reserves what seems to be the most authoritative view of men and women to a personal reflection of Birkin, in which the "lovely state of free proud singleness" is praised.[6] At the end of the novel, with the death of his friend Gerald Crich, with whom he has cultivated and tried to sustain a homoerotic relationship presumably to balance his relationship to Ursula, the debate between husband and wife continues. As in Richardson, we have a repetition of earlier debates, advanced only by the change in action. Similar tensions are aroused and explored. The novel concludes with a final exchange between them over Gerald:

> "Having you, I can live all my life without anybody else, any other sheer intimacy. But to make it complete, really, happy, I wanted eternal union with a man too; another kind of love," he said.
>
> "I don't believe it," she said. "It's an obstinacy, a theory, a perversity."
>
> "Well – " he said.
>
> "You can't have two kinds of love. Why should you? "
>
> "It seems as if I can't," he said, "Yet I wanted it."
>
> You can't have it, because it's false, impossible," she said.
>
> "I don't believe that," he answered.[7]

The novel does not tell us whether Birkin and Gerald's failure is personal to them – or whether, under other circumstances, such a relationship can exist in "strange conjunction." Indeed, the question cannot be answered, for as in Richardson the sense of fatality – Gerald will die for whatever reason, and has been marked for death like other members of the Crich family – remains constant, almost the single unexplained motive.

Character is not at issue. We have had merely a change of fortune in Gerald, occurring because he could not and does not accept an idea that may or may not have altered his own unbalanced relationship to Ursula's sister, Gudrun. His qualities and decisions are fixed from the beginning of the novel, in the depiction of the will to power as a form of dying.

Lawrence offers in the Foreword to *Women in Love* what is to him a profound explanation of human behavior. The novel presumes only to give an account of the writer's inner experiences: "Nothing that comes from the deep, passional soul is bad, or can be bad."[8]

6. *Women in Love*, Compass edition (New York: Viking, 1960), p. 247.
7. Ibid., pp. 472-73.
8. Ibid., viii.

Given this view, it is obvious why there can be no advance in character or change of thought, regardless of what pieties or philosophical ideas the novel purveys. Passional feeling is absolute: it is the primary experience. More significantly, the most enduring and constant feelings provide evidence of a superior or mystical realm; the passional self for Lawrence exists in a realm beyond the human. It is here that Birkin looks for "singleness."

2

Consistent with this general view of character is an antifeminism: the view in both Richardson and Lawrence that women tend to be inconstant and rebellious (even murderous), once they lose sight of their proper social and domestic role. To Richardson, as we have seen, they are encroachers when, like Miss Howe and Charlotte Grandison, they demand to rule in marriage. Lawrence rationalizes his view of women in mystical terms: the women is the hub of the marriage, not the axle, he states in the remarkable "Study of Thomas Hardy": "Until eternity, there shall be this separateness, this interaction of man upon woman, male upon female, this suffering, this delight, this imperfection. In eternity, maybe, the action may be perfect. In infinity, the spinning of the wheel upon the hub may be a frictionless whole, complete, an unbroken sleep that is infinite, motion that is utter rest, a duality that is sheerly one."[9] Lawrence refines this view in numerous ways. In his famous essay "Nottingham and the Mining Countryside," he blames "the nagging materialism of the woman" for the destruction of feeling: "The colliers were deeply alive, instinctively. But they had no daytime ambition, and no daytime intellect. They avoided, really, the rational aspect of life. They preferred to take life instinctively and intuitively."[10] Though more than ten years separate *Women in Love* from *Lady Chatterley's Lover,* the psychology of women is the same.

We should not be surprised, then, to discover that Richardson and Lawrence imagine their women as moral types, and make them the basis of psychological displacements – displacement that may shift from scene to scene. They do for this reason seem to emerge into a semblance of "roundness," for displacements usually entail sustained

9. *Phoenix,* pp. 443.
10. Ibid., p. 136.

inside views. We can accept in Richardson's women possibilities of experience that we would find incredible in B. and Grandison (not Lovelace, who is feminized). We could not accept B. dreaming as Harriet does. Her dream – developed at length – has the effect of deepening an impression of character introduced at this point in the novel – and deepening it without advancing our understanding of qualities we have previously observed. The same is true of Ursula, whose meditation at the end of *The Rainbow* is imagined independently of what we have seen earlier in the novel. Indeed, Lawrence is able to create a wholly new character in the Ursula of *Women in Love,* apparently without concern for obvious inconsistencies. These similarities suggest that character is perceived at a deeper level.

Displacement is particularly strong in the earlier *Sons and Lovers,* a novel that has been judged a failure for inconsistency of character, though it contains some of Lawrence's finest insights into the character of women. No novel of Lawrence is more revealing of the turn sentimental tragedy took in the novel following Richardson.

In what is still in my opinion the best critique of *Sons and Lovers,* Mark Schorer in his 1948 essay "Technique as Discovery" comments on "meanings confused by an impatience with technical resources." His reasons are worth reviewing in detail: Lawrence simultaneously "condemns" and "justifies" Mrs. Morel; Miriam, Paul's sweetheart, is made her "scapegoat"; "Paul is unable to love Miriam wholly, and Miriam can love only his spirit. These contradictions appear sometimes within single paragraphs, and the point of view is never adequately objectified and sustained to tell us which is true."[11] In short, Lawrence conceals his norms of character at the cost of a consistent narrative and psychological coherence.

In his psychoanalytical study of *Sons and Lovers,* Daniel A. Weiss shows that these consistencies may be explained as shifting tensions generated by an Oedipal fantasy. Miriam Leivers and Clara Dawes represent dual aspects of the Oedipal mother – Miriam, the virginal image that Paul wishes to preserve but nevertheless forces into sexual intercourse as a way of separating her from that identification; Clara, the "harlot." "With her [Miriam] as with his mother, Paul cannot act out the desired incest. His relationship with Clara, on the other hand,

11. *The World We Imagine* (New York: Farrar, Straus and Giroux, 1968), pp. 12-14.

succeeds and fails in turn because his repressed image of the beloved mother is realized in every essential."[12] When Mrs. Morel dies, Paul's incestuous fantasies "sicken and die with her. The pleasantly deathly consummation with Miriam and the Nirvana-like 'impersonality of passion' with Clara resolve themselves in Paul's horror at the coldness of his mother's lips, a horror he inverts and feels in Clara when he lies with her."[13]

Let us look more closely at how displacement and condensation are managed in *Sons and Lovers,* in comparison to similar modes of characterization in Richardson. The capacity of Lawrence's characters for undirected feeling – that is, for merely exploring their feelings and responding to experiences and ideas – defines them as people, regardless of what Lawrence may say about them, and permits displacement and condensation to occur. Mrs. Morel and Miriam – who are not merely antagonists but counterparts through most of the novel, as Weiss notes – are richly drawn yet, in their representation, inconsistent with statements that have the ring of normative truth. Thus Lawrence suggests in numerous passages that Miriam is sexually inhibited and given to sublimate her feelings into a love of nature:

> With Miriam he [Paul] was always on the high plane of abstraction, when his natural fire of love was transmitted into the fine stream of thought. She would have it so.
>
> To her, flowers appealed with such strength she felt she must make them part of herself. When she bent and breathed a flower, it was as if she and the flower were loving each other. Paul hated her for it.[14]

Eventually Miriam submits to sexual intercourse, believing that her "sacrifice" will satisfy Paul's restlessness and give her control over his life. With only slight alteration of tone, these same statements might describe Mrs. Morel, particularly in early passages that contrast her with Morel: "She was puritan, like her father, high-minded, and really stern. Therefore the dusky, golden softness of this man's sensuous flame of life, that flowed off his flesh like the flame from a candle, not baffled and gripped into incandescence by thought and

12. *Oedipus in Nottingham: D. H. Lawrence* (Seattle: University of Washington Press. 1962), p. 59. Cf. Simon O. Lesser, *Fiction and the Unconscious* (Boston: Beacon Press, 1957), pp. 173-78.

13. Ibid., p. 65.

14. *Sons and Lovers,* ed. Julian Moynahan (New York: Viking, 1968), p. 173. Subsequent references in the text are to this edition.

spirit as her life was, seemed to her something wonderful, beyond her" (p. 10). If the reader does not imagine Mre. Morel as a flaccid character in later scenes, the reason is that Lawrence focuses on episodes in which she *feels* victimized by Miriam's great feeling for Paul. In the same way, our impression of Clarissa's vitality is inseparable from our impression of her growing sensitiveness to Lovelace's grossness of moral feeling. Furthermore, we are given Paul's belief that, in the early days of her marriage, his mother has been able to ripen, as Miriam has not, because she found in her husband "the real, real flame of feeling through another person" (p. 317).

Any such vitality – and we are shown little of it in the early scenes – has been directed into material concerns and domestic passions. Incapable of maintaining her relationship with Morel at the same sexual threshold and of accepting his masculine habits and friendships that exclude her, she thwarts him at every opportunity. His response in their most violent encounter, occurring during the time she is pregnant with Paul, is to put her out of the house – in effect, momentarily depriving her of protection from genteel domestic arrangements she has tried to impose on him. In the garden behind the house, in a much-discussed scene, she falls under the spell of tall white lilies and grows dizzy from their scent. But this erotic experience is momentary; as her sexual excitations begins to wane, she masters her feelings by relating them to the morning-time domestic world in which she is dominant. She succeeds as Clarissa does: sexual feeling is moralized, directed into new pieties to which Lawrence grants authority.

Her relation to Paul is best understood through similar scenes in which mother and son retreat from Eros. In the most important of these, she complains to Paul that Miriam is taking him from her; she has, in her words, "never had a husband – not really." As he strokes her hair, his mouth touching her throat, Morel totters drunk at the doorway and mutters venomously to his wife, "At your mischief again? " (p. 213) When the shamed woman rejects Paul's appeal that she not sleep with her husband, Paul experiences first "a fury of misery," then, in the thought that he is her true lover, "the bitter peace of resignation" (p. 215).

A double displacement has been occurring in the novel. In an earlier episode, Paul makes a similar accusation when he observes Miriam trying to win the love of her young brother by swaying him in her hands: he angrily asks her why she is making a fuss. He behaves here as his father does in the later scene, but there is no basis as yet for Paul's complete identification of Miriam with his mother. The episode does prepare for this later identification. This displacement to Miriam of qualities earlier associated with Mrs. Morel is possible because the two women are shown to be *capable* of the same feelings.

We quoted Lawrence's comment on Mrs. Morel's puritan upbringing. Lawrence adds that despite her awakening erotic feeling she devotes herself, in the early days of her marriage, to rescuing her husband from what is to her a degrading world. This effort is "now a religious instinct," her fanatical love now associated with this effort (p. 16). Similar feelings are later attributed to Miriam, who doubts whether she can give herself sexually to Paul as fully as he wishes. She believes that she has to look forward not to happiness but "tragedy, sorrow, and sacrifice." Her pride will be in sacrifice, her strength in renunciation, "for she did not trust herself to support everyday life" (pp. 215-16).

Paul's confusion of his mother with Miriam becomes apparent when, immediately after Mrs. Morel rejects his appeal not to sleep with her husband, he attacks Miriam through her love of flowers. She does not want to love, he tells her, but to be loved – to "absorb" as if satisfying an "eternal and abnormal craving." The reason is that she is suffering "a shortage somewhere" (p. 218). It is their love of nature, of flowers in particular, that binds mother and son; the criticism is applicable to her and not to an adolescent girl trying to please a hypersensitive boy. These and other parallel scenes show that Paul has confused in Miriam – who dramatizes her spirituality – what he senses to be his mother's "shortage" or deficiency of feeling, which thwarted him (and his father early in the marriage) at the moment his sexual feeling for her was most intense. In this way Paul is able to maintain a relationship with his mother that is remarkably free of the anger and scorn he pours on Miriam.

Through such displacement and condensation in Miriam of various negative qualities shown in other women in the novel, the mother grows into a vital figure, like Clarissa after the rape – a potential sexual object in Paul's imagination – and she remains so to the end of the novel. Tragically, Paul can express his feelings following the crucial encounter with his father only through a contest for sexual power. When he turns temporarily from Miriam to Clara Dawes, whose estranged husband resembles his father in several ways, one reason is that Miriam offers him no real contest. Frustrated and confused, he tells Miriam that he is capable only of friendship. Their relationship has become unbalanced, and he wishes to end it because he hates "a toppling balance" (p. 221). In these scenes with Miriam, Lawrence anticipates the scenes between Birkin and Ursula. Paul in this way frees himself momentarily of the sexually possessive mother, and he now intensely pursues Clara, partly because she has separated from her husband, and Paul enjoys the danger of courting her in public places. The battle with Clara's husband, Baxter Dawes, duplicates earlier confrontations between father and son; the rhythm of the novel is that of engagement and disengagement, ending in the defeat of both men. Morel has long before become a dim and ineffectual character.

We have seen that in Richardson the virtuous woman offers the greatest contest to the libertine; Lawrence's similar concentration on women able to offer such a contest and his willingness to explore widely ranging feelings help to explain why he occasionally shows Miriam in a different light. We are referring now to motives that, as in *Clarissa,* are located in fantasy. Thus when Paul tells Clara that Miriam wants a union of souls only, she responds that he has imagined this and has not tried to discover the truth. The scenes that follow, in the chapter "The Test on Miriam," explore Clara's view, at the same time that Lawrence gives the impression that Miriam and not Paul is to be faulted. Yet, in what seems a moment of insight, Paul admits to her that he is responsible for the failure of their love; he is the "spiritual cripple" (p. 281). Earlier he spoke of his deficiency in loving her (pp. 221-22), and he senses now that their mutual shyness was perhaps love in its "first fierce modesty" (p. 278) – an admission that if true would totally alter the judgment made about Miriam. But these insights are forgotten in later passages that stress her possessiveness and hypersensitivity – qualities that Lawrence stressed initially in the mother and must continue to stress in Miriam.

Lawrence, like Richardson, is thus able to maintain tensions (the fear of the mock-marriage in *Pamela,* fear of rape almost to the end of *Clarissa,* the possible revival of Mrs. Moral as Paul's real love), at the cost of delaying the denouement that, when it does come, comes precipitously. In both *Clarissa* and *Sons and Lover,* the oncoming death of Mrs. Morel and Clarissa is the realization of a fatality hinted at in the early parts of both novels. To lose her sons to the mine as she lost her husband is death to Mrs. Morel; she cannot even save her oldest son, William, whose burial is one of the chief emotional events of the novel. The identification of her with Miriam, which preserves her vitality as we have noted, also has the effect of preparing us for her real death from cancer – which Paul and his sister hasten through the morphine they administer. The rhythm of the novel thus is shaped, as in Richardson, by the need in the underlying fantasy to repeat painful experiences in memory, perhaps as a way of allaying anxiety that will not rest.

Character has been our chief concern in this examination of *Sons and Lovers*; the treatment of character, as we noted earlier, is identical in Richardson and Lawrence. Miriam, like Clara, exists for Lawrence as a sum of potentialities, any single one of which can be stressed to the advantage of a particular exploration of Paul's feelings. But where Richardson wishes to stress competing wishes and perceptions, Lawrence limits himself to one set of qualities in the working out of fantasy, without regard to a consistent action. Thus he can show Miriam to have become as clearsighted as Clara and able to engage in a sexual relationship despite her initial revulsion; if she cannot overcome a sense of guilt, the fault is mainly Paul's. As she comes to recognize this, she becomes increasingly aggressive and more truthful than Paul is able to bear. In a scene parallel to his mother's in the garden toward the beginning of the novel, at the height of his sexual engagement with Miriam he goes into the garden of his parents' house and is captured by the "brutal" scent of the lilies. Afterwards he tells his mother he will break with Miriam – who greets this announcement with unexpected anger: "It has been one long battle between us – you fighting away from me. . . . It has always been you fighting me off" (p. 297). Paul does not reject this view of their situation, as his subsequent thoughts show: "There had never been anything really between them; all the time he had been imagining something where there was nothing. And she had known. She had known so much, and had told him so little" (p. 297). The passage implies that Paul is to blame. But we cannot ask how "deep" Miriam's knowledge has been, for her accession of insight – virtually halted following these scenes – had been introduced only as a means of offering a contest to Paul. To the end, however, she fears the mystic in Paul, though she may speak of living in the spirit; like Ursula she senses there will be no place for her in the darkness of "the great Being" he wishes to melt into (p. 287). Her fear is justified, for his final rejection of her – following his mother's death – is motivated by his need to exercise power which he can best do apart from her. In hastening his mother's death, he has exercised power over her, too. With some differences the novel ends as does *Clarissa.*

In showing Miriam in having begun to change, then reversing this change. so that the identification with Mrs. Morel is complete in the final scenes (where she urges marriage upon Paul to protect him from other women), Lawrence almost totally gives up consistency of character. If the novel is not harmed by this inconsistency, the reason is that the focus is by the end almost entirely on Paul and his mysterious wish to join his mother in death. The narrative in most of the instances quoted or discussed is a forshortening of his thoughts, and it remains this in the final scene, in which he intuits "at the core a nothingness, and yet not nothing," and suddenly makes the decision not to "take that direction, to the darkness, to follow her" (p. 420). The reader is here free to decide for himself why Paul makes this decision: no reason is given in the surface rendering of his thoughts. The answer is, however, to be found in the continuous displacement we have been analyzing: Mrs. Morel lives in Miriam. In turning away from her, he is turning away from both women, at the same time commanding power over their happiness whether in life or in death. The foreshortened narrative keeps open the possibility of choice: the novel simply comes to an end, the feeling of the present moment having been spent, as in *Pamela* B.'s intense pursuit ends, to be succeeded by new interests and feelings.

This method permits greater possibilities of tonal evaluation than Richardson enjoyed in his restriction to an epistolary technique, yet it has the defect, as *Pamela* also sometimes displays, of calling attention to these imprecisions and inconsistencies. A. M. Kearney notes how Pamela's dual function as character and narrator tends to change our impressions of her reality and to create two voices, "the first manifesting itself in a direct and spontaneous manner, coming from the centre of experience itself, and the second a much more deliberate one, suggesting the impressions of the observer rather than the participant."[15] Kinkead-Weekes analyzes problems of voice as a

15. *Samuel Richardson: A Collection of Critical Essays,* p. 29.

personal one for Richardson, commenting on the awkwardness of Pamela's reports of praises for her: "... behind the deeper and more worthy reasons for the choric praise in the last section, may lurk the half-conscious need to surround his character with the same supply of admiration that he found necessary to his own wellbeing and happiness." He states later in this discussion: "Not only does Richardson seem to have believed too easily that self-congratulation could co-exist with true humility, but he also failed to see that there could be unamiable calculation behind the impulse to secure the moral approval of others." In general, Richardson's understanding of subtle moral changes and growth in character was often at odds with "congenial but less wholesome and humanly attractive attitudes," into which he subsided when imagination waned.[16] In Lawrence, too, change in voice marks a change in valuation of character and action. Commenting on Paul's ambivalence toward his parents, Schorer argues that Lawrence failed to control his characterization: "This is a psychological tension which disrupts the form of the novel and obscures its meaning, because neither the contradiction in style nor the confusion in point of view is made to right itself."[17]

Yet, as we saw earlier, such shifts in voice and point of view, as in the penknife scene in *Clarissa,* can make possible fuller exploration of emotional experience, in all of its nuances and turns of feeling, than is possible in a consistent and wholly decorous narrative. The alleged failure of *Sons and Lovers* is attributed to an unreliable narration which presumably confuses the reader. A plain authorial commentary such as Richardson employs in letters of Belford and Miss Howe, to clarify motives and moral points, would have clarified what remains obscure in Lawrence, but at the cost of an emotional depth achieved through a concealment (or confusion) of norms. For Lawrence what Miriam says she feels is more important for many readers than what she does; a conventional commentary tends in Lawrence to carry little rhetorical weight beside the assertion of feeling a character makes at a key moment. This is true of Richardson, also.

Lawrence tends also to move to symbolic action in which tensions are explored at two levels simultaneously, the actual event often seeming less "real" than the passions or underlying motives exposed momentarily. Such stories as "The Prussian Officer," "The Rocking-

16. *Samuel Richardson: Dramatic Novelist,* pp. 102-04.
17. *The World We Imagine,* pp. 13-14.

Horse Winner," and "Tickets, Please" – in which a womanizing tram inspector is trapped in the depot by female tram conductors he has flirted with and is attacked by them, like the god Dionysius in the ritual mutilation – illustrate the method Lawrence carried into the novels with varying success. The ending of *Sons and Lovers* expresses unnameable gratification and also bewildered feelings and intentions – an inconsistency achieved through the focus on potential feeling, on something to follow in the life of the hero, suggested in Paul's turning his steps "towards the faintly humming, flowing town," but still indefinite and without resolution.

It is the present moment of feeling that matters, not the future. As in Lovelace's dying wish to be joined with Clarissa, Lawrence through the symbolic interplay of light and darkness points to bewilderment that will remain a continuing state of mind. Even as feeling and insight develop in a character like Paul, into whom the reader is given intensive views, they do not change character. Lovelace remains the character he was at the beginning of *Clarissa*, regardless of what possibilities for change are suggested in his final statements.

3

What matters in the psychological novel is the continual discovery of feeling, not necessarily the hero's discovery of motives or his "real" character. Conrad's Jim, in choosing to meet his death at the hands of Doramin, seeks to prove what he wishes his real character to be. As he tells Jewel, who wants him to run from the village and not sacrifice his life for an unattainable ideal, "should not be worth having" had he done so. Conrad ends *Lord Jim* without telling us whether Jim is flawed in character; he dies, Marlow reports, with "a proud and unflinching glance," yet "he passes away under a cloud, inscrutable at heart, forgotten, unforgiven, and excessively romantic."[18] Jim is complex, as Lovelace is, in his awareness of what he may be, in awareness of his potential character.

Conrad's psychological realism, which conceals the core of character, owes much to Henry James, who shows characters probing for unrealized potentialities for feeling and action. Numerous stories and novels provide examples. In the famous opening scene of *The Wings*

18. *Lord Jim,* ed. Thomas Moser (New York: Norton, 1968), pp. 251-53.

of the Dove, Kate Croy moves restlessly about the sitting room in her sister's house, waiting for her father, and aware of confinement and poverty – a world she can escape from only at the price of personal freedom. The motive of her feeling is not so important as her sounding in these moments to a "deeper depth" feelings she is trying to fix but cannot: "She tried to be sad, so as not to be angry; but it made her angry that she couldn't be sad. And yet where was misery, misery too beaten for blame and chalk-marked by fate like a 'lot' at a common auction, if not in these merciless signs of mere mean, stale feelings? " (Book 1, Chapter 1). What matters to James in this scene is potential, not actual, feeling – the something to be discovered that marks the adventures of James's characters from Isabel Archer to Strether and Milly Theale, who becomes Kate's rival in love. The greatest adventure is to be found in the potential for feeling created by the discovery that one is dying: much in *The Wings of the Dove* turns on Milly watching herself make this discovery, as Kate watches herself in the opening scene. So important is this kind of action that important events in the plot are not shown or are undisclosed, like Milly's last letter to Densher which Kate destroys. The novel ends as it begins, with concern for what might be felt by Kate and Densher, now doomed lovers, not for what is: "It had come to the point, really, that they showed each other pale faces, and that all the unspoken between them looked out of their eyes in a dim terror of their further conflict" (Book 10, Chapter,8). A few moments later the two discover further nuances of feeling that they spend the remainder of the scene trying to define. In the final pages, it is not what Kate does or will do that holds Densher's attention but the power of feeling she displays: "Strange it was for him then that she stood in his own rooms doing it, while, with an intensity now beyond any that had ever made his breath come slow to him, he waited for her act."

The psychological interest of scenes like this in James is not in Kate's motive – which can be named, and is known early in the novel – but in hidden powers of feeling, in which character inheres for James. It is the half-conscious moment and developing perception that interests him, as in Strether's gradual discovery of his baffled feelings about Chad and Mme. de Vionnet, in *The Ambassadors,* and Maggie Verver's watchfulness as she slowly realizes that her husband is acting upon feelings unknown to her. What the Prince is "doing" the reader already knows: and it has little importance to the novel itself. The same is true of the contents of Milly's letter to Densher.

The pictorial method that permits James to keep actual feeling concealed, and the descent of the curtain at the point of revelation – these direct attention from plot to action. "The sense of a single character" was the beginning of the novel for him, James states in the Preface to *The Portrait of a Lady,* – not "any conceit of a 'plot,' nefarious name, in any flash, upon the fancy, of a set of relations, or in any one of those situations that, by a logic of their own, immediately fall, for the fabulist, into movement, into a march or a rush, a pattern of quick steps . . . ."[19] Later in the same preface, James refers to "the high price of the novel as a literary form – its power not only, while preserving that form with closeness, to range through all the differences of the individual relation to its general subject-matter, all the varieties of outlook on life, of disposition to reflect and project, created by conditions that are never the same from man to man . . . but positively to appear more true to its character in proportion as it strains, or tends to burst, with a latent extravagance, its mould."[20]

The process of discovery in the psychological novel is thus endless: relations must remain unfinished. The complex technique of psychological novels like *Lord Jim,* with its multitude of reflector characters, or Ford Madox Ford's *The Good Soldier,* in which madness and suicide keep motive and feeling mysterious, is a response to this need of straining to discover "all the varieties of outlook on life." Ford, in a memoir of Conrad and James, describes the new form of the novel in precisely this way. The Impressionists – Flaubert, Maupassant, Turgenev – insisted that "once the suggestion was taken hold of, it should be turned over and over in the mind until the last drop of suggestion that could come from the original idea was squeezed out of it." They aimed for "progressions of effects." Conrad and James, following their lead, saw that ". . . a Novel was the rendering of an Affair: of one embroilment, one set of embarrassments, one human coil, one psychological progression. From this the Novel gets its Unity. No doubt it might have its caesura – or even several; but these must be brought about by temper-

19. Henry James, *The Art of the Novel,* ed. R. P. Blackmur (New York: Scribner's, 1950), p. 42.
20. Ibid., pp. 45-46.

amental pauses, markings of time when the treatment called for them. But the whole novel was to be an exhaustion of aspects, was to proceed to one culmination, to reveal once and for all, in the last sentence, or the penultimate; in the last phrase, or the one before it – the psychological significance of the whole."[21] The reader, this statement implies, is made aware of both the significance of feeling and how feeling is perceived from outside and from within. Praising Conrad's achievement in *Chance,* a novel as complex in its narrative as *Lord Jim,* James refer to the "fusion between what we are to know and that prodigy of our knowing which is ever half the very beauty of the atmosphere of authenticity."[22]

Kinkead-Weekes, who argues that Richardson's art "so radically depended on being taken over by his imaginative projection," draws this conclusion: "Yet his final affinity is rather with the Jamesian concept of the artist [than that of Conrad, Faulkner and Kafka, who forsake a final encompassing point of view], precisely because of his struggle to contain all the different ways of looking within an inclusive and definitive vision, allowing for all, but not reducible to any, or to relativity. He offers, as James does, the final illusion that 'the author' at his most imaginative, and 'the ideal reader' at his most perceptive, will meet at their fullest extension beyond the relativities, absolutely, and objectively."[23] The view developed in this study departs from this statement only in holding the psychological novel to be unfinished in its exploration of character. More than this, character is perceived at the deeper levels of fantasy – which can never be finished. This openness of the psychological novel may serve as one final defense for writer and reader, keeping identifications from becoming total. The experience of the psychological novel includes the awareness of artistry (a legacy of the eighteenth century): of how the story is being told and discoveries made, of how feeling is perceived and sometimes acted upon.

4

A work of Lawrence close to Richardson in form and characterization, and illustrating these general features of psychological fiction, is the novella *The Fox.* More so than in Richardson, the

21. *Thus to Revisit* (New York: Dutton, 1921), pp. 42, 44.
22. *Notes on Novelists* (London: Dent, 1914), p. 275.
23. *Samuel Richardson: Dramatic Novelist,* pp. 454-55.

characters are continuously perceived at two levels, the deeper sadistic fantasy providing our understanding of characters whose surface character is merely sketched, not analyzed from scene to scene as in *Sons and Lovers.*

In the story two friends, Nellie March and Jill Banford, are trying to run a farm in England during the World War. Trained in carpentry and similar skills, March becomes "the man about the place" and takes care of the unrobust Banford, who is little able to cope with her new life. Banford is, however, open and generous, showing none of March's complex and unnamed feelings – "so odd and absent in herself. . . ."[24] Contrary to the usual interpretation of their relationship, Lawrence does not state or suggest that it is overtly lesbian.

Some three years pass, and one day a young soldier, Henry Grenfel, comes to the farm looking for his grandfather, who had once lived on it; Banford invites him to stay with them instead of in the village. Almost at once March identifies Henry with a marauding fox that she has been hunting – to protect the farm fowl. There is, indeed, a physical resemblance, for his face is reddish and his blue eyes are "very bright and sharp." His "fine, fair hairs, like a down" give him "a slightly glistening look" (p. 228). Receiving his "long, steady, penetrating looks" as she watches him silently, March seems from the beginning marked as his prey. But through the awakening feelings of the three characters Lawrence raises an implicit question: Who is the predator, and who is the victim? Which of the three is the most cunning?

As in Richardson, initial statements and impressions are not a reliable indication of potentialities of character and action. Lawrence shows that March, like Clarissa, seems passive and withdrawn because her feelings become ambivalent toward a man she imagines is predatory before she has reason to know that he is. She is also much less conscious of her feelings than Banford and Henry are of theirs. Banford's need to hold March is not at first apparent to either woman; Banford is aroused to jealousy only by the surprising discovery that she may lose March to Henry in marriage. As her possessiveness intensifies, March grows even more ambivalent – a change Lawrence

24. *The Portable D. H. Lawrence,* ed. Diana Trilling (New York: Viking, 1947), pp. 221-22. Subsequent references in the text are to this edition.

suggests in her habit of vacant watching and musing, in her rapt mood screwing up her mouth into a sardonic look, or taking on a pinched look as though something has hurt her.

It is a crucial irony of the story that March feels herself possessed by the fox before Henry's arrival. Seeing the fox looking up at her, or glancing at her as he moves away, "half-inviting, half contemptuous and cunning," she does not know what it is she seeks in the woods. In this dreamlike experience, erotic feeling awakens. Seeing his "brush held smooth like a feather" and "his white buttocks twinkle," she walks through the woods, her cheeks faintly flushed, trying to find him. After Henry's arrival at the farm, her musings become increasingly erotic: "In a sort of semi-dream she seemed to be hearing the fox singing round the house in the wind, singing wildly and sweetly and like a madness" (p. 249). Watching Henry on the first night from "the shadow of the corner," she feels "she need not any more be divided in herself, trying to keep up two planes of consciousness. She could at last lapse into the odour of the fox" (p. 234). That night she dreams about the fox; "She stretched out her hand, but suddenly he bit her wrist, and at the same instant, as she drew back, the fox, turning round to bound away, whisked his brush across her face, and it seemed his brush was on fire, for it seared and burned her mouth with a great pain" (p. 236).

Henry does possess qualities of the fox. When Banford invites him to stay at the farm rather than in the village, "A smile like a cunning little flame came over his face, suddenly and involuntarily. He dropped his head quickly to hide it and remained with his head dropped, his face hidden" (p. 239). Under the spell of erotic feeling himself, he grows conscious of his role as huntsman, in this quality bearing striking resemblance to Lovelace. Ironically, he thinks of himself as a fatalist, and ingenuously tells March how fate guides the hunter as he stalks his prey. He is thus at first, like Lovelace, less cunning than he at first seems. With remarkable subtlety Lawrence reveals how Henry gradually assumes qualities in the fox that already have captured March's attention. His stealth and teasing intensify and become sinister as he catches the scent of his new rival – Banford. His qualities are ironic because he is also shown to be ingenuous. Though he sees himself as huntsman and not farmer, like Lovelace he exerts less control over events and is more directed by March's will than he is able to realize. The resemblance between Richardson and Lawrence is greatest in the tension between unconscious wishes and conscious attitudes and defenses – a much different tension from James.

Lawrence calls attention more than once to the conflict in March between her unconscious wishes and conscious fears – precisely what we see in Clarissa – as she grows increasingly aware of Banford's awakened possessiveness and hated of Henry. When Henry urges her to marry him, she reacts in a half-conscious way, then hysterically, as if she had been killed. Though her fears and bafflement deepen as Banford increasingly takes on the look of a hunted bird, she continues to look sardonic and shrewish, and vague and startled, and she secretly takes enjoyment in the heated atmosphere generated by building antagonism. Like Richardson, Lawrence makes dream the vehicle of ultimate psychological revelation. When Henry finally shoots the fox, March in a second dream puts Banford in her coffin and comforts her with the fox-skin – the symbol of her destroyer. We see her ambivalence when she awakens from the dream in tears. The next day, when she touches the belly of the dead animal and gets blood on her hand, she too takes on its destructive spirit – though she will continue to exhibit the same combination of shy ingenuousness and shrewishness that fascinates Henry. He does not realize how much she, too, has become the fox, as in a rage he watches her stride down a slope after Banford, and then run: "See her leap a ditch, and run, as if a house was on fire, just to get to that creeping dark little object down there! " (p. 271)

The final represented action completes the exploration of unconscious wishes. After Henry leaves for army camp without having married March, she writes him an ingenuous yet cunning letter that drives him to act against Banford: "We have a life together. And even if it can't last for ever, it is a life while it does last. And it might last as long as either of us lives. Who knows how long we've got to live? She is a delicate little thing, perhaps nobody but me knows how delicate. And as for me, I feel I might fall down the well any day" (p. 287) He returns to the farm, to find the two women trying to cut down a dead tree, Banford's father watching them. When Henry asks to finish the job, March hands him the axe, unconscious of her wish to destroy Banford – as her wild shriek at the sight of Banford lying on the ground, having been struck by the falling tree, shows. Henry's wish is conscious: "And his heart held perfectly still, in the terrible pure will that she should not move" (p. 297).

We need not look for greater consistency of character in March than we found in Harriet when she revealed unexpected hostility toward Grandison. March's ambivalent feeling for Banford is consistent, however, in the whole story. Her seeming passivity is not the whole truth about her nature. Like the fox she is a creature of instinct; she may be determined to find the fox, but she does not understand why she wants to. She is drawn to Banford, wishing to protect her, at the same time as she desires to escape from a safe but unproductive existence which increasingly frustrates her – indeed from any entrapment that threatens her freedom. In these ways, she is more like the fox than Henry, who though cunning and resourceful is at least conscious of the role he desires to play. The parallel between these lovers and Clarissa and Lovelace is striking: Clarissa's strength like March's is hidden and aggressive. Like Lovelace, Henry is ultimately ineffectual in dealing with ambivalent feeling.

The dead fox becomes symbolic of the prey they both seek. Banford, whose warmth and generosity are stressed at the beginning of the story, at the discovery that she will lose March takes on the qualities of a hunted animal. Fox-like, she watches the lovers furtively. In death, her neck and head lying in a pool of blood, she resembles an animal – "a little twitching heap" (p. 297). As in Richardson, the failure to achieve sexual dominance ends in a sadism turned upon the self and thus in a wasting of the spirit or else symbolic self-mutilation.

In the final pages Lawrence shows this defeat of Eros in Henry. How little he has controlled the events of the novel is evident in the way March draws him back to the farm and makes him the instrument of her will. He is to learn after Banford's death that if he has "won" March he has not "got" her. Both have been wasted by the passion of the hunt; Henry is less attractive to her because he no longer seems dangerous. Her twisted smile gone, her new smile is that of a woman whose old way of love has died. March tells herself that she cannot accept "submergence," and rationalizes that she must become passive and not exert herself in the effort to love: "She had to be like the seaweed she saw as she peered down from the boat, swaying for ever delicately under water, with all their delicate fibrils put tenderly out upon the flood, sensitive, utterly sensitive and receptive within the shadowy sea, and never, never rising and looking forth above water while they lived. . . . Beneath the wave they might have powerful roots, stronger than iron, they might be tenacious and dangerous in their soft waving within the flood. Beneath the water they might be stronger, more indestructible, than resistant oak trees are on land" (pp. 300-01).

As in Richardson, there is no joy except where there is struggle for dominance. Submerged, she may become tenacious and dangerous like the roots beneath the waves. Yet immediately afterwards she thinks of the "awful mistake of happiness": happiness is a "fatal flower," its calyx a "horrible gulf," "the bottomless pit." Erotic feeling is the fatality, once aroused. It is this view we find expressed in different ways in Richardson.

Like the characters of Richardson, March, Banford and Henry are revealed in their discovery of Eros; their confusion and ambivalent emotions are conveyed through the complex, multifaceted symbol of the fox, representing their furtive yet powerful desires. Innocence, cunning, power, beauty, pain directed into sheer destructiveness – these qualities are most completely realized in March, and with somewhat less intensity in Henry. Richardson develops the same complex view of life. Where the passions are allowed free play, outside of marriage or within, the result must be disaster. Friendship in marriage is best.

The Fox ends with Henry's bitterness that he will never possess March, who is "dying with the strain of her own wakefulness" (p. 304). One of his final thoughts is that he should have left the two women to kill one another. And that has been the point of the story from the beginning. Beautiful Eros – diverted by tension and ambiguity into sadism and destruction, innocent yet as cunning as the fox – cannot in these circumstances produce normal, lasting happiness. When obstacles to love are created through ambivalence and fear, a natural course for Richardson but not necessarily for Lawrence, the experience of love becomes meaningless when obstacles cease to exist. Like Lovelace, the predator is his own victim, once his passion is spent. Richardson, however, shows erotic feeling to be unwaning, and diverted into dying when no other avenue of expression is open to it.

5

In Richardson and Lawrence character exists at two levels – the social self and the unconscious self. Though Richardson gives more attention to the first, and indeed creates a more consistent semblance of personality, character as in Lawrence is invested in eroticized motives that momentarily break into consciousness and are realized in action. Lawrence's characters are portrayed almost always as they see themselves; so are Richardson's. Since erotic states are discrete, absolute moments of being, the narrative comprises an action that circles back upon itself, as Paul's involvement with Miriam must return to earlier conflicts since with Miriam he is playing out the unceasing Oedipal drama. In Lawrence, there is no advance to real self-understanding and change in character. Dream and daytime fantasy are the reality: this is why Lawrence's characters so often seem to stand apart from the world with which Lawrence identifies them in the beginning. The shift gradually from realistic settings such as we find in *Sons and Lovers* to symbolic settings and landscapes, even in *Lady Chatterley*, shows Lawrence's awareness of how little his characters are to be understood through their social origins and present world. The relation of character to social circumstance is almost always problematic: Mrs. Morel, Gerald Crich, Gudrun in *Women in Love,* and numerous other characters act from motives that cannot be accounted to social tensions and circumstances rendered with so much care. Lawrence's analysis of Hardy's characters applies, with slight qualification to his own: "Nowhere, except perhaps in Jude, is there the slightest development of personal action in the characters: it is all explosive. Jude, however, does see more or less what he is doing, and acts from choice. He is more consecutive. The rest explode out of the convention."[25]

Richardson, by contrast, begins with social character and social arrangements. But the setting of character soon becomes the backdrop of intense drama, as his women are removed from the protection of family into an environment in which sadistic desires and masochistic responses can be given full play. In the first three novels, the family group is restored only partially in the surface plot: Pamela's marriage is shown to involve the gradually forming family circle (including visitors like Miss Darnford); Clarissa dies with surrogate brothers and parents in attendance (Belford, Morden, Mrs. Lovick among them). The enlarging family circle is central to the underlying fantasy of *Grandison.* One important difference between Richardson and Lawrence is that Richardson's worlds of reality and fantasy are

25. *Phoenix,* p. 410.

never so divergent that the characters are removed from their initial setting; they do not really become allegorical figures, divorced from specific situations in which a wide range of feelings have been given free play. But even when Lawrence's characters move into an almost wholly symbolic world, as in *Women in Love,* they are guided by the same inner fatality as we find in Richardson. Nevertheless, the representation of erotic feeling, in both, is so intense that characters do act autonomously. Clarissa wills her death, as March wills the death of Banford. Lawrence's suggestion of a demonic force acting from without has little play beside the powerful psychological forces he shows at work.

Richardson disguises the powerful wishes of his heroine by moralizing her character, that is, making her the embodiment of piety, cleanliness, and Christian fortitude. Faults of character are cancelled in the final pages. In general, this kind of sentimentality is, psychologically, regressive, that is, Richardson retreats into the infantile fantasies associated with moral masochism. Lawrence's fantasy is, by contrast, sadistic – as March's final reflection shows. And so is Henry's, wishing at the end that he had left the two women to kill each other.

One result of these regressive fantasies is the bafflement of sexual feeling. Richardson and Lawrence follow the same course, the sacrifice of masculine striving through death or its substitute. Men assertive in love – Paul Morel in the scenes with Miriam and Clara Dawes, Gerald Crich, Henry Grenfel, to name only a few – are defeated or dying men after battling for power. These characters, and Richardson's B. and Lovelace, show evidence of obsessional neurosis as Freud describes it in *Inhibitions, Symptoms and Anxiety.*

At the beginning of the latency period, during which the Oedipus complex is weakened or dissolved and the ego and superego are strengthened and mature, castration anxiety plays an important role. "In obsessional neuroses these processes are carried further than is normal. In addition to the destruction of the Oedipus complex a regressive degradation of the libido takes place, the superego becomes exceptionally severe and unkind, and the ego, in obedience to the superego, produces strong reaction-formations in the shape of conscientiousness, pity and cleanliness." Infantile masturbation attaches itself to anal-sadistic, that is, regressive ideas as a way of escaping the condemnation of the superego. "There is an inherent contradiction about this state of affairs, in which, precisely in the interest of masculinity (that is to say, from fear of castration), every activity belonging to masculinity is stopped" (S.E., XX, 114-14).

This account is a perfect description of Lovelace: turning to repetitive and anal-sadistic behavior as a response to threats from authority and parental figures, of whom Clarissa becomes one. The long and exceedingly complex preparations for the rape, and the rapid descent into death, suggest motifs of the castration complex as Freud analyzes them. In Lovelace and his counterparts in *Grandison,* in Paul Morel and Henry Grenfel, the dream of love is pursued at the price of their erotic lives. Indeed the sentimental experience is ultimately the sacrifice and moralization of erotic experience as represented in fictional guise. Possibly the imaginative enactment of this sacrifice – often the most completely imagined scenes in sentimental fiction of many types – is necessary to preserve sexual potency – that is, to relieve castration anxiety. The sentimental solution, in psychoanalytic language, is a kind of reaction-formation originating in psychic masochism.

6

A final word may now be said about the problem for criticism discussed toward the beginning of this study. W. K. Wimsatt, in his definition of the "concrete universal," the highly complex work of art, states a premise of the New Criticism and incidentally of much twentieth century criticism of Richardson: "the rhetorical structure of the concrete universal, the complexity and unity of the poem, is also its maturity or sophistication or richness or depth, and hence its value. Complexity of form is sophistication of content."[26] "Sophistication of content" is a way of saying that the literary work is "true" in the sense that it presents "what is" or "what should be" according to a norm of civility and well established public truths. Yet the truths held by critics of any persuasion are often hard to piece out; few critics today refer to truths that have not been transformed by irony or point of view. Social and moral values, historically centered, provide a convenient test instead, and this is particularly true of criticism that rejects or minimizes the value of psychological interpretations of Richardson. Why the writer and his characters should

26. *The Verbal Icon,* p. 82.

"*respond* to a totality of inner and outer conditions" – to quote Frederick Crews – is not of concern.[27]

If Richardson's novels are thought to be successful because they do not lack in social and moral sophistication, it is obvious why psychological interests are minimized or interpreted in historical terms. I have tried to show chiefly through an analysis of defensive strategies and underlying trends of character that the ideal reader and the rhetoric postulated by many critics is neither Richardson's nor Lawrence's. Though they introduce characters who challenge the explicit moral and social norms of the work, their rhetoric is employed to express concealed meanings and disguise alterations and inconsistencies in characterization in such a way that character is increasingly revealed in symbolic action.

To argue that norms of character are inconsistent is, in fact, to assume that consistent characterization is a necessary condition of a sustained, though perhaps not integrated, literary experience. Richardson's novels show that character need not satisfy either requirements to be powerful in effect, granting that the writer who fantasizes as Richardson did may achieve a much different effect from what he intends – in dislocations of character arising in the course of the novel. Freud's statement in "Some Character Types Met With in Psychoanalytic Work" is worth quoting again. In cases where double or multiple motives are suggested for a character, "a deeper motive comes into view behind the more superficial one. Laws of poetic economy necessitate this way of presenting the situation, for this deeper motive could not be explicitly enunciated. It had to remain concealed, kept from the easy perception of the spectator or the reader; otherwise serious resistances, based on the most distressing emotions, would have arisen, which might have imperilled the effect of the drama." The impossibility of grounding effect in a well established *ethos,* in the modern psychological novel at least, is suggested by Lawrence in his study of Thomas Hardy: "The vast, unexplored morality of life itself, what we call the immorality of nature, surrounds us in its eternal incomprehensibility, and in its midst goes on the little human morality drama, with its queer frame of morality and its mechanized movement; seriously, portentously, till some one of the protagonists chances to look out of the charmed

27. *Psychoanalysis and Literary Process,* p. 27.

circle, weary of the stage, to look into the wilderness raging round."[28]

In brief, the rhetoric of Richardson and Lawrence makes certain questions about the roots of character and the displacements that occur impossible to ask. Through such a rhetoric each was able in his own way to explore areas of human experience and entertain solutions in fantasy that could not be assented to, undisguised. The result is occasionally a confusion of ethical norms – but not a confusion that harms the work if the characters are understood symbolically. In the words of F. C. Prescott, "In poetry, as in dreams, the most confused portions doubtless often have the greatest emotional intensity."[29] Rhetoric may achieve its goal by concealing the limits of judgment, not by defining them. This is the condition of experiencing many works great in their own way and of their own kind.

28. *Phoenix*, p. 419.
29. *The Poetic Mind* (Ithaca: Cornell University Press, 1922), p. 186

Appendix

FREUD'S THEORY OF MASOCHISM

1

Though Freud states in his 1928 essay "Dostoevsky and Parricide" that a person may be a complete masochist without being neurotic, he was concerned with the neurotic type in his writings. One reason is that his theory of masochism developed as part of the theory of sadism and later played a crucial role in the reformulation of the theory of instincts in the 1920's.

In the *Three Contributions to the Theory of Sexuality,* published in 1905, sadism is described as an "aggressive component" of the sexual instinct – needed in courtship to overcome the sexual object – which becomes independent of the sexual instinct and displaces it. By contrast, ordinary masochism compromises those passive traits encountered in sexual life; in its perverse form, it is further removed from normal sexual activity in being a transformation of sadism and often "an extension of sadism turned round upon the subject's own self" which substitutes for the sexual object (S.E., VII, 158). An important feature of Freud's theory is that active and passive aspects are usually found in the same person: sadism and masochism occur together, though one may be more highly developed than the other. The sadist takes pleasure in inflicting pain in sexual relationships – and also in receiving pain. In singling out sadism and masochism as perversions, Freud does not distinguish the abnormal from the normal man: one of his essential ideas is that normal sexual activity contains perverse elements. The perversions are universal rather than exception (VII, 159-60).

The chief alteration in Freud's theory came about through his puzzlement over the phenomenon of repetition-compulsion which he came upon in patients who were re-experiencing trauma in their dreams. In his early theory of mental life, Freud postulated that mental processes seek to lessen and stabilize tensions; consistent with the operation of this "pleasure principle," dreams (even punishment dreams) are essentially wish-fulfilling (IV, 122-33; V, 550-72). But the compulsion to repeat the painful experience exhibits exactly the opposite phenomenon, the maintenance and increase of tension. This discovery contradicted the purpose of dreams, and Freud wondered what impulse could be gratified by the repetition of traumatic experiences (XXII, 28). His solution was to go "beyond the pleasure principle" and revise the earlier libido theory by suggesting a duality in instinctual life. The new theory of masochism emerged as evidence of such a duality.

In the *Three Contributions,* Freud expressed doubt that a primal or original masochism existed. The dual instinct theory – developed in *Beyond the Pleasure Principle* (1920) and *The Ego and the Id* (1923) – changed this view. Freud now proposed the sexual and the death instincts, Eros and Destructiveness (Thanatos), which intermingle and fuse in the course of normal development, to the extent that neither is observable by itself. Because of this fusion, the two instincts remain heuristic ideas in analysis. One of the three kinds of masochism Freud now distinguished – in the 1924 essay "The Economic Problem of Masochism" – provided the decisive evidence for the fusion of the two instincts. This was moral masochism, to which we will return shortly. Freud's general view is that, when the instincts are suppressed in the interests of civilization, sadism turns upon the self. This "turning back" of the death instinct is experienced in the ego as a heightened or secondary masochism, for Freud had also postulated a primary or erotogenic masochism. In *Civilization and its Discontents* (1930), Freud defines masochism as "a union between destructiveness directed inwards and sexuality – a union which makes what is otherwise an imperceptible trend into a conspicuous and tangible one" (XXI, 119). This is the formulation Freud held to and applied in his thinking about masochism.

2

The change in Freud's conception of libido occurred partly through his earlier reformulation of narcissism. Primary narcissism – infantile sexual libido taking itself for object – hae been one of the postulates in *Three Contributions.* In *The Ego and the Id* Freud develops the controversial theory that superseded the original conscious-preconscious-unconscious classification of mental processes: ego is defined as a "precipitate of abandoned object-cathexes" (XIX, 29), that is, of attachments of psychic energy to external objects that offer libidinal gratification. The new theory involves a series of complex exchanges. The ego identifies with the external object to satisfy the demands of the id, which refuses to surrender the external love object, and simultaneously the demands of the external world that the object be surrendered. The result is that object-libido stored by the id flows into the ego (ego-libido), this energy undergoing desexualization or sublimation. The erotic instincts, Freud suggests, are more "plastic" and displaceable than the destructive instincts; furthermore, the displaceable libido is in the employ of the pleasure principle, following whatever path of discharge possible. In these processes, the ego works against Eros and puts itself in the service of opposing impulses (XIX, 46).

The investment of ego-libido – termed "secondary narcissism" – is basic to the formation of superego, the introjection of parental imagos in the id following the dissolution of the Oedipus complex. Freud states in "The Economic Problem of Masochism" that the superego represents the id and the external world simultaneously since it originates in the introjection of parental imagos to which libido had first been attached (XIX, 167).

The relation of superego to sadism and masochism, and ultimately to the idea of Fate is explored in this essay. Freud begins with a review of the formulation of the death instinct in *Beyond the Pleasure Principle.* The "tendency to stability" or, to give this tendency another name, "the Nirvana principle," turns out not to be identical with the pleasure principle, as we noted. To repeat his reasoning, the identification cannot be made because pleasure arises not merely from the lowering of tension, as the Nirvana principle demands, but from its increase, as in the repetition-compulsion of punishment dreams and in sexual pleasure. It follows that the Nirvana principle must have been transformed by the sexual instinct itself into the pleasure principle as the outlet of sexual libido. (Though the term *libido* is commonly used in the sense of sexual libido, the aggressive instincts are also libidinal, thus the idea of aggressive libido. The fusion of sexual and aggressive libido makes them ultimately indistinguishable, Freud states in *Civilization and Its Discontents.*) The death instinct is manifest in the aggressive impulses which, in normal development, are neutralized as threats to the individual through their diversion to the outer world by means of the muscular and skeletal system. A part of the death instinct directly serves the sexual function as a "true sadism."

That part of the death instinct excluded from this displacement is "bound" libidinally in the organism through attendant sexual excitement, taking the subject for object. This residue – which Freud terms "erotogenic masochism" – may be reinforced by sadism failing to serve the sexual instinct (as a means of overpowering the love object, as noted earlier) and as a result defuses from it. In these circumstances there takes place regression to the sadistic-anal phase of psychological development (in which sadism originates), this introjected sadism constituting a secondary masochism. Instinctual defusion is consequently the source of the strengthened superego. After sublimation. Freud states in *The Ego and the Id,* sublimation arising from identification with the father imago in the dissolution of the Oedipus complex, Eros no longer can keep bound the destructiveness joined with it: "This defusion would be the source of the general character of harshness and cruelty exhibited by the ideal – its dictatorial 'Thou shalt.' " (XIX, 54-55).

Erotogenic masochism, which underlies feminine and moral masochism, passes through the developmental phases of the sexual libido. The result is the generation of fantasies associated with feminine masochism in men: beating at the hands of the father (derived from the anal-sadistic phase); castration (a precipitate of the phallic stage, the period of the Oedipus complex); coitus and childbirth (derived from the post-Oedipal stage). Depending on the development stage at which fixation occurs, the feminine masochist may be impotent, his fantasies ending in onanistic gratification, or constituting the sexual gratification, or, as Freud indicates in the essay " 'A Child Is Being Beaten' " (1919), he may succeed in uniting masochism with normal sexual functions (XVII, 196-97). The punishing figures in the conscious fantasy of the feminine masochist are invariably women.

The masochistic beating fantasy, he explains in the same essay, is preceded by an unconscious one, originating in the phallic stage, in which the boy is beaten by the father. Eventually the normal "incestuous" fixation to the father underlying the fantasy is repressed, and the mother is substituted in the subsequent conscious fantasy. The beating endured thus expresses the disguised wish to undergo what are presumed to be the typical sexual experiences of women. Freud concludes that the boy escapes homosexuality by repressing and reshaping his unconscious fantasy; he adds that in successive stages later conscious fantasies express a feminine attitude without "a homosexual object-choice" (XVII, 199).[1]

The situation of the girl is more complex, Freud continues in " 'A Child Is Being Beaten.' " Her unconscious Oedipal fantasy begins with the familiar positive Oedipal fixation; in her transition to the conscious fantasy, however, she imagines the father as the person performing the beating. The originally masochistic situation is transformed ultimately into a sadistic fantasy through repression, the sexual quality erased without the assumption of the active masculine role; the girl becomes a man in fantasy – and merely the spectator of the activity which replaces the sexual act. By contrast, the boy, "who has tried to escape from a homosexual object-choice, and who has not changed his sex, nevertheless feels like a woman in his conscious phantasies, and endows the women who are beating him with masculine attributes and characteristics" (XVII, 200).

To return to Freud's account in "The Economic Problem of Masochism," a sense of guilt originating in Oedipal wishes is characteristic of feminine and moral masochism. The essential difference is that, in moral masochism, suffering is endured for its own sake rather than because it is administered by the loved one; indeed, it may be administered by impersonal forces or Fate. The moral masochist also differs from the ultra-moralist, in whom the intense sadism of the superego is pronounced. In the moral masochist, the masochism in the ego is pronounced – seeking punishment from the superego or from external parental figures. Another difference is that the sadism of the superego is experienced consciously, accounting for the ultra-moralistic attitude, whereas the masochism in the ego is not. The unconscious factor in moral masochism explains certain puzzling features: namely, that the ethical sense may be strong or may disappear, and that the masochist also may be tempted to per-

1. Seeking to explain this apparent contradiction, Bergler speculates that the child undergoes a sadistic phase arising from loss of the pre-genital Oedipal mother's breasts; resulting guilt causes him to turn this aggression upon himself and substitute his buttocks for the mother's breasts in the unconscious fantasy. Bergler suggests that the father is only partially eliminated in the conscious fantasy because "the father was a palliative for the all too sadistically conceived phallic mother." Edmund Bergler, "Phases of the Masculine Beating Fantasy," *Psychoanalytic Quarterly*, 7 (1938), 532.

form acts demanding punishment by the sadistic conscience or Fate. The sense of fatality – the sense that one is fated for bad luck – stands behind the wish of the masochist to destroy his chances of success in the world, and also to destroy his very existence. Fenichel's interpretation of this phenomenon is worth quoting: "In defending itself against the demands of the sadistic superego, the ego may use a countersadistic rebellion as well as submission (ingratiation), or both attitudes simultaneously or successively. Sometimes the ego seems willing to take upon itself punishments, acts of expiation, or even torture to an astonishing degree. This 'moral masochism' appears to be a complement to the 'sadism of the superego,' and this submission may be performed in the hope of using it as a license for later instinctual freedom."[2]

Still, the enormous power of moral masochism seems inexplicable in the absence of a strong libidinal component. It is precisely such a component that Freud now introduces. The "unconscious feeling of guilt," originating in the need for punishment from the parent figure, is a "regressive distortion" of the wish for sexual relations with him: "If we insert this explanation into the content of moral masochism, its hidden meaning becomes clear to us. Conscience and morality have arisen through the overcoming, the desexualization, of the Oedipus complex; but through moral masochism morality becomes sexualized once more, the Oedipus complex is revived and the way is opened for a regression from morality to the Oedipus complex" (XIX, 169). The loosening of moral masochism from sexuality is thus only apparent; the trends of feminine and moral masochism, complex as they seem to be, are related to Oedipal wishes incompletely sublimated in the genital stage.

We noted that the feminine masochistic attitude may result in impotence, according to Fenichel based on a continuing, unconscious fixation on the mother.[3] It may be total, perhaps as a result of "feminine identification," or partial, as a result of the phenomenon analyzed by Freud in the essay of 1912, "On the Universal Tendency to Debasement in the Sphere of Love." In one type of erotic experience tenderness in early childhood is directed toward family members who provide care. These erotic feelings are strengthened at puberty, but owing to the incest prohibition the child finds substi-

2. *Psychoanalytic Theory of Neurosis,* pp. 292-93.
3. Ibid., p. 170.

tute love objects that conform to the imagos of the forbidden parents; these new objects are invested with sensuality and tenderness simultaneously. This is the meaning of Freud's famous statement that in normal love tender and sensual feelings unite (XI, 180).

This achievement is prevented if the new object choice is frustrated or the infantile ties to the parents are too strong to be broken. Having rejected reality, libido is drawn into fantasy, intensifying imagos of the original sexual objects, to which it is fixated. The same substitution prevails even when new objects are substituted for the original ones, under these circumstances. The sensual current is unconsciously attached to incestuous objects, i.e., love objects that do not awaken memory of the incestuous object. Sensuality and tenderness are in this way dissociated: "The whole sphere of love in such people remains divided in the two directions personified in art as sacred and profane (or animal) love. Where they love they do not desire and where they desire they cannot love. They seek objects which they do not need to love, in order to keep their sensuality away from the objects they love . . . . the strange failure shown in psychical impotence makes its appearance whenever an object which has been chosen with the aim of avoiding incest recalls the prohibited object through some feature, often an inconspicuous one" (XI, 182-83).

3

The theory of dual instincts met with little acceptance by psychoanalytic writers close to Freud or by rival schools. In the course of this study we have referred to a number of theorists – among them Theodor Reik, Otto Fenichel, Karen Horney, Victor N. Smirnoff – who take various positions on the theory and the associated theory of masochism. Though many of them develop Freud's ideas in new directions, others have proceeded on different premises, occasionally arriving at similar conclusions. Fenichel, for example, rejects the death instinct yet accepts virtually the whole of Freud's description of masochistic behavior in the later writings.[4] By contrast, Horney

4. Fenichel attacks the inconsistency of the theory, arguing that the "constancy principle" applies equally to all instinctual drives (e.g., hunger). "It seems rather as if aggressiveness were originally no instinctual aim of its own . . . but rather a mode in which instinctual aims sometimes are striven for, in response to frustrations or even spontaneously." Ibid., p. 59.

rejects the libido theory and certain other ideas of Freud; she sees masochism as shaped by sociocultural influences that Freud neglected.[5] Her analysis proceeds from her view of neurosis as an alienation from self and the consequent overdependence on other people in setting goals. Masochism is a weakening as the only defense against the world.[6] In general, opinions on masochism divide according to views on the later theory, though some theorists ignore the death instinct, or, like Melanie Klein and Karl Menninger, use it as a heuristic idea.

To cite one recent writer, Angel Garma suggests that the death instinct helps explain how memories of infantile submissiveness are awakened and strengthen destructive behavior.[7] He also relies on the related idea of primary masochism. Proceeding from Freud's early view that the sadist is simultaneously masochistic and identifies with his victim, Garma argues that primary masochism is a necessary condition of this identification. Sadistic behavior is masochistic in aim because the possibility of erotic gratification is destroyed.[8] Under these circumstances sadism strengthens primary masochism.

One evidence of masochistic behavior is the submission of the ego to the sadistic superego in manic behavior, which shows "elation, hyperactivity, search for objects, flight of thoughts, increased self-esteem, feelings of impotence."[9] The Don Juan figure illustrates these qualities: "While he apparently shows complete freedom from genital prohibitions in his many affairs with women, he really shows his submission to these prohibitions by his inability to obtain any deep pleasure from his conquests. In Don Juan there is not only object hunger but also a flight from objects, similar to the flight of ideas. Don Juan, persecuted by his internalized parents, must always flee from his women in search of another woman. He has a manic

5. Karen Horney, *New Ways in Psychoanalysis* (New York: Norton, 1939), p. 189. In her essay "The Problem of Femine Masochism," she summarizes the phenomena that condition masochism in women, including absence of ways to express sexuality, presumed inferiority, economic dependency, social and cultural restrictions, restriction on the possible number of children, and the surplus of marriageable women. *Psychoanalytic Review,* 22 (1935), 255.

6. *New Ways in Psychoanalysis,* p. 274.

7. "Within the Realm of the Death Instinct," *International Journal of Psycho-analysis,* 52 (1971), 152-53.

8. Ibid., 151.

9. "The Deceiving Superego and the Masochistic Ego in Mania," 63.

need to make more and more conquests, but part of his purpose is that the woman shall suffer for having sought genital fulfillment. He wants to make them realize that it is wrong to try to free themselves from the prohibitions of their superegos and that this will have bad consequences. In this Don Juan is following faithfully the dictates of his superego."[10]

In contrast to Garma, Reik admits the profundity of the death instinct as a philosophic idea but finds it to be neither refuted nor confirmed by psychological investigation; instead he proceeds according to Freud's earlier formulation, namely that masochism is a late-developing transformation of a sadistic trend. In "Instincts and Their Vicissitudes," Freud states that before sadism turns completely into masochism, "The active voice is changed, not into the passive, but into the reflexive, middle voice" (XIV, 128). Possibly drawing on this formulation, Reik suggests that masochism develops in the intermediate or "reflexive" stage of development, during which the active instinctual aim is transformed into a passive one. The ego plays both the active and passive part, the victim participating in the enjoyment of his sadistic partner – forgetting that the aggression is directed against himself, and at the same time returning imaginatively to his childhood when, as a dependent child, he became active and sadistic. True masochism begins following this stage when the ego substitutes for the original love object and the fantasy of violence against the object becomes unconscious; in masochistic fantasies aggression rarely occurs undisguised.[11] Reik summarizes the characteristics of the masochist in these words: "The masochist is a person of strongly sadistic disposition, who has been diverted from its instinctual aim by the vision of punishment. This anxiety prevents his achieving satisfaction, and in his conflict between anxiety and urge for pleasure, he finally decides to get rid of his anxiety by that flight forward. He consequently does not strive for discomfort and punishment as such. He asks for them because they mark the only possible way to untroubled pleasure."[12] This "flight forward," to which we referred in discussing the masochism of B. and Lovelace, has much in common with the impatience and restlessness that Garma stresses in the masochist. Reik interprets this quality more specifically as a defense-

10. Ibid., 75.
11. *Masochism in Modern Man,* pp. 33, 174, 178, 180, 188-89.
12. Ibid., p. 191.

mechanism through which anxiety is overcome by meeting a feared event halfway.[13]

His account of feminine and moral (what he terms "social") masochism mainly supplements Freud's observations. Perhaps the chief addition is his idea that the masochist who plays the feminine role in his fantasies distorts the role enough so that identification with the woman is incomplete, his aim being to demonstrate to his love-object how he wishes her to behave – namely as a passive, suffering person; he does not seek to undergo the experiences of women for their own sake. Indeed, he secretly fears being used as a woman. His wish accords with his infantile idea of how women are ordinarily treated. Thus the feminine masochist plays a masculine and feminine role simultaneously in fantasy, his pleasure intensified by the contrast between consciously realized masculine strength and obvious submissiveness and weakness.[14]

Like Garma, Reik emphasizes the primacy of the sadistic instinctual trend: the sadistic fantasy precedes both feminine (sexual) and social masochism. If the aim of the masochist is sadistic possession, the result is the social form. Social masochism, in fact, is a later formation and can replace the sexual; it is not, however, a secondary formation.[15] As Freud points out in stressing the resexualization of moral masochism, its pleasure is entirely unconscious and is achieved through inherited social fantasies "retransformed into egoistical daydreams of individuals."[16] Like Bergler who stresses the prevalence of psychic masochism, Reik considers social masochism to be a pervasive phenomenon, so pervasive as to be normal in human nature. Perhaps most importantly, he emphasizes that the masochistic attitude is one of unconscious defiance, originating in the repression of hostility toward the love-object. The masochist thus is an unwavering optimist. Reik concludes: "The masochistic characters are weak on the psychic surface only. There is a powerful urge in them to prove that they are right and their enemies wrong.

13. Ibid., p. 122.

14. Ibid., pp. 127. 197-204, 212.

15. "The transition from sexual to social masochism is the result of a process of thoroughly unmixing of instincts. The erotic component is concerned, but the cruel and aggressive one rules the field." Ibid., p. 309.

16. Ibid., p. 314.

They have to prove it and defy their opponents, even if it is the last thing they do on earth. And often it is."[17]

The origin of masochism accounts, then, for what are taken to be the dominant characteristics of the masochist. This feature of the theory is to be found in another important writer, Berliner, who similarly stresses the influence of an early sadistic love object. Basing his argument on the premise that the death instinct is really "the infantile love instinct which makes the ego willing to offer suffering and death as a price for its gratification,"[18] he suggests that the cause of masochism is the need of the person to be loved by those hostile childhood figures who have been introjected and are reprojected later in life.[19] Berliner adds that masochism increases the worthiness of the victim to be loved by these introjected figures.[20]

Bergler and other writers stress pre-genital experiences. Partly agreeing with Nacht, who argues that biological masochism originates in the pre-objectual phase during which the infant cannot distinguish himself from the mother's breast, and with Rado, who argues that masochism originates in the oral stage, Bergler traces masochism to a single neurosis deriving from oral conflict. The single neurosis is for Bergler the only neurosis that exists, moral masochism serving as its single manifestation.[21]

17. Ibid., p. 324.

18. "Libido and Reality in Masochism," 333.

19. Ibid., 332. H. Hartmann, Ernst Kris, Rudolph M. Lowenstein suggest that aggression and sadism are not synonymous, aggression engaging in a wider field of activity and not always libidinal. "Notes on the Theory of Aggression," *Psychoanalytic Study of the Child,* 3-4 (1950), 22. Sylvan Keiser suggests that the death instinct is actually the "all-pervading drive toward unconsciousness that simulates a drive for death," integrated with "the expectation of rebirth, of continuing to live." Basic to the sexual act is the urge for "loss of self." Fearing loss of self, the masochist's castration anxiety increases during intercourse, for he must assure himself that he is losing nothing. He aims, thus, for a pseudo-orgasm, without giving himself completely to his partner. In essence the masochist cannot submit passively to intercourse. *International Journal of Psycho-analysis,* 30 (1949), 167-69.

20. "The Role of Object Relations in Moral Masochism," *Psychoanalytic Quarterly,* 27 (1958), 46.

21. Edmund Bergler, *The Basic Neurosis* (New York: Grune and Stratton, 1949); S. Nacht, "Le masochisme," *Revue française de Psychoanalyse,* 10 (1938); Sandor Rado, "Fear of Castration in Women," *Psychoanalytic Quarterly,* 2 (1933).

A third group of writers analyze masochism in relation to defense mechanisms. Grunberger argues that, since the aim of the masochist is pleasure through introjection of the father's penis sadistically obtained, that is, through castration, masochism is pre-genital; for in the Oedipal stage the killing of the father and not his castration is the central fantasy. Since the wish necessitates defense in face of the father's anger, the masochist demonstrates that he has been castrated by the "bad mother," on to whom he also projects his wish against the father. The woman inflicts punishment in the beating fantasy precisely because she is the castrating figure; and for this reason, too, she exhibits certain masculine attributes insofar as she condenses father and mother into a single figure. In demonstrating that he is a victim, the masochist is addressing mother and father simultaneously: "The provocative attitude is intended to induce ill-treatment by the former, while the demonstration of what is taking place is directed at the latter. In the last resort, it is the frustrating mother who is the source of all the rejections, privations and ill-treatment of which the patient feels himself to be victim, whether the ill-treatment of the patient feels himself to be the victim, whether the ill-treatment is handed out by his love partner or by his employer, by society or by God, by the stars or by the universe as a whole; and all the sufferings which she inflicts on the masochist are displayed for the benefit of the father. The masochist's ever-present interlocutor, whether real or imaginary, is a condensation of the mother and father figures."[22] Moral masochism is the demonstration to the superego that identification with the castrating mother is impossible. The moral masochist continues to defend against anxiety in this way and to sacrifice pleasure, in contrast to the masochist who achieves orgasm by concealing his introjection of the father's penis in masochistic behavior.[23]

In stressing the pre-genital origins, Grunberger arrives at Reik's view that the masochist is unconsciously defiant, though his behavior

22. Bela Grunberger, "Psychodynamic Theory of Masochism," pp. 193-94.

23. Ibid., p. 204. Emphasis on defense-mechanism is found in Charles W. Socarides, who stresses introjection and reaction-formation as a means of balancing libidinal and aggressiveness, and emphasizes the powerlessness and deprivation felt by the masochist owing to his introjection of the sadistic mother's view of him. "The Function of Moral Masochism," *International Journal of Psycho-analysis,* 39 (1958), 587-97.

is apparently docile and submissive. In a recent discussion, Smirnoff confirms this observation but presents another interpretation: "The masochist is not seeking to be killed or destroyed, but to be branded. Not by the absolute power of the other, but by the fictitious power that he himself has bestowed on the executioner: a power that the victim has, by way of contract, forced on the executioner, who can exercise it only at the victim's order."[24] Rejecting the view that suffering is the basis for a definition of masochism, Smirnoff argues that the masochist seeks "the arrangement of a certain immutable setting" and therefore a contract which guarantees that no element of masochistic experience will be improvised (the sadist seeks precisely the opposite guarantee).[25] The purpose of the masochistic contract is to stipulate which of two roles the woman is to play; for another feature of male masochism is the dual feminine ideal – the good and the evil woman (the good mother and the castrating mother of other theories). If the ideal woman is unavailable, the masochist turns to her opposite. These two figures coexist for him even though he cannot imagine them simultaneously. "Such is the masochist's tragedy: he must love the cold, inhuman image in order to be loved by the other one."[26]

4

A unified theory of masochism remains to be formulated. I have focused in this brief account of several influential theories on the origins of masochism in order to suggest that, whereas differences are often theoretical, descriptions of masochistic behavior are often in agreement. In the preceding analysis of Richardson's novels, I called attention to the following observations:

1. Masochistic behavior is sometimes manic. Garma stresses "elation, hyperactivity . . . increased self-esteem, feelings of omnipotence." Reik is concerned with similar qualities in his analysis of the "flight forward": "It is independent of masochism and can be observed in situations which have no relation to this perversion and

24. Victor N. Smirnoff, "The Masochistic Contract," 668.

25. Ibid., 666. Smirnoff adds later in the essay: "To institute and enact the endless repetition of this denial, masochism can only be based on a contract that is also an alliance. By instituting such a ritual, with all the compulsive elements included, the executioner must be part of the masochistic position, not an outside figure" (670).

26. Ibid., 669.

in which there is only an overwhelming drive, to get rid of an unbearable anxiety tension. It does not need to be only anxiety that is overcome in that way, but just as well the expectation of severe suffering or inescapable blows of destiny. This way will often be chosen when an end with terror is preferred to a terror without end."[27] It should be noted that Smirnoff distinguishes the masochist from the sadist on the basis of absence of such a quality: "The sadistic fantasy contains its own sequence: every detail must be commanded and performed according to the sadist's whim and will, in an almost improvised sequence of events. Everything is built up little by little, detail by detail, minutely arranged; as things go on, orders are issued, precise instructions given and a constant rearrangement of the procedure takes place while the performance proceeds. This sadistic happening can be compared with a rehearsal, where everything is being set in order to lead to a final and definitive version, but it never goes beyond these rehearsals: the final performance is delayed forever."[28]

2. The masochist may participate in the sadistic enjoyment of his partner, forgetting that he is the victim. Reik states that in masochistic fantasies feelings of aggression are usually disguised.

3. Reik adds that the feminine masochist distorts the feminine role somewhat, for his real aim is to demonstrate to the love-object how he wishes her to behave. He thus plays the masculine and the femine roles simultaneously – his pleasure intensified by the contrast in these roles.

4. Though the masochist often feels powerless and deprived, he is actually defiant, owing to his hostility toward the love-object (Reik, Grunberger, Smirnoff).

5. The masochist may hold to a dual feminine ideal: the good woman and her opposite, the bad or castrating woman, coexisting yet not imagined simultaneously. The "masochistic contract," which guarantees the immutable conditions of the masochistic experience, stipulates which role the woman plays (Smirnoff).

6. The masochist remains under the influence of an early sadistic love object (Berliner, Reik). The woman is the punishing figure in the masochistic fantasy precisely because she is the castrating mother (Grunberger).

27. *Masochism in Modern Man,* p. 122.
28. "The Masochistic Contract," 668.

BIBLIOGRAPHY

I. SAMUEL RICHARDSON, THE NOVEL, LITERARY CRITICISM

Aldridge, A. O., "The Pleasures of Pity," ELH, 16 (1949), 76-87.

Booth, Wayne C., *The Rhetoric of Fiction.* Chicago: University of Chicago Press, 1961.

Boyd, James, *Goethe's Knowledge of English Literature.* London: Oxford University Press, 1932.

Burke, Edmund, *A Philosophical Enquiry into the Origin of our Ideas of the Sublime and Beautiful,* ed. J. T. Boulton. London: Routledge and Kegan Paul, 1958.

Burke, Kenneth, *The Philosophy of Literary Form,* revised edition. New York: Vintage Books, 1957.

– *A Rhetoric of Motives.* Berkeley: University of California Press, 1969.

Carroll, John, ed., *Samuel Richardson: A Collection of Critical Essays.* Englewood Cliffs, New Jersey: Prentice Hall, Inc., 1969.

Crane, R. S., "Suggestions Toward a Genealogy of the 'Man of Feeling,' " ELH, 1 (1934), 204-30.

Crews, Frederick, ed., *Psychoanalysis and Literary Process.* Cambridge, Massacusetts: Winthrop Publishers, Inc., 1970.

Doody, Margaret Anne, *A Natural Passion: A Study of the Novels of Samuel Richardson.* Oxford: Clarendon Press, 1974.

Downs, Brian W., *Richardson.* London: George Routledge and Sons, Ltd., 1928.

Eaves, T. C. Duncan and Ben D. Kimpel, "The Composition of *Clarissa* and Its Revision before Publication," PMLA, 83 (1968), 416-28.

– *Samuel Richardson: A Biography* (Oxford: Clarendon Press, 1971.

Eissler, K. R., *Goethe: A Psychoanalytic Study.* Detroit: Wayne State University Press, 1963.

Fiedler, Leslie, *Love and Death in the American Novel.* New York: Criterion Books, Inc., 1960.

Goethe, Johann Wolfgang von, *The Sorrows of Young Werther*, trans. Victor Lange. New York: Holt, Rinehart, and Winston, 1949.

Golden, Morris, *Richardson's Characters.* Ann Arbor: University of Michigan Press, 1963.

Holland, Norman, *The Dynamics of Literary Response.* New York: Oxford University Press, 1968.

James, Henry, *The Art of the Novel.* ed., R. P. Blackmur. New York: Charles Scribner's Sons, 1950.

Kinkead-Weekes, Mark, "*Clarissa* Restored?", *Review of English Studies* (New Series), 10 (1959), 156-71.

– *Samuel Richardson, Dramatic Novelist.* Ithaca: Cornell University Press, 1973.
Konigsberg, Ira, *Samuel Richardson and the Dramatic Novel.* Lexington: University of Kentucky Press, 1968.
Kris, Ernst, *Psychoanalytic Explorations in Art.* New York: Schocken Books, 1964.
Kuhn, Albert J., ed., *Three Sentimental Novels,* Rinehart, and Winston, 1970.
Lawrence, D. H., *Phoenix: The Posthumous Papers of D. H. Lawrence,* ed. Edward D. McDonald. London: William Heinemann Ltd., 1936.
– *The Portable Lawrence,* ed. Diana Trilling. New York, The Viking Press, 1947.
– *Sons and Lovers,* ed. Julian Moynahan. New York: The Viking Press, 1968.
– *Women in Love.* New York: The Viking Press, 1960.
Lesser, Simon O., *Fiction and the Unconscious.* Boston: Beacon Press, 1957.
– "A Note on *Pamela," College English,* 14 (1952), 13-17.
McIntosh, Carey, "Pamela's Clothes," *ELH*, 35 (1968), 75-83.
McKillop, Alan D., *Samuel Richardson: Printer and Novelist.* Chapel Hill: University of North Carolina Press, 1936.
– *The Early Masters of English Fiction.* Lawrence: University of Kansas Press, 1956.
Phillips, William, ed., *Art and Psychoanalysis.* Cleveland: World Publishing Company, 1963.
Pierson, R. C., "The Revisions of Richardson's *Sir Charles Grandison," Studies in Bibliography,* 21 91968), 163-89.
Praz, Mario, *The Romantic Agony,* second edition. New York: Oxford University Press, 1970.
Richardson, Samuel, *Clarissa,* 4 volumes. London: J. M. Dent, 1932.
– *The Correspondence,* ed. Anna Laetitia Barbauld. London: 1804.
Pamela, 2 volumes. London: J.M. Dent, 1962.
Selected Letters, ed. John Carroll. Oxford: Clarendon Press, 1964.
Sir Charles Grandison, 3 volumes. Edited by Jocelyn Harris. London: Oxford University Press, 1972.
Slattery, William C., ed., *The Richardson-Stinstra Correspondence and Stinstra's Prefaces to Clarissa*. Carbondale: Southern Illinois University Press, 1969.
Steele, Richard, *The Tender Husband,* ed. Calhoun Winton. Lincoln: University of Nebraska Press, 1967.
Stoll, Elmer Edgar, *From Shakespeare to Joyce.* Garden City, New York: Doubleday and Company, Inc., 1944.
– *Shakespeare Studies.* New York: The Macmillan Company, 1927.
Van Ghent, Dorothy, *The English Novel: Form and Function.* New York: Harper Torchbooks, 1961.
Wasserman, Earl, "The Pleasures of Tragedy," *ELH,* 14 (1947), 283-307.
Watt, Ian, *The Rise of the Novel.* Berkeley: University of California Press, 1957.
Weiss, Daniel A., *Oedipus in Nottingham: D. H. Lawrence.* Seattle: University of Washington Press, 1962.
Wendt, Allan, "Clarissa's Coffin," *Philological Quarterly,* 39 (1960), 481-95.

Wimsatt, W. K., *The Verbal Icon.* Lexington: University of Kentucky Press, 1954.

Wolff, Cynthia Griffin, *Samuel Richardson and the Eighteenth-Century Puritan Character.* Hamden, Connecticut: Archon Books, 1972.

II. THE THEORY OF MASOCHISM

Abraham, Karl, "Rescue and Murder of the Father in Neurotic Phantasies," *International Journal of Psycho-analysis,* 3 (1922), 464-74.

Bergler, Edmund, *The Basic Neurosis.* New York: Grune and Stratton, 1949.

– "Phases of the Masculine Beating Fantasy," *Psychoanalytic Quarterly,* 7 (1938), 514-36.

– "Voyeurism," *Archives of Criminal Psychodynamics,* 2 (1957), No. 2, 211-25.

– *The Writer and Psychoanalysis.* New York: Doubleday and Company, Inc., 1950.

– "Writers of Half-Talent," *American Imago,* 14 (1957), 155-64.

Berliner, Bernhard, "Libido and Reality in Masochism," *Psychoanalytic Quarterly,* 9 (1940), 322-33.

– "The Role of Object Relations in Moral Masochism," *Psychoanalytic Quarterly,* 27 (1958), 38-56.

Bieber, Irving, "The Meaning of Masochism," *American Journal of Psychotherapy,* 7 (1953), 433-48.

Brenman, Margaret, "On Teasing and Being Teased and the Problem of 'Moral Masochism,'" in *Psychoanalytic Psychiatry and Psychology.* New York: International University Press, 1954.

Feldmann, Sandor, "On the Fear of Being Buried Alive," *Psychiatric Quarterly,* 16 (1942).

Fenichel, Otto, *Collected Papers: Second Series.* New York: W. W. Norton and Company, Inc., 1954.

– *Outline of Clinical Psychoanalysis.* New York: Psychoanalytic Quarterly Press and W. W. Norton and Company, 1934.

– *Psychoanalytic Theory of Neurosis.* New York: W. W. Norton and Company, 1945.

Ferenczi, Sandor, "The 'Family Romance' of a Lowered Social Position," in *Further Contributions to the Theory and Technique of Psychoanalysis.* New York: Basic Books, Inc., 1952.

Freud, Sigmund, *Standard Edition of the Complete Psychological Works.* 24 volumes. London: The Hogarth Press, 1954-74.

Frosch, John, "Transference Derivations of the Family Romance," *American Psychoanalytic Association Journal,* 7 (1959), 503-22.

Garma, Angel, "The Deceiving Ego and the Masochistic Ego in Mania," *Psychoanalytic Quarterly,* 37 (1968), 63-78.

– "Within the Realm of the Death Instinct," *International Journal of Psychoanalysis,* 52 (1971), 145-54.

Grunberger, Bela, "Psychodynamic Theory of Masochism," in *Perversions:*

Psychodynamics and Therapy, ed. Sandor Lorand. New York: Gramercy Books, 1956.

Hartmann, Heinz, Ernst Kris, and Rudolph M. Loewenstein, "Notes on the Theory of Aggression," *Psychoanalytic Study of the Child,* 3-4 (1950), 9-36.

Horney, Karen, *New Ways in Psychoanalysis.* New York: W. W. Norton and Company, 1939.

– "The Problem of Feminine Masochism," *Psychoanalytic Review,* 22 (1935), 241-57.

Kamiat, Arnold, "Male Masochism and Culture," *Psychoanalytic Review,* 23 (1936), 84-91.

Keiser, Sylvan, "The Fear of Sexual Passivity in the Masochist," *International Journal of Psycho-analysis,* 30 (1949), 162-71.

Menaker, Esther, "Masochism – a Defense Reaction of the Ego," *International Journal of Psycho-analysis,* 12 (1931), 123-40.

Rado, Sandor, "Fear of Castration in Women," *Psychoanalytic Quarterly,* 2 (1933), 425-75.

Reik, Theodor, *Masochism in Modern Man.* New York: Farrar and Rinehart, Inc., 1941.

Smirnoff, Victor N., "The Masochistic Contract," *International Journal of Psycho-analysis,* 50 (1969), 665-71.

Socarides, Charles, "The Function of Moral Masochism," *International Journal of Psycho-analysis,* 39 (1958), 587-97.

Sterba, Richard, "Aggression in the Rescue Fantasy," *Psychoanalytic Quarterly,* 9 (1940), 505-08.

Wittels, Fritz, "The Mystery of Masochism," *Psychoanalytic Review,* 24 (1937), 139-49.

INDEX

COSTERUS. Essays in English and American Language and Literature.

Volume 1. Amsterdam 1972. 240 p. Hfl. 40.–
GARLAND CANNON: Sir William Jones's Translation-Interpretation of Sanskrit Literature. SARAH DYCK: The Presence of that Shape: Shelley's *Prometheus Unbound.* MARJORIE ELDER: Hawthorne's *The Marble Faun:* A Gothic Structure. JAMES L. GOLDEN: Adam Smith as a Rhetorical Theorist and Literary Critic. JACK GOODSTEIN: Poetry, Religion and Fact: Matthew Arnold. JAY L. HALIO: Anxiety in *Othello.* JOHN ILLO: Miracle in Milton's Early Verse. F. SAMUEL JANZOW: De Quincey's "Danish Origin of the Lake Country Dialect" Republished. MARTIN L. KORNBLUTH: The Degeneration of Classical Friendship in Elizabethan Drama. VIRGINIA MOSELY: The "Dangerous" Paradox in Joyce's "Eveline". JOHN NIST: Linguistics and the Esthetics of English. SCOTT B. RICE: Smollett's *Travels* and the Genre of Grand Tour Literature. LISBETH J. SACHS and BERNARD H. STERN: The Little Preoedipal Boy in Papa Hemingway and How He Created His Artistry.

Volume 2. Amsterdam 1972. 236 p. Hfl. 40.–
RALPH BEHRENS: Mérimée, Hemingway, and the Bulls. JEANNINE BOHLMEYER: Mythology in Sackville's "Induction" and "Complaint". HAROLD A. BRACK: Needed – a new language for communicating religion. LEONARD FEINBERG: Satire and Humor: In the Orient and in the West. B. GRANGER: The Whim-Whamsical Bachelors in Salmagundi. W. M. FORCE: The What Story? or Who's Who at the Zoo? W. N. KNIGHT: To Enter lists with God. Transformation of Spencerian Chivalric Tradition in Paradise Regained. MARY D. KRAMER: The Roman Catholic Cleric on the Jacobean Stage. BURTON R. POLLIN: The Temperance Movement and Its Friends Look at Poe. SAMUEL J. ROGAL: Two Translations of the Iliad, Book I: Pope and Tickell. J. L. STYAN: The Delicate Balance: Audience Ambivalence in the Comedy of Shakespeare and Chekhov. CLAUDE W. SUMERLIN: Christopher Smart's A Song to David: its influence on Robert Browning. B.W. TEDFORD: A Recipe for Satire and Civilization. H. H. WATTS: Othello and the Issue of Multiplicity. GUY R. WOODALL: Nationalism in the Philadelphia National Gazette and Literary Register: 1820–1836.

Volume 3. Amsterdam 1972. 236 p. Hfl. 40.–
RAYMOND BENOIT: In Dear Detail by Ideal Light: "Ode on a Grecian Urn". E. F. CALLAHAN: Lyric Origins of the Unity of 1 Henry IV. FRASER DREW: John Masefield and Juan Manuel de Rosas. LAURENCE GONZALEZ: Persona Bob: seer and fool. A. HIRT: A Question of Excess: Neo-Classical Adaptations of Greek Tragedy. EDWIN HONIG: Examples of

Poetic Diction in Ben Jonson. ELSIE LEACH: T. S. Eliot and the School of Donne. SEYMOUR REITER: The Structure of 'Waiting for Godot'. DANIEL E. VAN TASSEL: The Search for Manhood in D. H. Lawrence's 'Sons and Lovers'. MARVIN ROSENBERG: Poetry of the Theatre. GUY R. WOODALL: James Russell Lowell's "Works of Jeremy Taylor, D.D.'

Volume 4. Amsterdam 1972. 233 p. Hfl. 40.–
BOGDDY ARIAS: Sailor's Reveries. R. H. BOWERS: Marlowe's 'Dr. Faustus', Tirso's 'El Condenado por Desconfiado', and the Secret Cause. HOWARD O. BROGAN: Satirist Burns and Lord Byron. WELLER EMBLER: Simone Weil and T. S. Eliot. E. ANTHONY JAMES: Defoe's Autobiographical Apologia: Rhetorical Slanting in 'An Appeal to Honour and Justice'. MARY D. KRAMER: The American Wild West Show and "Buffalo Bill" Cody. IRVING MASSEY: Shelley's "Dirge for the Year": The Relation of the Holograph to the First Edition. L. J. MORRISSEY: English Street Theatre: 1655–1708. M. PATRICK: Browning's Dramatic Techniques and 'The Ring and the Book': A Study in Mechanic and Organic Unity. VINCENT F. PETRONELLA: Shakespeare's 'Henry V' and the Second Tetralogy: Meditation as Drama. NASEEB SHAHEEN: Deriving Adjectives from Nouns. TED R. SPIVEY: The Apocalyptic Symbolism of W. B. Yeats and T. S. Eliot. EDWARD STONE: The Other Sermon in 'Moby–Dick'. M. G. WILLIAMS: 'In Memoriam': A Broad Church Poem.

Volume 5. Amsterdam 1972. 236 p. Hfl. 40.–
PETER G. BEIDLER: Chaucer's Merchant and the Tale of January. ROBERT A. BRYAN: Poets, Poetry, and Mercury in Spenser's Prosopopia: Mother Hubberd's Tale. EDWARD M. HOLMES: Requiem For A Scarlet Nun. E. ANTHONY JAMES: Defoe's Narrative Artistry: Naming and Describing in Robinson Crusoe. MICHAEL J. KELLY: Coleridge's "Picture, or The Lover's Resolution": its Relationship to "Dejection" and its Sources in the Notebooks. EDWARD MARGOLIES: The Playwright and his Critics. MURRAY F. MARKLAND: The Task Set by Valor. RAYMOND S. NELSON: Back to Methuselah: Shaw's Modern Bible. THOMAS W. ROSS: Maimed Rites in Much Ado About Nothing. WILLIAM B. TOOLE: The Metaphor of Alchemy in Julius Caesar, PAUL WEST: Carlyle's Bravura Prophetics. GLENA D. WOOD: The Tragi-Comic Dimensions of Lear's Fool. H. ALAN WYCHERLEY: "Americana": The Mencken – Lorimer Feud.

Volume 6. Amsterdam 1972. 235 p. Hfl. 40.–
GEORG W. BOSWELL: Superstition and Belief in Faulkner. ALBERT COOK: Blake's Milton. MARSHA KINDER: The Improved Author's Farce: An Analysis of the 1734 Revisions. ABE LAUFE: What Makes Drama Run? (Introduction to Anatomy of a Hit). RICHARD L. LOUGHLIN: Laugh and Grow Wise with Oliver Goldsmith. EDWARD MARGOLIES: The American Detective Thriller & The Idea of Society. RAYMOND S. NELSON: Shaw's Heaven, Hell, and Redemption. HAROLD OREL: Is Patrick White's Voss the Real Leichhardt of Australia? LOUIS B. SALOMON: A Walk With Emerson On The Dark Side. H. GRANT SAMPSON: Structure in the Poetry of Thoreau. JAMES H. SIMS, Some Biblical Light on Shakespeare's Hamlet.

ROBERT F. WILLSON, Jr.: Lear's Auction. JAMES N. WISE: Emerson's "Experience" and "Sons and Lovers". JAMES D. YOUNG: Aims in Reader's Theatre.

Volume 7. Amsterdam 1973. 235 p. Hfl. 40.–
HANEY H. BELL Jr.: Sam Fathers and Ike McCaslin and the World in Which Ike Matures. SAMUEL IRVING BELLMAN: The Apocalypse in Literature. HALDEEN BRADDY: England and English before Alfred. DAVID R. CLARK: Robert Frost: "The Thatch" and "Directive". RALPH MAUD: Robert Crowley, Puritan Satirist. KATHARINE M. MORSBERGER: Hawthorne's "Borderland": The Locale of the Romance. ROBERT E. MORSBERGER: The Conspiracy of the Third International. "What is the metre of the dictionary? " – Dylan Thomas. RAYMOND PRESTON: Dr. Johnson and Aristotle. JOHN J. SEYDOW: The Sound of Passing Music: John Neal's Battle for American Literary Independence. JAMES H. SIMS: Enter Satan as Esau, Alone; Exit Satan as Belshazzar: *Paradise Lost,* BOOK (IV). MICHAEL WEST, Dryden and the Disintegration of Renaissance Heroic Ideals. RENATE C. WOLFF: Pamela as Myth and Dream.

Volume 8. Amsterdam 1973. 231 p. Hfl. 40.–
SAMUEL I. BELLMAN: Sleep, Pride, and Fantasy: Birth Traumas and Socio-Biologic Adaptation in the American-Jewish Novel. PETER BUITENHUIS: A Corresponding Fabric: The Urban World of Saul Bellow. DAVID R. CLARK: An Excursus upon the Criticism of Robert Frost's "Directive". FRANCIS GILLEN: Tennyson and the Human Norm: A Study of Hubris and Human Commitment in Three Poems by Tennyson. ROBERT R. HARSON: H. G. Wells: The Mordet Island Episode. JULIE B. KLEIN: The Art of Apology: "An Epistle to Dr. Arbuthnot" and "Verses on the Death of Dr. Swift". ROBERT E. MORSBERGER: The Movie Game in Who's Afraid of Virginia Woolf and The Boys in the Band. EDWIN MOSES: A Reading of "The Ancient Mariner". JOHN H. RANDALL: Romeo and Juliet in the New World. A Study in James, Wharton, and Fitzgerald "Fay ce que vouldras". JOHN E. SAVESON: Conrad as Moralist in Victory. ROBERT M. STROZIER: Politics, Stoicism, and the Development of Elizabethan Tragedy. LEWIS TURCO: Manoah Bodman: Poet of the Second Awakening.

Volume 9. Amsterdam 1973. 251 p. Hfl. 40.–
THOMAS E. BARDEN: Dryden's Aims in *Amphytryon.* SAMUEL IRVING BELLMAN: Marjorie Kinnan Rawling's Existentialist Nightmare *The Yearling.* SAMUEL IRVING BELLMAN: Writing Literature for Young People. Marjorie Kinnan Rawlings' "Secret River" of the Imagination. F. S. JANZOW: "Philadelphus," A New Essay by De Quincey. JACQUELINE KRUMP: Robert Browning's Palace of Art. ROBERT E. MORSBERGER: The Winning of Barbara Undershaft: Conversion by the Cannon Factory, or "Wot prawce selvytion nah? " DOUGLAS L. PETERSON: Tempest-Tossed Barks and Their Helmsmen in Several of Shakespeare's Plays. STANLEY POSS: Serial Form and Malamud's Schlemihls. SHERYL P. RUTLEDGE: Chaucer's Zodiac of Tales. CONSTANCE RUYS: John Pickering–Merchant Adventurer and Playwright. JAMES H. SIMS: Death in Poe's Poetry: Varia-

tions on a Theme. ROBERT A. SMITH: A Pioneer Black Writer and the Problems of Discrimination and Miscegenation. ALBERT J. SOLOMON: The Sound of Music in "Eveline": A Long Note on a Barrel-Organ. J. L. STYAN: Goldsmith's Comic Skills. ARLINE R. THORN: Shelley's *The Cenci* as Tragedy. E. THORN: James Joyce: Early Imitations of Structural Unity. LEWIS TURCO: The Poetry of Lewis Turco. An Interview by Gregory Fitzgerald and William Heyen.

New Series. Volume 1. Edited by James L. W. West III. Amsterdam 1974. 194 p. Hfl. 40.–
D. W. ROBERTSON, Jr.: Chaucer's Franklin and His Tale. CLARENCE H. MILLER and CARYL K. BERREY: The Structure of Integrity: The Cardinal Virtues in Donne's "Satyre III". F. SAMUEL JANZOW: The English Opium-Eater as Editor. VICTOR A. KRAMER: Premonition of Disaster: An Unpublished Section for Agee's *A Death in the Family*. GEORGE L. GECKLE: Poetic Justice and *Measure for Measure*. RODGER L. TARR: Thomas Carlyle's Growing Radicalism: The Social Context of *The French Revolution*. G. THOMAS TANSELLE: Philip Gaskell's *A New Introduction to Bibliography*. Review Essay. KATHERINE B. TROWER: Elizabeth D. Kirk's *The Dream Thought of Piers Plowman*. Review Essay. JAMES L. WEST III: Matthew J. Bruccoli's *F. Scott Fitzgerald a Descriptive Bibliography*. Review Essay. JAMES E. KIBLER: R. W. Stallman's *Stephen Crane: A Critical Bibliography*. Review. ROBERT P. MILLER: Jonathan Saville's *The Medieval Erotic Alba*. Review.

New Series. Volume 2. **THACKERY. Edited by Peter L. Shillingsburg.** Amsterdam 1974. 359 p. Hfl. 70.–
JOAN STEVENS: *Vanity Fair* and the London Skyline. JANE MILLGATE: History *versus* Fiction: Thackeray's Response to Macaulay. ANTHEA TRODD: Michael Angelo Titmarsh and the Knebworth Apollo. PATRICIA R. SWEENEY: Thackeray's Best Illustrator. JOAN STEVENS: Thackeray's Pictorial Capitals. ANTHONY BURTON: Thackeray's Collaborations with Cruikshank, Doyle, and Walker. JOHN SUTHERLAND: A *Vanity Fair* Mystery: The Delay in Publication. JOHN SUTHERLAND: Thackeray's Notebook for *Henry Esmond*. EDGAR F. HARDEN: The Growth of *The Virginians* as a Serial Novel: Parts 1–9. GERALD C. SORENSEN: Thackeray Texts and Bibliographical Scholarship. PETER L. SHILLINSBURG: Thackeray Texts: A Guide to Inexpensive Editions. RUTH apROBERTS: Thackeray Boom: A Review. JOSEPH E. BAKER: Reading Masterpieces in Isolation: Review. ROBERT A. COLBY and JOHN SUTHERLAND: Thackeray's Manuscripts: A Preliminary Census of Library Locations.

New Series. Volume 3. Edited by James L. W. West III. Amsterdam 1975. 184 p. Hfl. 40.–
SAMUEL J. ROGAL: Hurd's Editorial Criticism of Addison's Grammar and Usage. ROBERT P. MILLER: Constancy Humanized: Trivet's Constance and the Man of Law's Custance. WELDON THORNTON: Structure and Theme in Faulkner's *Go Down, Moses*. JAYNE K. KRIBBS: John Davis: A Man For His Time. STEPHEN E. MEATS: The Responsibilities of an Editor of Correspon-

dence. Review Essay. RODGER L. TARR: Carlyle and Dickens *or* Dickens and Carlyle. Review. CHAUNCEY WOOD: Courtly Lovers: An Unsentimental View. Review.

New Series. Volume 4. Edited by James L. W. West III. Amsterdam 1975. 179 p. Hfl. 40.–
JAMES L. W. WEST III: A Bibliographer's Interview with William Styron. J. TIMOTHY HOBBS: The Doctrine of Fair Use in the Law of Copyright. JUNE STEFFENSEN HAGEN: Tennyson's Revisions of the Last Stanza of "Audley Court". CLIFFORD CHALMERS HUFFMAN: *The Christmas Prince*: University and Popular Drama in the Age of Shakespeare. ROBERT L. OAKMAN: Textual Editing and the Computer. Review Essay. T.H. HOWARD-HILL: The Bard in Chains: *The Harvard Concordance to Shakespeare.* Review Essay. BRUCE HARKNESS: Conrad Computerized and Concordanced. Review Essay. MIRIAM J. SHILLINGSBURG: A Rose is a Four-Letter Word; or, The Machine Makes Another Concordance. Review Essay. RICHARD H. DAMMERS: Explicit Statement as Art. Review Essay. A. S. G. EDWARDS: Medieval Madness and Medieval Literature. Review Essay. NOEL POLK: Blotner's Faulkner. Review.

New Series. Volume 5–6. **GYASCUTUS. Studies in Antebellum Southern Humorous and Sporting Writing. Edited by James L. W. West III.** Amsterdam 1978.
NOEL POLK: The Blind Bull, Human Nature: Sut Lovingood and the Damned Human Race. HERBERT P. SHIPPEY: William Tappan Thompson as Playwright. LELAND H. COX, Jr.: Porter's Edition of *Instructions to Young Sportsmen.* ALAN GRIBBEN: Mark Twain Reads Longstreet's *Georgia Scenes.* T. B. THORPE's Far West Letters, ed. Leland H. Cox, Jr. An Unknown Tale by GEORGE WASHINGTON HARRIS ed. William Starr. JOHNSON JONES HOOPER's "The 'Frinnolygist' at Fault" ed. James L. W. West III. SOUTH CAROLINA WRITERS in the *Spirit of the Times* ed. Stephen E. Meats. A NEW MOCK SERMON ed. James L. W. West III. ANOTHER NEW MOCK SERMON ed. A. S. Wendel. The PORTER-HOOPER Correspondence ed. Edgar E. Thompson.

New Series. Volume 7. **SANFORD PINSKER: The Languages of Joseph Conrad.** Amsterdam 1978. 87 p. Hfl. 20.–
Table of Contents: Foreword. Introductory Language. The Language of the East. The Language of Narration. The Language of the Sea. The Language of Politics. *Victory* As Afterword.

New Series. Volume 8. **GARLAND CANNON: An Integrated Transformational Grammar of the English Language.** Amsterdam 1978. 315 p. Hfl. 60.–
Table of Contents: Preface. 1) A Child's Acquisition of His First Language. 2) Man's Use of Language. 3) Syntactic Component: Base Rules. 4) Syntactic Component: Lexicon. 5) Syntactic Component: Transformational Rules. 6) Semantic Component. 7) Phonological Component. 8) Man's Understanding of His Language. Appendix: the Sentence-Making Model. Bibliography. Index.